Advance Praise·

" . . . tough and funny and touching and harrowing."
—John Barth

"Rutkowski is one of the most original writers in America today. Once you've read his low-key, continually surprising fiction, the world will look different to you."
—Alison Lurie

"I took great joy watching this author drive home his strong and deceptively simple sentences like a craftsman, hammering nails straight and with a trained aim, working his trade. The writing strikes true and therefore beautiful. Rutkowski here builds a solid story, a kind of memoir/bildungsroman, telling of a biracial kid stunned in an emotional and psychological crossfire between his crazed and cryptic Polish father and cool-headed Asian mom. There are episodes that skirt magic realism and others, deadpan funny and straightforward, that acknowledge the magic in the simplest acts of growing up, school, love, being a victim of parents and finally a parent oneself. Recommended!"
—James Robison, author, Whiting Award winner and recipient of a
    Rosenthal Award from the American Academy of Arts and Letters

"Story by story, Thaddeus Rutkowski snaps into place the puzzle of a mixed-race kid playing dumb in *Guess and Check*'s Appalachia. Much more than the postmodern sum of its parts, *Guess and Check* is spare, subtle and deadpan, Charles Simic married to Joyce Carol Oates. A beautifully constructed delicate narrative, a near dream of a book, a place 'vulnerable to anyone who wants to break through the glass.'"
—Terese Svoboda, author of *Bohemian Girl*

"In a disarming style, Rutkowski has written a moving, often disturbing, yet ultimately optimistic, story full of irony and wit. With prose that is frequently stunning, Rutkowski creates a troubling world that is often absurd and sometimes beautiful. It is a vivid portrait of a world where, as for the memorable hero, things rarely mesh. Rutkowski recounts how—through intellect, cunning, a sense of humor, and just making do—the hero negotiates the dysfunctions, dangers and oddities of his existence. Guided by a gifted writer, we also learn a thing or two about negotiating the painful and the strange—and that despite it all, things might turn out well."

—Sanjay Nigam, author of *The Snake Charmer* and *Transplanted Man*

Guess and Check

by Thaddeus Rutkowski

Arlington, Virginia

Published by Gival Press, an imprint of Gival Press, LLC.
For information please write:
Gival Press, LLC
P. O. Box 3812
Arlington, VA 22203
www.givalpress.com

First edition ISBN: 978-1-940724-11-9
eISBN: 978-1-940724-12-6
Library of Congress Control Number: 2016948934

Cover art: *Rise* © 2016 by Shalom Neuman.
Design by Ken Schellenberg.

For Randi Hoffman and Shay Rutkowski

Contents

Part 1

Painted Ladies

Early in the day, my parents dropped me off at my grandparents' house—a wooden two-story on a once-prosperous street. When we arrived, my grandfather was "out doing his business," my grandmother said.

I lay on the couch in the living room and watched morning television shows while my grandmother did housework. Her mother—my great-grandmother—sat without moving in a straight-backed chair. The older woman, as far as I could tell, did not speak English. She spoke Polish, and broke from it only to call me "stupid" when I got up and ran around the room.

My grandmother told me her mother was born in Trzaski, a village in Pomerania. "You know," she said, "that's where Pomeranian dogs come from. My mother came to this country because she'd heard that women here live the life of a dog. They lie around all day and do nothing."

*

Shortly after my parents brought me home, my mother announced that she had to go to the hospital. The reason was, she was going to have a baby.

I thought babies arose spontaneously. When it was their time to arrive, they just appeared. I didn't know why my parents were hurrying to leave. I didn't see the emergency.

On their way to the hospital, my parents dropped my sister and me off at my grandparents' house. As before, our great-grandmother was sitting in her chair. My sister and I watched a TV show featuring a man named after a marsupial. This man had a military title. Basically, Captain Kangaroo was a teddy bear. My sister and I laughed along with the studio audience until our great-grandmother interrupted us with a sharp "Stupid!"

*

When our baby brother came home, my sister and I started calling him by his first name. Our father discouraged us, saying we should call him by his middle name. The first name was for his baptism. The middle name was what my father wanted.

My mother, on the other hand, gave the baby a Chinese name, Da Wei, meaning Greatly Accomplished, but that name didn't stick. We children didn't call each other by our Chinese names. My mother was the only one called by her Chinese name, Chia In, except that no one could pronounce it correctly. We said, "Jeye Een," without any intonation. We forgot that the name meant "Good Tidings." Her American friends and my father's relatives called her Irene.

*

In the afternoon, I followed my father to an overgrown lane. "We'll find some butterflies here," he said.

The lane was two dirt tracks made by tires through a patch of woods. We walked onto the pathway and were soon surrounded by gnats.

"I'm not a businessman, like my father," my father said. "I want to live in nature. The capitalists started the rat race. I'm part of the human race."

I could hardly swing the cloth net my father had given me. The handle was too long, the torque too great. At one point, we saw a butterfly on the ground. Its wings were folded back, and it didn't move when my father picked it up.

"Look," my father said, pointing to the orange, black and silver markings, the delicate circles and waves. "It's a painted lady. That's the common name. It means lady of the night, someone who paints her face and walks the streets.

"It's not alive," he added as he tossed it away.

*

I took my bicycle for a ride. It was a small bike, with 16-inch wheels, suitable for a 6-year-old. I went along the lane my father had shown me and came out on the other side. I found myself on a paved street lined with houses. I had the idea that a boy in my class lived in this neighborhood. I rode to a house I thought was his, but no one was home.

On my way back through the woods, a bee flew into my ear as I was riding. I could hear it buzzing next to my skull. I took a hand from the steering bar to bat the insect away and lost control of the bike. The front wheel hit a stone, turned sharply and carried me into the brush. I put out a forearm to stop myself, and my wrist hit a branch. I went down in a tangle of twigs and leaves.

When I walked my bicycle out of the bushes, I noticed that my wrist was injured. It hurt when I turned it. I felt pain shooting from my forearm through my hand. When I let my arm hang limp, the wrist felt better.

A woman who lived in a house I was passing called to me: "You're Irene's son, aren't you? Are you all right?"

I nodded yes and kept walking.

*

The next time I saw my great-grandmother, she was living in a nursing home. Again, she was sitting in a chair, this one next to her bed, and she didn't say much, but she seemed to have learned a new English word: "Yankee." Instead of calling me stupid, she called everyone around her Yankees.

When my mother asked her how she liked her roommates, she said, "Yankees."

*

Soon afterward, my great-grandmother passed away. I didn't go to the memorial service, but I heard my grandmother talking to my mother about her.

"She was 96," my grandmother said.

"So old!" my mother said.

"Not in her mind," my grandmother said. "She insisted she was 72 until the day she died."

"She lived a long time."

"In her youth, she was beautiful, a glamour girl, a made-up lady."

*

My wrist took a long time to heal. While I waited for it to get better, I was still able to ride my bicycle. I took it to the lane through the woods and came to the neighborhood on the other side. I looked for the boy who was my classmate. I didn't find him, but I spotted a number of painted lady butterflies. They were alive. They started up when I came through; they flitted over the weeds.

Guess and Check

My brother and sister and I took my mother to a parking lot to teach her to ride a bicycle. We rolled a child's bike along with us. The bike had one gear, and its brake was built into the pedals. When we got to the paved area next to the local school, we helped our mother onto the bike. "Go for it," we said. "Pump."

"I don't know how to pedal," she said.

We gave her a push, and she coasted down the slight hill of the parking lot. As she rolled, neighbor children stood and watched her.

"I don't know how to stop," she called.

"Use the brakes!" we yelled.

"Where are the brakes?"

"In the pedals! Stand on the pedals!"

She worked the pedals, but she pushed them forward, not back. She picked up speed for a few yards, then pitched over onto her side. She ended up at a right angle to the bike. She got up but didn't lift the bicycle—she let it lie on the ground. "I don't think I can learn," she said.

The neighbor children stood there, watching.

*

On our way home, we walked past a house that had a dog in its backyard. When the animal sensed our presence, it started to bark.

"I don't want to go near it," my mother said.

We couldn't tell if the dog was loose or tied, so I went to the edge of the yard to see. The dog rushed forward and shot into the air. A chain attached to its collar jerked it back like a shock cord.

"You can walk past," I called to my mother.

She went around the house in a large half-circle.

"Where I grew up," she said, "dogs weren't pets. They were wild animals. If they were larger than knee-high, they could be taken away from you. If you had more than one dog, you had to give up all but one. After Mao took over, all dogs were banned. They were seen as bourgeois."

At home, our two pet dogs jumped at my mother's legs. She wasn't afraid of them, but she wasn't happy to see them, either.

"I don't like these dogs," she said. "I don't like them rubbing their fur against me. I wish we could bring them to a shelter."

*

In the evening, my mother helped me with my algebra homework. The idea was to isolate x on one side of an equation, but the first equation I was given was complicated. It contained parentheses, positive and negative numbers, and repeated multiplications and divisions.

I started simplifying. I divided by 2 on both sides of the equals sign; I subtracted 6; I divided by x. I was able to isolate x on one side of the equation—I knew it didn't matter which side. On the other side, there was a load of numbers—that was acceptable, too. In my solution, x equaled $2(x-6)$, all over 4.

My mother looked at the same problem, worked for a minute and came up with an answer. For her, x simply equaled 4. According to the workbook, her answer was correct.

"How did you get that?" I asked.

"I can't explain it in English," she said. "I know the language of numbers."

"Maybe I'll just guess and check," I said. "I'll guess at an answer; then I'll check to see if it works out."

When my father saw what we were doing, he said to my mother, "Don't coddle him. What do you want him to be, a mama's boy?"

I had several more problems to solve. The assignment would take a long time, with no guarantee of success. I had a lot of guessing and checking to do. I started looking at the equations, plugging in numbers like 6.5 and 17, but luck was not with me. The random answers didn't work out.

*

My siblings and I rode in the back seat while my father tried to teach my mother to drive. In the passenger seat, my father kept hitting the floor with his foot, as if stamping on a brake.

"Let up," he said, as he tried to release an imaginary gas pedal with his toe. "Don't gun it."

My mother responded and the car lost some speed, but its momentum carried it forward.

"Accelerate," he said as my mother went around a curve.

"I don't know what you want me to do," my mother said.

"When you go around a turn, you want more traction. Give it the gas."

My mother accelerated and the car left the road. It shot across the gravel shoulder and into a wheat field. The car ran softly over the plants. I could see the tops of the stalks sweeping across the side windows. The car encountered nothing solid, and my mother kept going. She accelerated as she turned. Eventually, she brought the car back across the shoulder and onto the pavement.

"That's it," my father said. "From here on, you can take lessons from a professional."

*

On the school bus, no one wanted to sit next to me. When the seat beside me was the last vacant spot, a boy sat there, but he didn't speak to me. I pretended I didn't notice him during the half-hour ride to school, and he did the same with me.

In class, I sat hunched over a pile of books on my desk.

"Egghead," someone whispered.

"Nerd," someone else said.

"Dork," said another student.

In the hallway, a tall girl approached me. "Just act like you're stupid, and you'll do OK," she said. "See those other guys? That's what they do, and they're popular."

*

When I came home from school, I saw my father sitting at the kitchen table; he was drinking a beer and smoking. He didn't notice me, or he seemed not to.

"Is there anything to eat?" I asked as I went to the refrigerator.

"Why do you always interrupt me?" my father asked. "I can't do anything with you around. I always have to stop what I'm doing to serve you."

He got up and heated milk, then poured it into cups for hot chocolate. He called my brother and sister, and the three of us sat at the table, looking down into the cups.

"Drink!" our father shouted. "Now!" He slammed his hand on the table, and the cups jumped.

We drank reluctantly. As we sat there, our father lectured us. "My work requires full concentration," he said. "I might look like I'm doing nothing, but I'm thinking. I'm figuring out how to start a revolution. That's what Lenin did. That's what Mao did. They didn't spend their time taking care of children."

*

Our father banished my siblings and me from the house.

We went out to the yard, but we had little to do there. We looked for stones, picked them up and threw them. We could heave a few over the telephone wire strung between houses. But we soon tired of this activity.

We stood around until our mother got home from work. She spent some time inside, presumably listening to our father speak, then came out to talk to us. "If my parents had a disagreement, they wouldn't argue," she said. "They would put the issue aside and bring it up after the children were asleep. Then they would discuss the problem calmly and come to an agreement."

"Why did you marry him?" one of us asked.

"I was in a new country," she said, "and I didn't have many friends. I ate in the college cafeteria. Two boys also ate there. One was an artist; the other was a mathematician. Both of them liked me. For some reason, I picked the artist."

At night, I could hear my father yelling. I couldn't tell what he was saying. Nevertheless, the sound of his voice—the volume and cadence—made my stomach sink.

*

Later in the night, I could hear a storm blowing against the windows. The wind made the frames rattle. The air pressure was dropping with each gust. I imagined that whole trees were being knocked over. I could picture pines lying on their sides. I heard dripping, and I thought water was coming through the ceiling, through a crack in the plaster.

I could hear myself crying, but there were no tears. There was just a rhythmic huffing sound as the air left my lungs. I could have been laughing.

When I woke in the morning and looked outside, all of the trees were standing. There was no water dripping through the ceiling. But the nearby stream had overflowed. A large, shallow lake covered what had been a cornfield. I saw that the dirt lane through the field was still above water. I could walk along that lane to get to higher ground. I could cross the flooded field and walk up the hill on the other side. The problem was, there was nothing but brambles and tall grass on the other side.

I put on my insulated boots and got ready to go out. I didn't know what I would find. I would have to guess and check.

Out of Fashion

In school, I wore bell-bottoms made of brushed felt. The pants were tight around the thighs, but the bells—with fringes—were very loose around the ankles. I kicked the fringes when I walked. For a top, I wore an orange corduroy shirt.

I walked alone in the hallways. No one wanted to walk beside me. If I happened to be walking toward someone, the student stared at me as I passed.

*

I had one teacher—a Spanish teacher—who was a perv. He would notice any girl who wore a miniskirt. The school had a dress code—one of the rules was that the hem of a skirt had to touch the floor when the wearer was kneeling.

Whenever this teacher had any doubt about the length of a skirt, he would have the girl student kneel on the tiles, and if the fabric of her skirt touched the floor, she would be allowed to take a seat and the class would resume. If not, the teacher would dress her down, in Spanish.

When I walked into the classroom wearing my bell-bottoms, the teacher looked at the fringes brushing the floor and shook his head. He waved a finger, then rubbed one finger over the other as if to say, "Shame on you."

"Tomás," he said, addressing me by my Spanish name. "Tomás, we don't wear those *pantalones* here."

*

My math teacher didn't care what kind of clothing his students wore, but he was a sadist nonetheless. He said he would raise students' grades on one condition. "If you take a whack," he said, "I'll give you a higher letter."

He opened a closet door to reveal a collection of paddles. He had flat wooden bats in various shapes, some with holes drilled through them for greater sting.

Students lined up around the classroom, waiting to be paddled. The line included girls as well as boys. One by one, they went to the front of the room. Each of them took a swat, except for one boy, whose grade was too low for the paddle. He had to accept a kick. The teacher hauled back and booted the boy. The force of the blow sent the boy hopping forward, but he didn't make a sound.

Only a few students were doing well enough not to get whacked. I was one of them. When the teacher noticed me sitting at my desk, he said, "You, Mouse, come up here. You're next. You also get one—that's a real number, 'positive one'—just for being here."

I rose from my seat and went forward.

*

At home, I put on hip boots to go fishing. My brother called the rubber wear "hippie boots." I walked to the creek with the tops of the boots folded down. When I was ready to wade, I pulled up the tops and buckled the rubber straps around my belt.

As I walked through the fast-moving water, I realized the boots weren't really necessary; the creek was only about two feet deep. I could have waded wet and made my casts. I could have fished without stepping into the water at all.

I put away my hippie boots when I returned from the stream. I decided that the next time I went out, I would wear sneakers.

*

My father took my family to see the movie *Alice's Restaurant*. The movie was rated R, and I looked forward to seeing some sex, but there was next to none in the film. There was some nudity when the main character was given a physical exam for induction into the military. There was drug use among the people who were living communally. There was some swearing. That was it.

*

Later, my father became angry about a scene from the movie. In that sequence, a junkie gets high on drugs and swings around on some kind of apparatus, maybe a chandelier. As he hangs like a monkey, he says repeatedly, "I am an artist!"

"That guy was no artist," my father said. "He was a horse's ass."

After a few drinks, my father called me to where he was sitting. "I'm a real artist," he said. "I'm serious, too serious for the rest of these clowns. But you don't give me my due. You treat me like your social organizer. My job is not to entertain children!"

*

My mother brought home a small box from the hospital where she worked. The box held greeting cards. "Look," she said. "It's a drawing by your father."

I looked at the sepia-colored drawing on the front of the cards. It showed the county's only hospital, where my mother was a lab technician. Every edge of the building was sharp; every angle followed perspective. The roof of the carport jutted over the area where ambulances arrived. The windows of the rooms looked new and clean.

I could see that my father had exceptional eye-hand control. I couldn't understand how his hand could be so steady, after years of drinking.

*

My sister embroidered an image from one of my father's paintings onto a lapel of my jacket. In light- and dark-blue thread, she created an antique bottle, the kind with a stopper instead of a twist cap. It looked like one of the bottles my father had dug from a dump in the woods. He'd cleaned the antique glass container and set it up as a still life.

The bottle floated there, against the tan color of my cotton jacket. I wore the jacket to school, and some students noticed the splotch of color in the shape of a bottle, but no one asked me what it was.

*

I tried writing a piece in the manner of a book I was reading. The book was ostensibly about fishing for trout in America, but it was really about a character named Trout Fishing in America. He did some fishing, but he did many other things as well.

My piece had a beer wino in it. This wino drank only beer, which he bought by the case. He would start drinking in the afternoon, and he would continue until he fell asleep in front of a television test pattern at night. He drank beer like a wino.

Somehow, my father saw my story. After he'd read it, he said, "Is this all you can do? Write funny stories? Why don't you go to your room now and write another funny story. Don't come out until you're done."

*

I went out to the porch, where there were hooks in the ceiling that had once held a wooden swing. The swing must have broken and been taken down. Or maybe it hadn't been broken, and had just been taken down. Perhaps my father took it down. Maybe he just didn't like the idea of rocking in a swing on the front porch, chanting that he was an artist. It might have signaled boredom to him, as if people who sat in swings had nothing better to do. He had his ways of relaxing—sitting on a porch wasn't one of them.

Most of our neighbors did, however, have porch swings. I would see them sitting there on summer evenings, looking out from their front porches. They wouldn't be talking. They would just be staring. When I walked by, they wouldn't talk to me. They wouldn't wave, even if I waved. So I didn't wave. I avoided eye contact when I passed by.

The last thing I wanted was to have a swing on our porch. I didn't want to rock back and forth in it and chant, "I am an artist." That would have been an embarrassing thing to do.

The Catfish Fog

I was in the yard next to my family's house when a boy walked in from the street. I hadn't seen him before, though I knew all of the other children in town. He looked like he was a teenager. He was not tall, but he was thick and doughy, and he had small, pink eyes. He sat at the picnic table under the butternut tree, the largest tree in the yard. He didn't move and didn't say anything.

My father must have seen him from inside the house, because he brought the boy a drink in a plastic cup.

"Do your parents know where you are?" my father asked.

When the boy didn't answer, my father went back inside.

My brother and sister joined me, and we continued "playing" in the yard. We walked around the patch of grass, picking up nuts that had fallen from the tree. My sister gathered them into a pile; my brother and I threw them over the hanging telephone wire.

The boy looked at us but didn't speak. I had the idea that he couldn't speak.

After what seemed a long time, he said something to me. He mumbled the word, and at first I didn't understand. "Jerry," he said and pointed to himself, and I understood he was telling me his name.

Then he said, "Chinese" and pushed out another word, "Mother," and I realized he was asking if my mother was Chinese.

Then I understood that he was not asking a question; he was making a statement. I didn't have to reply.

*

Later, my father said to my mother, "We saw that disabled kid from down the street."

"Jerry," my mother said, as if she were trying to remember. "He never leaves his house."

"Maybe they let him out," my father said. "Maybe he escaped."

"How old is he?" my mother asked.

"He looks like he's fifteen but he could be thirty."

"What was he doing?"

"He was wandering by himself."

"I hope he's OK by himself. I hope he wasn't lost," my mother said.

"He'll be OK. If he's not, they'll come after him."

*

In school, I took my report card around to my teachers to get my grades. In each classroom, students went in turn to the front desk and held out their cards. The teacher would fill in a grade on a grid by hand. Most teachers said nothing as they gave a grade, but one, my math teacher, was a wise guy. "If you want to raise your grade," he said, "you can take a swat with my paddle."

A few of the students, even a couple of the girls, accepted his offer. One gathered her skirt around her knees as she bent over. She flinched when the paddle hit, but she didn't make a sound.

I decided to stick with my grade as it was.

When I brought home my report card, I expected approval from my parents. My grades were good, except for physical education. I received a Satisfactory, equivalent to a C, in gym class.

My mother made an exclamation when she saw my card. "Very good!" she said.

I left my card for my father to pick up later. When he got home, he came to where I was sitting on the couch and said, "I guess you can't do much better than that, except for this 'S' grade in phys. ed. What are you, some kind of fairy?"

I could tell he was three sheets to the wind.

*

I went into my parents' bedroom and opened my mother's trunk. She had brought it from China on a boat, first to Honolulu, then to San Francisco. She had taken a train from the West Coast to college in the East, where she met my father.

I had never seen my mother wear the silk dresses she kept in the trunk. I'd seen her wear those dresses only in pictures—photos taken at her wedding. I opened the heavy lid, and there the dresses were, along with "cash" coins on strings. The coins had square holes in the middle and embossed characters. There were a couple of sandalwood fans, which smelled good when I unfolded them.

I wasn't tempted to try on the dresses, though I liked the feel of the fabric on my fingers. I did try on a pair of high-heeled shoes, however. My feet slid down in the shoes until my toes were pressed against the tips. When I tried to walk, I tilted forward. I teetered around on the shoes, imagining life as a cross-dresser. It would have to be a secret life—I didn't think I could walk around openly in woman's heels and gain the respect of people around me. Oh, there might be a few fellow transvestites who would welcome a half-Asian dragon girl. But the idea seemed weird. Aside from the weirdness, the pain in my ankles and toes wasn't worth it. I didn't care how attractive they made me seem; I didn't want to learn to walk in those shoes.

*

Jerry returned on a morning when there was fog in the valley. It covered everything below the tops of the mountains, which were really no more than hills. Again, he sat at the picnic table in our yard. My brother and sister and I were inside, but we could see his shape through the fog. He stayed there for a long time; he didn't seem to need to interact with anyone.

Eventually, I brought him a glass of water. Inside, my mother stood at a screened window, where she could see and hear us, but she didn't come out.

Jerry looked at me and said a word I couldn't understand.

"What?" I asked.

"Catfish."

I understood "catfish" but didn't know why he said it. He pointed at the air around him and said, "Swimming."

I thought, "Swimming catfish," but still didn't get his point.

He made a motion with his hands and said, "Swimming in fog."

"Really?" I asked.

"Thick enough for fish to swim in," he said.

I looked around to see if I could spot any catfish. I knew they were a hardy breed—they could live a long time out of water. Why wouldn't they be swimming through the fog? I could picture a whiskered fish gliding toward me through the cloud. It would look me in the face, with its forward fins waving and its tail sweeping. It would hover there, wondering what I was doing in its element. In that event, would I try to catch it? Or would I let it swim by?

"Do you think we can catch these catfish?" I asked Jerry.

I didn't expect an answer, and he said nothing for at least a couple of minutes. Then he looked at me with complete comprehension and said, "I doubt it."

*

In my next phys. ed. class, all of the boys had to participate in a fitness test. We had to throw a ball, run six hundred yards, and do a standing broad jump. We were tested in the empty football stadium. Some boys could throw a softball the length of the field.

I was weak in all of the events, especially running. After dragging myself around the perimeter, I came in next to last. I was faster only than a boy who was too fat to jog.

But I could do the broad jump. I stood at the starting line, bent my knees, got low to the ground, and sprang. I landed solidly, without shifting my feet. The coach measured the distance from the starting line to my heels. I had covered eight feet, four inches.

"Good jump, Mouse," the coach said. "The world record is only eleven feet."

I was no mouse. I was a grasshopper, or a frog. I outjumped most of the other boys in the class. I was no fairy; I was a kangaroo. However, the fitness test result was a combination of all events. I received no award.

*

On a clear day—without morning fog—my mother told me Jerry had been taken away.

"Where?" I asked.

"To a community of disabled people. He has a job there."

"What is it?"

"Shredding paper."

"Oh." I pictured him feeding documents into a machine that hummed as it spit out strands of paper confetti. "I hope he's safe."

"He likes it. He especially likes dressing up for parties. They have parties regularly."

"What does he dress up as?" I asked.

"A fisherman, of course."

Animal Sightings

I had to watch the evening news as extra credit for my social studies class. But I couldn't get involved in it; I wasn't interested. There was a war in Vietnam, but the comments of the officials didn't engage me. I heard the body counts. The United States won every battle, but no resolution was reached. The conflict looked like it would never end.

I did the required reading in my textbook—about the organization of counties in our state—but that was all I did.

The next day, the social studies teacher gave a quiz on the assigned reading, and I knew the answers. I could name the capital of every county in our state. But the extra credit part stumped me. The question was, who is the president of the United States? The answer had to include the president's first, middle and last names. All I could think of was Johnson.

Later, the teacher said, "For the extra credit, I accepted Lyndon Baines Johnson, Lyndon B. Johnson or L.B. Johnson. But I didn't accept just Johnson."

*

My father opened a drawer in the dresser he shared with my mother and showed me his medals from the Army. One medal was for marksmanship; it was a cross with a circle in the middle. The four arms of the cross seemed to point to a bull's eye.

He picked up a cloth patch with the words "Hell on Wheels" and said, "This was for the Second Armored Division. I was with them in Seattle. On clear days, I could see Mount Rainier. I never made it out of the country."

He pulled out a pair of dog tags, threaded on a beaded chain. "When I die," he said, "you can send these to the veterans' department. The government will supply a headstone, with engraved dates and the name of the war I served in."

*

Later, my father said to me, "I could march 50 miles a day in the Army. It wasn't easy, but all of the men did it. You and I are going on a hike."

I put on heavy boots and a wool coat. My father gave me a hunting gun, and we trudged out the door. We headed straight for the nearest mountain. We crossed farm fields and arrived at a line of trees. We followed a path straight up the slope.

"If you see anything worth eating, shoot it," my father said.

I didn't see any game animals, but I did see, near the top of the mountain, a porcupine sleeping in a tree.

"Should I fire?" I asked.

"We could eat it if we were desperate," my father said. "We could build a fire and throw the whole thing in. The quills would burn off, and we'd have a cooked porcupine."

We left the animal alone. We hiked until the sun went down. We walked along the top of a ridge, down into a gap, up onto another ridge. Then we stumbled downhill and headed home.

"How many miles did we cover?" I asked when we got back.

"About three," my father said.

*

When my history teacher asked, "Where is the Isle of Rhodes?" I extended my arm, but the teacher called on someone else.

"Between Connecticut and Massachusetts," the other student said.

"No," the teacher said, "that's Rhode Island. This is the Isle of Rhodes, where the Colossus stood in the Classical Age."

The teacher recognized me, and I gave the right answer. "Next to Turkey," I said.

After class, a girl said to me, "You know, more kids would like you if you were dumber."

*

I started paying attention to the stupid guys in school. Actually, they were smart; they just acted stupid. When they were questioned in class, they would say, "Doh!" If surprised, they would say, "Dah-ee!" If pressed, they would say, "Whoa!" They were popular with both boys and girls.

I stopped raising my hand in class. When called on, I responded by saying, "Huh?"

I waited for my classmates to come to me as friends.

*

At home, I tried to do my homework while my father drank beer and complained about the weather. "It always rains here," he said. "I haven't seen the sun for days.

"It reminds me of Seattle," he continued. "Moss grows on everything there."

I pictured houses with soft, green exterior walls, cars with tendrils floating off their roofs.

"That's not right," my father added. "Moss grows only on the *north* side of everything."

My mental picture changed to houses with only one green side, cars only partially covered by green clumps of vegetation.

"Here," my father said, "mold grows on your bones. But it won't stop me. I can do anything in the rain. I can hike 50 miles with a full pack. And when I'm done, I'll be ready to make my art. I'm going to print broadsides and give them away. I'm going to tell the masses what's happening. I'm going to do what the Bolsheviks did. It's called propaganda."

He walked out the door then, in the direction of the local bar.

*

My mother showed up at the side of my bed when I was trying to sleep. She squatted so her face was on the level of mine. "We learned about the monkey king when I was a child," she said. "In Chinese, his name is Sun Wukong."

She said the words with a particular intonation. "Say it," she said.

I couldn't duplicate the sounds.

"Say it," she said more loudly, but I still couldn't.

"The monkey king is strong and fast," my mother said, "able to transform himself into other animals. He's a fighter. He has power in every strand of his hair. The only thing he can't do is change into a human, because he can't hide his tail.

"Your father is like that," she continued, "like a drunken monkey king. And like the king, he'll have to travel very far to find enlightenment."

We heard the door bang downstairs, signaling that my father had returned from the bar. "I'd better go," my mother said. "He'll want to talk to me."

*

The next time I watched the evening news, my father joined me. When a government official came on, my father said, "Those war mongers just want to make money. You know that copper-and-brass factory in our county?"

I nodded.

"That's a munitions factory. Everyone there is making casings for M-16 shells. The workers love the war.

"Someone's got to go there and tell them what's really happening," he continued. "I'll go there and hand out leaflets. The workers will mutiny."

My father put my brother and sister and me into his car and drove us to the factory. He couldn't get past the gate, so he parked on an access road. We all stood there as people drove past. My siblings and I looked at the ground while our father waved leaflets in the air. No one stopped to talk to us.

*

In social studies class, my teacher said to me, "I heard you were at the brass factory yesterday. What were you doing there? You're one of my best students. Your brother and sister will be good students after you.

"You should be leading a full life. Instead, you're part of a local Gang of Four. What are you going to do, re-educate everyone?"

*

At home, I studied a map of our state. We lived in Appalachia, where the mountains defined parallel valleys. Our state was between the South and the North; it was a swing state in the Civil War. After an hour of memorization, I was ready for a test in social studies class.

In the night, my mother didn't come to talk to me. I pretended to be asleep, but I wasn't. I could see the one street of the town through my window. It sloped downward from a point above our house. Below the house, it passed the hotel bar and the post office, then leveled out where Amish farms began.

While I was looking, an animal came over the rise in the street. The creature was shuffling along the middle of the pavement. It was as big as a bushel basket, but its features were indistinct. I couldn't make out its head. It didn't have fur: it had quills, which stuck straight out and dragged on the ground. It passed my window and moved downhill, toward the bar and post office.

Pushkin's Works

In English class, our teacher assigned books for a future report. The students could choose any book from a collection of titles that had been donated over the years. Most of the books were taken quickly. I waited until the end of the process, when one title remained. It was a thick book, with flimsy pages and tiny type.

"Who wants this one?" the teacher asked.

"I'll read it," I said.

"You can try it," she said.

*

Instead of reading the assigned book, I went into my father's "library"—the former dining room in our rented house. A drawing table was set up in front of one of the windows, and one wall was covered with bookshelves. I pulled out one of the books, a faded-red hardcover. I opened the front panel and saw a sheet of yellow paper folded twice, as if to fit in a business envelope. I saw that the letter was from my grandfather to my father.

The letter had been written before my parents were married. In it, the older man warned his son about marrying the woman he was engaged to. "You might love each other now," the letter read. "That might be fine for you. But think about your children. What will life be like for them?

"They won't have friends," the letter continued, "and they won't understand why. You're adults; you see things differently. What will happen with your kids?"

I put the letter back in the book and replaced the book on the shelf.

*

When my father caught me in his library, he said, "You have to read the Russians." He pointed to a group of books. They all had identical bindings, and the spines displayed the same title: *Pushkin's Works.*

"Alex Pushkin," he said, "was the greatest Russian poet. Did you know that? He fought and died for what he believed. Can you do that?"

I wanted to leave the room but couldn't. When I started for the doorway, my father said, "I'm not finished!"

I could have kept walking, but I stopped.

"I haven't read Pushkin myself," my father said, "because I haven't had time. Why haven't I had time? Because I'm always taking care of you! You and your brother and sister. An artist isn't meant to be caring for children. Was Pushkin a babysitter? No, he was a poet. He was a fighter. He wasn't a governess."

I stood in the doorway until my father said, "You can leave. Get out."

*

I asked my mother about her wedding.

"We had to take lessons before we were married," she said. "We had to write a letter to the Pope, promising not to use birth control."

"What was the ceremony like?" I asked.

"Not many people came," she said. "There were about seventeen people. Some came from the hospital lab where I was training. After the ceremony, they all went back to work."

"Where was it?"

"It was in a rectory, not the main church. We weren't allowed to have it in the main church. I don't know if that was a law or what. The rectory was on a cliff over a river. Below us was a house built for a French queen. She never came there. We could look over the cliff and see the house next to the river."

"Did you go anywhere afterward?"

"We went to Provincetown, where your father took lessons with a painter. They painted landscapes—the grass, the ocean, the dunes. I remember the town, from the paintings."

*

Over the next couple of weeks, I tried to read the book I'd chosen for class, but the prose was so complicated and archaic that I couldn't understand it.

I gathered that the setting was a house covered in cobwebs. An elderly lady lived there; she never moved from her chair. A boy came to visit her. At first, the two of them seemed unrelated, but the boy discovered his true identity by the end of the story. I plowed through almost the entire book before I realized what was going on. By the time the relationships became clear, the book was finished.

I wasn't clear or incisive when I gave my class presentation. I was nervous. I discussed what I thought was the author's approach, and I read some passages aloud. When I was done, I said, "That's the whole shebang."

As I was returning to my desk, a boy student said to me, "Zen, dude."

The teacher said, "You missed the author's point; obviously you weren't ready for this book—but you read well aloud."

*

At night, my father sat in my brother and sister's room and read to them as he sat on my sister's bed. I brought in a chair and listened.

I thought the material was compelling—it contained non-human characters in a fantastic world. These bipeds were of different species, yet they all coexisted in harmony—except for the slant-eyed ones who wanted to kill everyone else.

When I got tired, I went to my own bedroom to sleep.

In the morning, I walked past my brother and sister's room and saw that my father was still on my sister's bed. He was lying there, not sitting. The book he'd been reading was closed, beside him. My sister was sleeping next to him. My brother, in the neighboring bed, seemed unaware of what was going on.

*

I went into my father's library and scanned the shelves. I looked in the book where I'd found the letter from my grandfather and saw that the sheet of paper was missing.

Presently, my father appeared at the doorway. He had a bottle of beer in one hand and a lit cigarette in the other. "I was proud of my father," he said. "He went to night school, and he worked his way up. I went to school, too, but I didn't work my way up. That's because I got no help from the people around me. You don't understand me. You can't."

He left me there so that, I guessed, he could get another beer.

I didn't know what to do in the library. I picked up a volume of *Pushkin's Works*. There were passages in Russian, which meant nothing to me. The parts in English spoke of loss, loneliness, mortality, beauty, the passage of time, the impossibility of permanence.

The material was serious. It must have been what life was about, for a great poet. But it was alien to me.

*

At some point during the night, I had a dream. In it, I was going somewhere with my mother, brother and sister. My mother was moving us to a new house. At first, I didn't realize we were moving: I thought we were just visiting. Then I saw we'd brought some of our possessions—not many, but we wouldn't be able to go back for more. When I asked why we were moving, my mother said, "Something happened."

She meant our father did something. Maybe he said something. Or maybe he told us to do something, to leave. In any case, he wasn't around anymore.

In our new house, I took an upstairs bedroom. It had a closet and a couple of beds. I started to put together a stereo system by connecting sets of wires. It was hard, close work, but I managed it. Then I realized I wouldn't have the room to myself. I'd have a roommate, maybe my brother or sister. I didn't know which one.

I looked forward to getting the stereo working. I would put on a record, something in the blues-rock genre, and I would play the music loud, just like the album cover said to do.

The Mountain Man

I walked to the post office to pick up my family's mail. When I went through the swinging doors, I saw that the dusty room was empty. Presently, the postmistress came out of her living area and stepped behind the counter.

While she checked a pigeonhole for mail, I looked at the Wanted posters on the wall. They showed fugitives' faces and described their crimes. Some of the men were "armed and dangerous"; others were "extremely dangerous." I tried to memorize what they looked like, in case I saw one of them. If I did see one, there wasn't much I could do, because I had no weapon. I would just have to run as fast as I could in the opposite direction.

The postmistress handed me a roll of mail, and I left through the heavy wooden doors.

*

On my way home, I saw a couple of hunters outside the hotel bar. They were wearing plaid wool coats and fleece-lined boots. As I walked past, I saw a dead deer in the back of their pickup truck. The deer had no antlers. In buck season, it looked like an illegal kill.

In the truck cab, a gun rack held two rifles. Both of the guns had scopes and shoulder straps. I could imagine the hunters marching through the woods like soldiers, guns slung over their shoulders, barrels pointing into the air.

One of the men noticed me and asked, "Doing any hunting this season?"

I shook my head no and walked on.

*

At the dinner table, my father spoke while my brother and sister and I listened. "There's a mountain man on the loose in Shade Gap," he said. "He kidnapped a teenager. The FBI went after him with a dog. First, he shot the dog; then he shot an agent. That man has courage."

"All these guns," my mother said from her post by the stove.

"He was lonely, so he took her," my father said. "They'll never catch him. He knows the mountains and the hollows, just like I know the land around here."

"Why do you need to know it?" my brother asked.

"If they come for me," my father said. "I'll know where to go."

"What will you do for food?" my sister asked.

"I'll be armed. I'll hunt for food."

"I saw a deer without antlers on a truck," I said.

"Enough!" my father shouted. "I've had enough of you kids for a while."

My siblings and I finished our meal in silence.

*

After dinner, my father left the house. While he was gone, my siblings and I watched television and did our homework.

At a late hour, my mother picked up the phone and made a call. I could tell she was talking to the bartender down the street.

She said my name and handed me the phone.

"Come down here," my father said. "There are a couple of guys who want to talk to you."

I had to get partly dressed in order to go out—sweat pants, shoes but no socks, a coat but no shirt. When I walked into the hotel bar, I saw the same two hunters I'd seen earlier.

My father introduced me by saying, "This is my son. Soon to be my drunken son."

"You know," one of the hunters said, "we didn't poach that deer."

"No," said the other. "The deer jumped in front of the truck."

"If you want poachers," the first said, "go up the road. Those guys cut wood in the day and poach at night."

"Have a drink," my father said.

I was too young to drink, so I had a soda. When I was finished, my father showed no sign of leaving the bar. I left by myself.

*

During the night, I woke to the sound of my father's voice. I couldn't discern most of what he was saying. Among the sharp sounds, I heard, "I can't make art with kids around. I go into my workroom, and soon enough I get interrupted. I have to stop what I'm doing and entertain children."

"They learn from you," my mother said.

"My oldest kid's a candy-ass. He'll never amount to anything. I'd give him a dollar to be good, but he'll be good for nothing."

When he started talking about me, I tried to stop listening.

*

A couple of days later, my family and I watched a news report on television. The mountain man had been on the run. Wherever he went, he took the teenaged girl with him. The two of them had climbed stony ridges and hiked through valleys. They stayed a step ahead of the authorities. Finally, they were spotted as they passed a farmhouse. An FBI agent was stationed there. A boy who lived on the farm and the agent both shot at the kidnapper. One of the bullets killed him—it turned out to be from the agent's gun. The teenaged girl had a chain around her neck, but she was unharmed.

After the report, my father said, "The FBI goes after a lot of people, but why did they have to shoot the mountain man?"

*

The next day, my father took my siblings and me with him to a beer distributor. He pulled his car into the loading area, under a large sign that read "Discount," and opened the car trunk. An attendant lifted two cases and put them down, and my father paid.

"I'm set now," he said as he drove home. "I don't need your company. I can drink on my own."

*

I went to my room to write some letters. The problem was, I didn't know who to write to. I had some relatives on the other side of the world—my mother's family—but I didn't have their addresses. Worse, I didn't know their language. I looked around and saw a coupon on a cereal box. I could write away for a prize, a plastic ring with a hidden compartment, but I had no money to pay for it. So I went to the post office empty-handed.

As the postmistress checked for my family's mail, I looked around the room at the other offerings. There was penny candy for sale at the counter, two loaves of bread next to the candy, and cigarettes on a shelf out of reach. Next to the mail window, there was the sheaf of Wanted posters. Some of the criminals were murderers, others were kidnappers. The mountain man hadn't been on the loose long enough to make it onto a poster. The faces meant nothing to me.

*

At dinner, my mother served a new food. It was the reddest meat I'd ever seen. It was so red; it didn't look cooked. "Your father brought it home," my mother explained.

"It's from that deer that was hit by the truck," my father said. "The hunters gave it to me. That deer is going to get two families through the winter."

He left the room. When he returned, he was carrying a couple of bottles of beer.

"I'm going into my workroom," he said. "I'm silk-screening a book about politics. But right now, I'm going to drink to the mountain man."

*

I walked up a dirt lane that led away from town. Shortly, I came to an abandoned house. Its walls were still standing, but its door and windows were missing. The remains of a chimney stood at one corner, and an old millstone lay on the ground.

I thought I could live in the house. I wouldn't have heat, but I could build a fire at the bottom of the chimney. I could survive on the food I'd find in the fields and woods. I'd get lonely, but there was a girl in my class at school who might come with me. If she didn't, I would have to fasten her to the millstone, which looked quite heavy. I would become the Mountain Boy.

Rings of Ice

Late at night, my father arrived home from the local bar. I was in bed but not asleep. I heard him shout, "Someone is coming to get me!"

My mother came out of the bathroom and walked past my open door. She was wearing a robe, and she had curlers on her head. I didn't know why she would want to twist her straight, black hair.

She walked downstairs and asked my father, "Who is it?"

"A guy from the bar. He didn't like what I said about the war. He thinks I'm a Communist."

My mother went out to the front porch. I looked through a window and saw the headlights of an approaching car, but I couldn't see who was inside.

I could hear my mother talking to the driver. "You wouldn't like it if someone shot your cat," she said, "so why do you want to shoot other people?"

My father stayed in the house.

"Where is he?" the driver asked.

"Life is simple," my mother said. "The Vietnamese aren't your enemy. Everything has beauty. That's what Confucius says."

"We'll get him next time," the driver said as the car rolled away.

When my mother came back inside, my father said, "'Confucius say, Confucius say.' I don't care what Confucius say. I'm going to teach my children what I say."

*

As I rode the school bus the next morning, I noticed a new boy getting on. He had light-brown hair that was short but wasn't shaved. The bus picked him up just after the road from my town ended. He lived along the highway, in a small house covered with green shingles. The house had no yard; a farm field came up to the outside walls.

I didn't talk to the boy because he didn't sit next to me. No one ever sat next to me unless there were no other empty seats. I was the last to be joined. On this day, the seat beside me remained empty, so I just glanced at the boy. Out the bus window, I saw fields of chopped cornstalks sliding by. Around the bases of the stalks were rings of ice.

*

When my father found out that new children were living nearby, he said, "I'm going to visit them."

He went out, and when he came back he had a girl with him. She was about my sister's age, maybe 8 years old. "Two kids moved in," my father explained. "I left her brother at home."

He brought the girl and my sister to his "studio," a side room filled with insects in boxes. When my brother and I tried to follow, he said, "You'll have to amuse yourselves" and shut the door.

Later, I asked my sister what they had been doing.

"There were pieces of colored paper on the floor," she said. "He told us to roll around on them, so we did. We rolled around, and he took pictures of us with his instant camera."

I went into the studio to see the pictures. All I found were some scraps in a wastebasket. The prints had been cut with scissors. I could make out a knee, an arm, a face, hair, but I couldn't put the pieces together to form a whole figure.

*

I took my bike onto the two-lane road outside our house. As I pedaled, cold air blew around my neck and through my gloves. I rode to the new boy's house and saw him outside. He greeted me, then said, "I want to show you something."

I went into the house and saw there was no furniture in the rooms. And there was no back door; there was only an opening in a back wall for a door. A sheet of heavy translucent plastic covered the opening. The house wouldn't hold much heat, if it had a source of heat.

The boy's younger sister walked past us. "I'm not going back to your house," she said to me. "Your father's a freak."

The boy opened a drawer and brought out a firearm—it was the largest handgun I'd ever seen. The "pistol" was about two feet long and had a bolt action. On top of the barrel was a scope. The grip allowed only one hand on it. When the boy gave me the gun, I could barely lift it.

"Is this yours?" I asked.

"My father gave it to me," the boy said, "before he left."

"Where is he now?"

"I don't know. Maybe Florida."

We took the gun to the field that surrounded the house. The boy pushed a cartridge into the chamber, lay on the ground, and set the handgrip on a rock. He sighted through the scope and fired. I covered my ears too late to muffle the explosion.

"Your turn," he said.

I took my turn. I didn't sight at a target. I shot toward where the field met the mountain.

*

At dinner, my father said, "I've had enough of capitalism. It's just a stage in history. Soon, we'll have socialism, then communism. We'll have them even sooner if we start a revolution."

"I'm tired of being the worker," my mother said. "Why don't you get a job?"

"I'm going to bring socialism," my father said. "That's my job."

"You do that," my mother said.

"I would do it, if you and your chink children weren't holding me back."

I heard what he said, but I made no response. I left the table to do my homework. My task was to build a model of the Tower of London. I didn't have a clear idea of how to proceed. I looked up a photo in an encyclopedia; then I found a cardboard box and started to cut it with scissors.

When my father saw what I was doing, he went into his studio and shut the door. By the time I went to bed, he hadn't come out.

*

My mother came to my bed and said, "Don't be hurt. Your father calls you names because you don't look like him. You look like me."

After she left the room, I tried to widen my eyelids so they would look Western. I pulled my eyelashes back with my fingers and held them. I hoped that if I stretched them enough, they would stay that way.

*

In the morning, I saw what my father had done. He had used the materials in his studio to build an exact replica of the Tower of London. He had constructed turrets and ramparts, and had punched openings for windows. He'd drawn details with India ink and laid a stone-like patina on the outside walls. He'd mounted the castle on a Homasote board and painted grass and bushes on the base.

My mother drove me to school so I could carry the model easily. As I rode, I glanced at her hair. I didn't see the effect of the curlers she wore at night. Her hair was perfectly straight.

In the classroom, the teacher said, "That's a very nice project your father made."

*

I rode the school bus home in the afternoon. As usual, the seat beside me was empty. I looked out the window at the mown fields going by. At the bases of the cornstalks were the same rings of ice I'd seen earlier.

I could see a line of trees that marked where a creek ran. At the edge of a field, next to the trees, a fox was running in the same direction as the bus. I could tell by its large tail that it was a fox, not a dog. If I had the new boy's gun, I could shoot at it. The handgun was a high-powered rifle, only with a shorter barrel. It could drop an animal at 300 yards. That's all I wanted to do: hold the gun and fire it. I didn't even need a target. The fox could go on its way. I wanted to work the bolt and pull the trigger. I wanted to be enveloped in the sound of the exploding gunpowder charge.

Under the Guns

My father took me to a "turkey shoot" in a field next to a firehouse. At the event, people didn't shoot turkeys, they fired at paper targets. They used shotguns, and the pellets that ripped the paper closest to the bull's eye won. Since it wasn't possible to aim a shotgun, winning was a matter of chance. The prize was a frozen turkey.

My father positioned me about thirty yards from a target and gave me a 20-gauge shotgun. "Go ahead. Blast away," he said.

I lifted the gun to my shoulder and looked down the barrel. When I pulled the trigger, the explosion was deafening. I felt the recoil in my arm and glimpsed a shock wave in the air. A man ran in front of me and yelled, "Clear!" as he took down the target I'd shot at.

My shot didn't make much of an impression—a couple of nicks were gone from the edges of the paper.

Shortly, my father said, "These cartridges are expensive, and we have to pay for each try. It's time to go."

I had fired once. We left the grounds without a turkey.

*

Later, my father took me to hunt for quail. We hiked through fields above the town, kicking at clumps of weeds to scare up game.

As I walked along the spine of a hill, I could see the valley stretching away. The ridges were parallel in this part of Appalachia, and the valleys ran straight for miles. Below me, I could see the town with its one paved street, and the firehouse lawn, where the turkey shoot had been held.

I had my shotgun ready at my side. With one hand I bore the weight of the gun, while I kept my other hand around the chamber. I rested one finger on the trigger guard and another on the safety. I could raise the firearm, release the safety and pull the trigger all in one motion.

As I walked, I saw many small birds, none of them fair game, and none of them quail.

Suddenly, I saw a brownish-colored bird fly up. I lifted my gun and shot the creature out of the air. The blast scattered the feathers.

My father came over to look. The bird was spotted black and brown, and it had a yellow chest.

"Is it a quail?" I asked.

"No," he said. "It's a meadowlark."

"Should we bring it home?" I asked.

"No. It's too small. After cleaning, it would be one bite."

We left the downed meadowlark in the field. Scavengers would find it sooner or later.

*

Another day, my father took me in his car to a stretch of highway that ran between fields. We weren't carrying guns. He parked on the gravel shoulder and unloaded photography equipment. I followed as he walked into a sea of grain stalks and set up an instant camera on a tripod. He pointed the lens at the striated fields—they lay in rows until they reached the nearest ridge. The fields were shades of yellow and brown, and the hill was dark purple. He took several frames of the fields, hill and sky.

"I'm going to make paintings from these photos," he said as he held the prints in the air to dry. "Then I'm going to turn the paintings into prints. I'll sell them for a couple of dollars each, so anyone can afford them."

I looked across the field and didn't see any game animals, or any animals at all, not even small birds. The farmland was totally barren.

At home, when I walked into my father's studio, I saw the photos he'd made; they were lying on a table. When I moved them to the side, I saw some images of my sister, nude from the waist up. I didn't know when these photos had been taken, and I didn't know why my sister had agreed to them.

*

After small-game season, my father marched me into the woods for deer. We both wore heavy boots, and I followed behind. He didn't call out the steps, but I could hear a cadence in my head: "To the left, to the left, to the left, right, left …" He found a likely place—next to a trail made by deer hooves—and stopped there. The idea was to stand in one place and wait for an animal to walk by. I found a tree to lean against, and my father took a spot out of my sight.

I got tired of waiting, so I played with the gun I was carrying—it was a .410 shotgun loaded with rifled slugs. I pretended I saw a deer running across my field of vision. I brought the gun up to my shoulder and swung the barrel as if leading the deer. I didn't pull the trigger; I didn't even take off the safety. But as I grew more bored, I became bolder. I pulled the gun up and slid the safety off, but I didn't touch the trigger. After a few more practice moves, the gun went off, startling me. I must have squeezed the trigger.

I liked the sound—I'd wanted to fire the gun. I'd been holding it for hours without shooting.

I took out the spent cartridge and buried it under leaves as my father came running. "Did you shoot?" he asked. "I heard a close shot."

"It must have been someone else," I said.

"A deer must have run through here, and someone must have seen it," he said.

Later, I gave back the cartridges he'd given me. He counted them and noticed one was missing.

"I must have dropped it," I said.

"Yeah," he said. "You must have dropped it."

At home, my father made me clean the guns. "Take this cloth and put oil on it," he said. "Run it through the barrels, then wipe down the metal parts. Get rid of the powder and rust. You're not done until the guns shine!"

I spent the evening wiping and polishing while my brother and sister watched television. My mother spent the time in the kitchen with her apron on. My father spent his evening at the local bar.

*

In school, a student asked me, "Did you hear about Bob?"

"Bob who?" I asked.

"The student council president. He skipped school to go hunting and got shot.

"How?"

"He was crawling under a barbed-wire fence, and he was holding his gun. It went off."

"Did it hit him?"

"It killed him."

I knew the boy, or knew who he was. Everyone knew who he was. That day, I noticed that students were quiet in the hallways and classrooms.

Later, I discovered that I'd forgotten my lunch. I didn't have money to eat in the cafeteria, so I went to the alternate lunch area—a storeroom—and sat at a long, Formica-topped table. When the kids around me noticed that I had no food, they gave me parts of their lunches. I got half of a peanut butter-and-jelly sandwich, one celery stick and one carrot stick. The food was good—much better than nothing.

*

My father presented me with one of the guns I'd cleaned. "I want you to have this," he said.

"I'll take it." I said, "so I can sell it."

"You can't do that," he said. He pointed to the metal that enclosed the chamber and trigger mechanism. "See," he said, "there's an engraving of a fox on one side and a grouse on the other."

"I still want to sell it."

"You won't want to give up this gun," he said, "even when you're my age."

I took the gun from him and put it in its canvas case. I brought the covered firearm to my bedroom and propped it in a corner, just behind the door. It balanced perfectly on its blunt end there.

At the Shore

In the summer, my family traveled by car to a beach. While we rode, my brother and sister and I amused ourselves by identifying passing license plates. At first, most of the tags were from Pennsylvania; later, those plates vanished and licenses from New Jersey appeared.

Between rounds of the game, I read a *Mad* magazine. The line I found funniest was "It's crackers to slip a rozzer the dropsy in snide." I understood the message: It was crazy to sneak a buzzing sound in a slippery place with a cynical attitude.

We traveled away from dairy farms into the pine barrens, where my father stopped along the road. All of us got out to walk on the shoulder. The ground, I noticed, had turned from loam to sand. My brother and sister and I looked for the biggest pinecones we could find—round ones the size of grapefruits.

When we arrived on an island between a bay and the ocean, I could smell brine and decaying sea life. At our motel, the parking lot was covered with pebbles, and the rooms were uniformly small and damp.

*

There was a pool in the middle of the motel parking lot. On the bottom was a painted red seahorse. The pool was just the right size for me. I could swim from one side to the other without stopping to breathe. When my siblings joined me, I jumped on them and pushed their heads under the water.

At night, a submerged floodlight illuminated the pool. I went in by myself and swam toward and away from the light repeatedly, torpedoing through the warm water.

*

At the beach, my father sat on the sand above the water line. He was wearing clothes but no shoes. The sand there was powdery and hot. In swimming suits, my mother and siblings and I huddled nearby. We had no sun umbrella.

"You have to bob in the waves," my father said to me.

I walked across the wet sand and into the surf. The waves were higher than my head, but I leaped just before they crashed.

I heard raised voices coming from where my family was sitting. When I looked toward the sound, a wave hit the back of my head and carried me forward. My face scraped against the sand. When I stood up, I could feel a rough patch from my forehead to my chin.

The brush burn didn't stop me. I returned to the water and bobbed in the waves.

Shortly, my mother and siblings arrived at the surf. "I didn't grow up near the ocean," my mother said. "But my city had a deep spring, where people thought a dragon lived. Boys would dive in and try to reach the bottom. They would leave a wish for the dragon there."

I walked out of the water and joined my father on the dry sand.

*

In the evening, my father took us to a local restaurant. White cloths covered the tables, and an assortment of silverware framed each place setting.

When we ordered, I asked for a special item. Shortly, the rest of my family received their food, but my dish didn't arrive. No one said anything about the oversight. I sat at an empty square of tablecloth while the rest of my family ate.

Noting my silence, my father said, "He's sulking again. That's what he does when he doesn't get his way. Who knows what he wants? He won't say."

I knew better than to comment. If I did, my father might have shouted at me.

My mother began cleaning the neck of a ketchup bottle with a napkin. It wasn't her job to do that, but she seemed to need to do something.

When everyone else was nearly finished eating, a waiter noticed my absent dish and brought it with an extra—a saucer of pasta.

*

My brother and sister and I rode with our father to a nearby bay. We took spinning rods out of the car trunk and walked to the water. We used pieces of frozen fish as bait. Soon, we were reeling in blowfish. They were small but had sharp beaks. If we didn't pull them out of the water fast enough, they bit through our lines and fell away.

We brought a couple of the fish back to the motel. We carried them in a bucket of water—they had blown themselves up to the size of softballs. "It's a delicacy where I grew up," my mother said, "but part of the fish is poison."

"I don't care if they're poison," my father said, taking out a scaling knife.

"Save the tails," my mother said.

My siblings and I watched television while my father butchered the fish.

*

Later, my father went out to the parking lot and tried to start his car. I could hear the engine turning over, without catching. He came back in and said, "I'm out of gas."

He went to the motel office and returned with a piece of plastic tubing. He opened a different car's gas cap, inserted the hose and sucked on the free end. When the gasoline reached his mouth, he slid the hose from his lips and covered the end with his thumb. He spit out the excess gasoline. He put the free end into the empty fish bucket and held the hose while the gas flowed. He poured what he'd siphoned into his own tank.

He started his car and tore out of the parking lot.

*

I woke when my father returned, but I didn't get out of bed.

He stumbled around, then put a hand on a wall to steady himself. "I went to a bar," he said to my mother, "and I stayed until it closed. No one talked to me. I didn't care; I had Mr. Beam for company.

"Then I went to the beach," he continued. "It reminded me of when I was in the Army. I was stationed on the coast. That's where I was when I heard my sister passed away."

"She had a heart attack," my mother said.

"No," my father said. "My parents said it was a heart attack. She killed herself."

"Why?"

"She said she was looking for a waveless bay, a place of calm. But that wasn't the reason. Her boyfriend was a Jew."

"I'm not a Catholic, either," my mother said.

"Vacations are for the middle class!" my father shouted. "We're not bourgeois! We're leaving tomorrow."

*

On our way home, we stopped at a convenience store. Inside, my father asked if I wanted a magazine. "Do you want a *Mad* or a *Cracked*?" he asked.

I didn't want a humor magazine. I picked up a publication that promoted the bachelor lifestyle and featured nude women, and took it to the counter. To my surprise, the cashier sold it to me.

*

At home, I took out my souvenirs from our trip: a pinecone from the barrens and the porn magazine. I put the pinecone on a shelf and examined the magazine's centerfold. A model was standing next to a gym locker with a white towel over her shoulder. She was looking back at me and smiling. The towel covered her front but not her behind.

I wanted to do some towel snapping of my own. I knew I was crackers. I wanted to slip something somewhere; I wanted to find the dropsy. I didn't care if I was being snide.

*

I couldn't sleep. I was anxious; I couldn't let my mind wander. I tried different sleep positions: on my back with my hands over my chest, like a mummy; on my side with my fists on the mattress, like a fetus. But no position was relaxing.

I got up and left my room. I walked around the two unused rooms upstairs. They were drafty and smelled like dust. The sound of my footsteps must have carried, because my father appeared. "You have to stop bothering me," he said as he escorted me back to my room. "You can take a walk, you can take an aspirin, you can drink a beer, or you can count a thousand sheep."

I just wanted him to leave my room, but I didn't say anything. I just lay there. Presently, he walked out.

On the Go

My father decided to teach me how to tie flies for fishing. "You should learn to make something useful," he said.

He clamped the point of a fishhook between the metal jaws of a vise so that the eye and shank of the hook were exposed. He wrapped a foil strip around the bare wire. Then he attached deer hair by holding it next to the wire and wrapping thread around it. He tied the thread and sealed the assembly with glue. "What does it look like?" he asked.

"A tuft of hair?" I asked.

"It's a bucktail streamer! A wet fly! It doesn't float. You make it swim like a minnow."

When my father wasn't around, I put the tip of one of my fingers into the vise and turned the handle. The jaws had ridges, and I could feel the metal digging into my skin. My fingertip would have burst if I'd kept going, but I stopped before that happened. When I loosened the jaws, I saw that my skin had serrated marks on it. Even my fingernail was dented.

*

I saw that the grass and weeds had grown tall in my family's yard. We owned a lawn mower, but no one wanted to use it. My brother and sister were too small to handle the machine, my mother was at work during the day, and my father was too hung over to exert himself.

I went into the back yard and took the mower from its shed. The machine was heavy, not easy to push. I flipped it onto its side and dislodged caked grass from the blade shield. Then I righted the mower and filled the small tank with gas from a spouted can.

I grabbed the handle of the starter cord and jerked it. After a couple of tugs, the engine caught. I engaged the gear, and the mower leaped away from me. I had to hold it back as it ate its way across the lawn. Where the grass and weeds were thick, I tilted the mower backward, so its front wheels were in the air. I placed the spinning blade over the stalks and brought it down. Homemade hay shot from the side chute.

What I really wanted to do was take the engine off the lawn mower and use it to power a go-cart. I'd seen a nice go-cart made from a metal frame and a rear-mounted engine. A classmate of mine had built it. He wanted to be an engineer, but instead of attending classes, he would tear around the fields next to the high school on his buggy.

When I came in from mowing the lawn, my father called me to his studio. He was sitting on a stool at a drawing board, but there wasn't any artwork in front of him. There was a pile of loose tobacco on the wood surface. On the nearby table was an open bottle of beer. "Manicured lawns are for the bourgeoisie," my father said. "Is that what you want to be—middle class, like everyone else?"

I looked at the floor and didn't say anything.

"I say, let the grass grow," my father said. "Let the spiders live. Let them weave orbs in the weeds. Let them catch flies!"

He played with the pile of tobacco with his finger, then rolled a cigarette. He lit the cigarette and picked bits of tobacco off his lips.

"I want a dune buggy," I said.

"Oh, you'll have a dune buggy," he said. "You'll have metal to ride on. All you have to do is build it.

"I've got other things to do," he added. "I'm just getting started. It'll take me the next twenty years, if you don't hold me back."

*

I didn't steal the engine from the lawn mower. What I did was, I removed the wheels and axles from a toy wagon and found some pieces of wood. I used a plank for the base of my go-cart and a square block for the seat.

I took the cart to the town's one street, to a point near the top of the only hill. I used my feet as brakes, then let go. I rolled past my house, the hotel bar and the post office. I didn't stop moving until I got to the empty carnival grounds. When I looked back, I saw my father coming out of the bar.

I dragged the cart up the hill with an attached rope. When I came within earshot, he said, "I don't think you're ready for the Soap Box Derby.

"Come in for a drink," he added.

I followed him into the bar and sat on a stool. The room was dark, and a television on a high shelf was playing.

My father got a bourbon for himself and a soda for me. We sat and watched the Miss America pageant on the TV. During the talent portion, one of the contestants led an orchestra with a small baton. "Congratulations to our young conductor!" the MC said.

"How much do you think she can conduct?" my father asked.

"What?" I said. I thought I hadn't heard him correctly.

"How much electricity can she conduct?"

I got up and walked into the large, empty dining room. I went to the jukebox and put in a coin. I listened to a song about seeing a seventeen-year-old girl standing there. The way she looked was beyond compare.

*

Later, I gave my brother and sister rides on my go-cart. We rolled down the one street and walked back up repeatedly.

"It's like a surfboard," my brother said.

"It's bumpy," my sister said.

Mostly, we rode solo, but sometimes we rode double. One time, I went down the hill with my sister, and when we were walking back up, she said, "I tried to tell them about our father at school."

"What about him?" I asked.

"About what he does to me."

"What did they say?"

"They didn't believe me.

*

At home, we tried to get our mother to take the cart for a spin, but she said, "I want to ride a tricycle. You know, one of the big ones with a basket. Since I can't ride a bicycle, I could get around on a trike. I could go shopping with it."

"I thought everyone rode a bicycle where you grew up," I said.

"There were more bicycles than cars," my mother said. "I saw bicycle jams on the roads every day. But I never learned to ride because I didn't need to. We had help-ers."

*

I went to the local creek alone. As I approached, I saw that the water was clear. The motion of my approach made fish shoot away, up and down the stream. I stood still, and after a few minutes two trout returned. They lay a few feet out from me. One was green, the other brown. Their coloring had changed to match the algae, or the sand, on the bottom of the stream, but I could see the speckles on their skin that distinguished them from the background. I stood there, throwing my bucktail wet fly downstream and working it back so it looked like a minnow.

Suddenly, I noticed that my father was beside me. I hadn't heard him arrive. He had his fishing gear with him, but he wasn't fishing. He was watching me. He crouched on the bank next to me as I cast my streamer into the water.

His presence made me uncomfortable, but I couldn't ask him to leave. I just kept fishing. After a while, he straightened up and walked away.

*

I caught one of the trout I'd been fishing for. I held the creature in one hand while I lined the bottom of my creel with wet grass. I put the fish into the sack. I could feel it flopping against my side as I walked along the stream. After a short while, the movement stopped.

I knelt beside the water, took the trout from my creel and sliced its underside with a pocketknife. I grabbed the gills with a finger and pulled out the entrails. I threw the guts onto the bank for raccoons to eat. I washed the blood out of the cavity, then replaced the fish on its bed of wet grass in my creel.

At home, I laid the fish in the sink in the kitchen. When my mother saw my catch, she made an exclamation of approval.

*

At night, I heard the television playing in the kitchen. I knew my father was down there, watching and drinking. The hour was late, but I was still awake.

I knew that my father would fall asleep without turning off the television. The programming would change from a show with actors, to the national anthem, to black-and-white "snow," and my father's head would be resting on the kitchen table.

Sweet Music

I brought home an assignment from music class. The task was to memorize the lyrics to the "Marines' Hymn."

When my father heard about the homework, he asked, "Why are you learning that song?"

"To serve my country?" I asked.

"No son of mine is going to be a leatherneck," my father said. "I'm pulling you out of that class.

"Your teachers are all gung-ho," he continued, "except one, Mrs. Sadowsky. She's from the old country. I'm going to take you to Mrs. Sadowsky's house for private music lessons."

"I don't want private lessons," I said.

"See this?" my father said, pointing to the table in front of him. There was a sketch on paper, next to an open bottle of beer. "This is my new series. I'm going to print these, and I'm going to distribute them like propaganda."

I looked at a drawing of a classical Greek shepherd, with curly dark hair and a thick beard, leaning on a crook. He was clothed in a white robe. In front of him, a boy in a similar robe was on one knee, playing a lyre. The boy's head was bowed over the instrument as his fingers touched the strings.

"After some lessons with Mrs. Sadowsky, you'll play music for me," my father said. "That's how we'll spend our evenings. I'll listen while you play. Now, get out of my sight."

*

My sister came along when my father took me to Mrs. Sadowsky's house. Off the highway, we followed a stream for a short while, then parked outside a ranch-style home. A dog with a collar and chain crouched in the yard. The dog appeared to be resting.

My sister approached the animal, and it charged at her. The chain attached to its collar was very long: the tether didn't stop the dog from reaching her. The mad animal sank its teeth into her calf.

I went inside while my father drove my sister to the hospital.

Mrs. Sadowsky said to me, "Our dog is usually harmless."

She changed the subject and asked, "You've come for music lessons. What are you learning to play?"

"The lyre," I said.

"I don't have a lyre," she said. "But I have a harp."

She sat at the huge instrument and demonstrated. "You can either pluck," she said, hooking her fingertips around the strings, "or you can make sweeping strokes. Now, you try."

I sat on a stool facing the harp and hit the strings a few times. The notes sounded good. We went through the lesson until my father and sister returned. My sister had a thick white bandage around her lower leg, but she was walking.

"I could have that dog's head," my father said. "I could have it tested for rabies."

"The dog is mean sometimes," Mrs. Sadowsky said, "but it's not infected."

*

My mother and father had an argument about the treatment for rabies.

"She should get the shots," my father said, "even though they're painful."

"Medical science knows very little about disease," my mother said.

"You're a lab technician," my father said. "You should know."

"I don't know," my mother said. "I just know how to do blood tests. I'll take a sample to the hospital."

"You can't find rabies that way."

"I can find some things."

My sister had to sit at the kitchen table with her arm out while my mother rubbed her skin to find a vein and jabbed a needle in.

*

I did my English homework on the living-room couch. The exercises went quickly, save for one, which contained a crossword clue: "An insect that won't quit." Part of the answer was already filled in: the word "QUIT" with blanks before and after it. I asked my mother, "What's the name of an insect with the word 'quit' in it?"

"I have no idea," my mother said.

I thought some more. "Mos-QUIT-o!" I said.

"Where I grew up," my mother said, "mosquitoes carried malaria. There were warning signs near water holes: 'If you see mosquitoes breeding here, tell the authorities!' I got bitten, but I didn't get malaria. All I got was scarlet fever."

"Did you almost die?" I asked.

"I don't remember. I was very young, 5 or 6. My skin turned red, and my throat got sore. I was sick for a long time."

*

I walked into my father's workroom when he wasn't there. I pulled a box from a shelf and saw that it contained beetles on pins. All of the exo-parts were intact: legs, antennae and shells. Some of the shells were iridescent blue; others had markings like hieroglyphics. The beetles were lined up in rows and grouped by size.

My father came in and saw me looking. "I collected all of those when I was a teenager," he said, "before I became an artist. I still have dreams about chasing butterflies. In my sleep, I'm running after big, colorful swallowtails, but they're just out of reach."

*

In school, I went to Mrs. Sadowsky's chorus practice. She didn't have us sing the "Marines' Hymn." Instead, she played piano accompaniment for "Blowin' in the Wind."

We all stood up to sing. A couple of athletic boys were positioned behind me. Instead of following the lyrics, they shouted, "Blow! Blow! Blow!"

*

When I got home, I walked across our cement porch and opened the door to the kitchen. I stepped onto a carpet. The linoleum floor was covered so that our dogs could sleep there. The two dogs lay under the table. On a cabinet top, a small black-and-white television flickered, but no one was watching. My mother wasn't home yet from her job at the hospital.

When I came into the living room, I saw my brother and sister.

"We're bored," my sister said.

"What should we do?" my brother asked.

I sat on the couch. On the windowsill next to me was an aquarium that held two inches of water. In it, three guppies swam around an aquatic vine.

"We could open the door to the kitchen," I said.

"Yeah," my brother said, laughing.

He opened the door, and the dogs ran into the living room. They pranced in front of us with their tongues out and tails wagging. Their nails clicked against the living room's linoleum floor.

*

My brother and sister and I took our dogs to a farm field and started to cross it. My sister still had the bandage on her leg.

Presently, we came to a pasture where sheep were grazing. The farm belonged to an Amish family.

We came to a sheep corral. Alongside the fence, we saw some sheep carcasses. When we looked farther, we saw other dead animals—chickens and ducks. The sight made the living sheep less cute and appealing.

*

Later, my mother reported on my sister. "She doesn't have rabies," my mother said, "and she doesn't have mononucleosis, either. She doesn't seem to be anemic. Her blood tests came out negative.

"But I want to take your blood," my mother said to me, "so I can see if you're using drugs."

I sat in a chair in the kitchen and extended my arm. My mother wrapped a rubber cord around my bicep and took out a syringe. She probed with the needle until she found a vein, then stuck the needle in.

*

At night, I played music for my father. I had no lyre or harp, but there was a ukulele in the house. I picked it up and started to strum. I didn't know any chords, so I put my fingers across all of the strings. The barre chords sounded like Delta blues.

My father leaned against the door frame of his studio with a beer bottle in his hand. "That's sweet music," he said. "You'll play the lyre for me yet. You'll be my muse."

I strummed faster and slid my fingers up the strings to make higher notes. I tapped my feet—first one, then the other. I played so hard the neck snapped off the body of the ukulele. But the strings were still attached to the tuning pegs and the bridge. I held the neck with one hand and strummed with the other. I moved the detached neck in and out for different sounds. The notes were discordant, but they were energetic and loud. I found a rhythm and brought the song back home.

In Our Nature

Our father took my brother and sister and me to the woods to hunt for mushrooms. We didn't see much on the ground as we walked, except for moss and wintergreen plants. In time, we came to a red-capped mushroom. "That's called the Sickener," my father said. "Its scientific name is *emetica*. It makes you vomit. But the Russians and the Poles like it. Cooking breaks down the poison." He picked the mushroom and put it in a canvas sack.

Farther on, we came to a white mushroom. "That's the death cap, the Deadly Angel," our father said. "It's scientific name is *phalloides*, from phallus."

He kicked the mushroom at its base, and the stem broke off at the ground. There were no roots on the end of the stem—just a white cup. We bent down to examine the gills and veil. "It's supposed to taste good," our father said. "Most people who eat it die."

We left the white penis alone and continued our hike.

We came to a mushroom that had a red cap covered with white spots. "That's the Fly Killer," my father said. "It's name is *muscaria*, same as the housefly. It's a hallucinogen when raw. Flies are drawn to it, but they don't hallucinate—they die. We should put it in milk and leave it out, like they did in the old days, to keep the flies away."

*

On our way home, we walked into a cemetery on a hill overlooking the town. On one side was the Ridge, on the other a mountain. The Appalachians were lower here than in the South. I guessed people were buried at this spot because of the pleasing view of fields and trees.

I saw a gravestone decorated with two cowboy boots, one on each side of the marker. One boot was larger, with pink plastic flowers attached to it; the other was smaller, a child's boot. Both were faded from rain and harsh weather. The grave belonged to a woman who'd lived till she was 63; the only description of her was "Mother." I imagined she had been a ranch hand, or at least had dressed like a ranch hand, though there were no ranches nearby. There were only dairy farms.

When my father saw me looking, he said, "She killed herself. Her daughter found her in the attic."

"Why?" I asked.

"I don't know. Her husband was cheating on her, but there was probably more to it than that."

*

When I walked into my bedroom, I heard flapping near the ceiling. I turned on the lamp and saw a brown creature tearing around the room. I thought it might be a giant silk moth, but by the sharpness of its wings—its hands, really—I could tell it was a normal-sized bat.

Was it a real bat? I'd heard about Dracula, but this creature was way too small to be the Romanian count in his bat phase. Either that, or this bat could turn into the count, and the nobleman would be about six inches tall.

I called to my father. He walked up the stairs and poked his head into the doorway, then left.

When my mother asked what the problem was, my father said, "He has a bat in his belfry."

"We had bats where I grew up," my mother said, "in the limestone caves where Buddhist monks lived. The monks would chant in the evening, and the bats would fly around their heads."

My father picked up a butterfly net, re-entered my room, and with one swing caught the bat in the mesh. I followed as he took the creature outside. The bat seemed dazed when my father shook it free. Slowly, the bat found the side of the house and crawled upward. It seemed to be gathering its strength. I was sure it was going to climb higher, point its head downward and launch itself into the air. Then it would fly across the moon on the way back to its castle.

*

In the morning, my father talked about a sound he'd heard. "I was sitting at my drawing table and drinking beer," he said. "Outside, it was pitch-dark. No one was awake. Across the fields, from the mountain, came this howling. It wasn't a coyote. It was a lion. The big cat was coming down the hill."

My mother walked by in her white uniform, ready to catch her ride to work. "Maybe it was a white tiger," she said. "The white tiger appears in China only when the emperor rules with virtue."

"Forget your myths," my father said. "The lions are not extinct! They were here then, and they are here now."

*

The next night, my father put me into his car and started to drive. He went fast, down the middle of the pavement. I wasn't frightened. I thought he would see the headlights of an approaching vehicle in time to get over to his side.

"We're going to find those big cats," he said as he rolled down his window. "Just listen for their yowls."

I opened my window but heard nothing but the noise of wind.

Presently, I was surprised to see a car blocking the road ahead of us. It was at right angles to the direction of traffic—it was sitting across both lanes. A couple of people were standing around the vehicle. Maybe they were trying to start its engine or getting ready to push it out of the way.

My father pressed the brake, and our car went into a skid. He steered while the tires were sliding. I heard the squeal of rubber against blacktop as we went off the pavement and onto the shoulder. He pulled around the stationary car, then kept skidding across dirt and gravel until he came back to the paved road on the other side.

"Roll down your window," he said, "and listen for the lions."

*

My father stopped at a house at the end of a long driveway in the woods. "Rose lives here," he said. "I'm going in for drinks."

I waited in the car for him. While I sat, I turned on the radio and listened to a local station. We were so far from the broadcasting antenna that the sound barely came through. Now and then, truckers' shortwave transmissions interrupted the music. I heard pieces of a conversation between a driver named Rubber Duck and a driver called Good Buddy. The duck was warning his pal about a Smokey Bear up ahead. The duck told his buddy to slow down until they passed Smokey.

When my father returned, he seemed intoxicated. His eyes were half-closed and he had trouble grasping the door handle. Behind the wheel, he fumbled with the ignition key. "I know Rose from the library," he said to me. "We had some drinks and looked at books. She has quite a collection."

I doubted he could drive, but I had no choice but to ride with him. When we got home, my brother and sister asked where we'd been.

"We went to visit his friend Rose," I said. "I waited in the car and listened to music."

My mother also asked where we'd been.

"We were looking for lions," my father said. "We found Rose."

During the night, I was awakened by the sound of my father's voice. He was yelling, and my mother was listening. "I want to be free," he was saying. "I have people to see, places to go."

At one point, I heard a small crash that indicated a dish had been thrown.

*

In the moments before dawn, I dreamed that I was living in a new house. It was nothing like the house I knew. My mother and siblings were there, but my father wasn't. At first, I didn't realize we'd moved; I thought we were just visiting a different place. Then I saw we'd brought some of our possessions—not many, but all we could carry. We weren't going to return for the rest.

All we had to eat were the mushrooms with red caps, but none of us wanted to taste them. None of us wanted to get sick.

My mother said our father had done something to disappoint her. But how did she know? I pictured her climbing up the outside wall of our former house to spy on my father through the windows. Then I pictured her climbing down quietly, like a bat.

Speaking Into the Microphone

At the end of a school day, I went to an empty classroom to talk to a teacher who'd summoned me. At first, her tone was light. "I want you to be honest," she said. "I don't want you to equivocate.

"I won't prevaricate," I said.

"I'm concerned about your sister," she went on.

My sister, who was younger than I, was in a class with this same teacher.

"She seems precocious, but not about her studies."

I didn't reply.

"Most students her age thinks oral sex means kissing," the teacher said, "but your sister knows more. Is something happening at home?"

"No," I said, but I was prevaricating.

The teacher switched the subject. "Are you going to the Freshman Frolic?" she asked. She was referring to the annual dance for ninth-graders.

"I'm not," I said.

"There's a girl who wants to go with you."

"I'm not going to change my mind," I said.

"You never change your mind," the teacher said.

*

I changed my mind. I asked the girl, and she said yes. But when I told my father about my plan, he didn't seem to like my decision. He didn't offer to give my date and me a ride to the dance. I had to arrange for other transportation.

On the big night, I rode with a classmate, his date and his father. I was wearing a tan leisure suit and carrying a corsage. When I met my date at her house, I noticed her height. She was always tall, but on this occasion she was taller than ever. She was wearing a long gown that might have concealed elevating shoes. I gave her the flower bunch and she pinned it onto her chest.

I sat out most of the dances, but I went onto the floor for one. I put my arm around my partner's waist and held her hand with my free hand. When I stepped forward and back, from side to side, she followed me. When I looked up, I was looking at her chin.

"I don't like being tall," she said.

"No problem," I said. "I just need a stepladder."

Later, she and I posed for a photograph. The idea was for me to stand behind her and put my arms around her waist. We turned sideways to face the camera.

When we arrived at her house after the dance, she said, "Good night." She got out of the car by herself and walked to her door. I didn't accompany her.

I didn't realize how rude I'd been until we dropped off my classmate's date. The boy got out of the car and walked his date to her door. He spoke to her before she went in. That was the polite thing to do.

*

Later, my teacher came to our house. No one knew why she was there. When I walked into the kitchen, I saw her sitting at the table. My mother, wearing an apron, was leaning against a counter. I looked into the sink——it held a freshly caught trout. I pointed to the fish, but the teacher didn't respond.

"Are our children doing well in school?" my mother asked.

"They have some ability," the teacher said.

"They have it easier than I did," my mother said. "When Japan attacked China, I had to ride in the back of a truck to get to school."

Shortly, the teacher left.

My father came into the room. "I know why she was here," he said. "She was spying on me!"

"She was just visiting," my mother said.

"Visiting!" my father said. "She was gathering information for the authorities. We're living in a police state. I'm going to that school, and I'm going there armed."

"You're making an earthly hell," my mother said. "That's what the Buddhists say. You have to rise to no-self."

"I don't need your Eastern advice," my father said. "Siddhartha was a sissy."

My father went on a rant. "I'm an artist," he shouted. "That's what I do. But I can't do what I do because of you!"

While he yelled, my mother, my siblings and I remained silent. When he paused, my mother said, "He's sick inside."

"Are you listening to me?" he shouted.

"Sick inside," my mother said to me and my siblings.

"I'm going to the bar," my father said, "and I'm going to drink until my money is gone."

*

I got my Freshman Frolic photo along with everyone else who'd attended the dance. The picture was an eight-by-ten glossy print. My date looked nice, draped in her gown. I was standing behind her, in a sort of piggyback position.

A student asked me how I liked my photo. When I didn't reply, the boy held a loose fist under my chin and said, "Speak into the microphone."

I leaned toward the offered hand, then stopped when other students started to laugh.

Suddenly, I realized the fist wasn't holding a microphone. It was holding an imaginary penis, and "speaking into the microphone" would be speaking into the penis, or worse than speaking. I didn't want to get any closer to the fist.

*

I was assigned a presentation on human behavior for my health class. To complete the task, I found an entry in an encyclopedia volume at home and rewrote what I'd read. I made very few changes.

In school, I explained what I'd learned about human needs. "Beyond the basics of survival," I said, "there has to be some stimulation."

A girl student interrupted me. "What do you mean by stimulation? Do you mean physical touching?"

I started to mumble. "I don't know," I said.

"Can you speak up?" the teacher said. "What we need is a microphone. You need to speak into a microphone!"

*

My sister spoke to me later. "That teacher came because I talked to people in the school office," she said.

"What did you say?" I asked.

"I told them about our father."

"What about him?"

"He was abusing me."

"What did they say?"

"They thought I was lying, but they sent the teacher."

*

At home, my father told my siblings and me to stay in our rooms. "You know the saying 'Children should be seen and not heard,'" he said. "Well, you should not be seen or heard."

In my bedroom, I sat by myself. There was nothing else for me to do. I had books, but I couldn't focus on reading. All I could think about was not being able to leave my room.

I picked up a reel-to-reel tape recorder I'd received as a birthday present. I plugged in the microphone and held it in my fist. I brought my lips close to the pickup and started talking. "I'm speaking," I said. "I'm saying something. Here's what it is."

Not Faking It

My father decided I should go to Sunday school. He announced his plan one morning over the kitchen table. "I want you to see how the other half lives," he said. He seemed only half-awake as he spoke. The remnants of the previous night's activity were scattered around him: bottles, a beer mug and a large ashtray full of cigarette butts.

I had no choice: I rode with him to the nearest sizable town, ten miles from where we lived.

The classroom was in a building attached to a church. Inside, a woman was telling the story of Zacchaeus, a Roman tax collector who was a cheater. When Jesus came to Jericho, he decided to stay with Zacchaeus. Needless to say, Zacchaeus had a change of heart after Jesus' visit. He refunded the money he'd stolen—he refunded it fourfold.

The teacher said, "Now, of course, Jesus can't physically come to your house anymore, but he can come in spirit. When you feel love, you feel his spirit."

I looked around the room and noticed a boy from my class—I had recently enrolled in a new, larger school.

The boy's hair was black and straight like mine, and it looked like he hadn't cut it in a while. I myself hadn't had a haircut in years. I'd stopped going to a barber as soon as I was old enough to refuse. I just let my hair grow, although sometimes I took scissors to it. Maybe this boy did the same. His hair hung down to his neck and had an even border all around. It was tucked into the sidepieces of his glasses.

Other than our hair, we didn't share many features. His nose was pointed; mine was flat. His face was thin, while mine was wide. Worse yet, he was taller.

The Sunday school teacher ended the session with an instruction: "Do not carve anything into the wood desks."

I saw that most of the desktops in the room had been defaced.

"How would your parents like it," the teacher asked, "if you carved an obscenity into your dining table at home?"

"My parents wouldn't like it," the boy said to me, "if I carved 'God is love' into our dining table."

When my father picked me up, he asked what I'd learned.

"You shouldn't cheat people," I said.

In my room, I took out a small knife. It had a spring-loaded blade, activated with a button on the handle. I opened and shut the blade repeatedly while I thought about carving words into my furniture with it. I settled on marking the top of my desk with my initials.

*

My father made a new announcement. "I've found a friend for you," he said to me. "That boy you met at Sunday school. His father's the church minister. You are going to socialize with him."

My father drove me to the boy's house, a red-brick structure with white trim, on a main street in town. Inside the house, the floors were decorated with woven rugs. A curved staircase led to the second floor.

Quickly, I met the boy's parents.

"So you're Jeep's friend," his father said to me.

"Jeep?" I asked.

"That's what we call him. When I was in the Army, I drove a small truck. My buddies said, 'When you have a child, if it's a boy you'll have to call him Jeep.'"

Jeep's mother said, "I don't know what we would have called him if he'd been a girl."

Jeep led me up the stairs to his room, a large space with few things in it. "I play the drums," he said.

I didn't see a drum set. Presently, Jeep brought out a wooden wedge with a rubber pad glued to it. He picked up drumsticks and hit the pad with the tips.

"What is that?" I asked.

"A roll," he said.

He tapped out another pattern. "A paradiddle," he said.

I brought out a record album I'd been carrying. On the cover was a 3-D photo of the band. Their faces changed as the cover was tilted. All of the musicians were wearing colorful costumes and hats. A temple stood in the background, and a red Saturn hung in the sky. We listened to one song, about a woman who resembled a rainbow.

"What kind of music do you like?" I asked.

"Hard classical."

Before I left, Jeep's father talked to me. "I used a pop song in a sermon," he said. "The lyrics went: 'I know I'm fakin' it. Not really makin' it.'

"That was the question I asked the congregation," he continued. "Are you making it, or are you just faking it?"

I didn't know the song, but the lyrics made me self-conscious. Did I lack what it took to really make it? Was I using pretense to get through whatever I had to get through in life? What would happen if I didn't start behaving in a genuine way? Would I end up like that Biblical tax collector who wouldn't change until Jesus visited him?

*

In study hall at school, I sat at a large table in the library. Across from me was a burly guy with a crew cut. I put my face into one of my textbooks and didn't look at him. Presently, Jeep came into the library and sat nearby.

The guy across from me wasn't reading. He was staring at me. "Why don't you get a haircut?" he asked.

I didn't respond.

"I said, 'Why don't you get a haircut?'"

"Why don't you keep your mouth shut?" Jeep asked him.

"Why don't *you* get a damn haircut?

"Why don't you keep your damn mouth shut?"

"Hey!" the library proctor said. "Keep it down over there!"

*

My father brought Jeep to our house. Inside, he led us to his workroom. The floor was covered with linoleum; a metal-topped table stood next to the window. On the table were jars filled with dead butterflies.

"How did you kill them?" Jeep asked.

My father opened a jar. "Carbon tetrachloride," he said, pointing to a wad of white fiber taped to the lid. "I soak the cotton with carbon tet."

All of the gassed butterflies had their wings folded up or down.

My father brought out glass-topped boxes of mounted butterflies. Most of the specimens were pinned right side up, though some were upside down.

"Look at this Question Mark," my father said. "On the bottom of its hind wings, there's a silver shape that looks like the punctuation symbol."

We looked closely at the tiny curlicues.

"Here's a related species," my father said, "called a Comma."

We examined a comma shapes on the butterfly's hind wings.

"Any questions?" my father asked. "No? Good."

*

While my friend was visiting, my mother stayed in the kitchen. I could see her through the doorway. She was wearing an apron and standing at the sink. When Jeep and I came into the room, she said, "I want to show you something."

She laid some papers on the table. "I'm working on a special number for the blood tests I do in the hospital lab," she said. "This is a universal coefficient, a factor that will make all the tests consistent. I call it 'my madness.'"

Jeep and I looked at some equations. They meant nothing to me.

"I'm going to send this to a medical journal," my mother said. "I want doctors to accept this standard for all lab tests."

Jeep adjusted his glasses and looked closely. "This is strange math," he said.

"It's Asian math," my mother said, "the kind I learned as a child. It's based on a place-value decimal system. We used the abacus for calculations."

"A couple of the decimals are in the wrong places," Jeep said.

My mother picked up the papers and said, "You're right. I'll make the changes; then I'll submit my madness."

*

My father took Jeep and me out to collect butterflies. My brother and sister came along. We walked from our house to an overgrown field. We stopped at a mud puddle and watched yellow and orange butterflies bounce over the water.

Suddenly, my father pointed and said, "Look, it's a regal fritillary. Get it!"

I waded into the field with my net. My friend, siblings and father stayed on the road as I chased the specimen through waist-high weeds.

"Don't run like a sissy!" my father called.

The butterfly flew ahead of me in a quick, erratic pattern. I plowed through the field and swung my net. In one swipe, I caught the fritillary.

On the road, my father put the butterfly into a killing jar. "I'm going to donate this to the university's collection," he said. "The biology department has specimens collected by Nabokov. Now, it will have specimens from Nabokov and me."

*

My guidance counselor called me into her office. "I want to discuss your standardized test scores," she said.

"How did I do?"

"Your scores aren't consistent, even on the same test given on different dates. How did this happen? Are you playing games?"

"Can I go to college?" I asked.

"Your friend Jeep aced everything. I'm advising him to leave high school early."

"What about me?"

"You'll have to stay till the end."

*

My father called me to his workroom, where he was sitting at the butterfly table. On the tabletop was an open bottle of whiskey. He lit a cigarette and started to talk.

"I had a dream about chasing a butterfly," he said. "If I were Nabokov, I would have caught it. If I didn't have a family, I would be Nabokov. He went into exile in Europe. I went into exile in Pennsylvania. He lost the only house he ever owned. I never owned a house.

"The problem was, I had kids," he continued. "Did Nabokov have kids?"

"I don't know," I said. I tried to make my voice low, not sissified, but it came out in a squeak.

*

Later, Jeep had an interview at an Ivy League university. Afterward, he told me how it went. "They asked what I would do if I were lost in the forest and had only a compass and a box of matches," he said.

"What did you say?"

"I said I'd walk downhill until I found water."

In time, I learned that Jeep had been rejected by that institution. But he was accepted at another prestigious place, and by the end of the school year he was gone.

*

Sometime later, I was working on a geometry problem. The angles weren't easy to see on the textbook page, so I brought out a straight edge and my spring-loaded knife and cut some shapes from tracing paper. I tried to remember an approach shown to me earlier. I ended up with two triangles joined at their apexes. I laid them over another sheet of paper, on which I'd drawn some lines. I wrote my proof below the shapes.

In class, I presented my solution. When I was finished, the geometry teacher asked, "Have you been talking to Jeep? Is he teaching now?"

I didn't know what my friend was doing at that point. "I'm just trying not to fake it," I said.

City Visit

When I first saw the city, I thought it was filled with hospitals. The buildings visible through our car's windshield were rectangular, with rows of identical windows. To me, they looked like the county hospital where my mother worked. "What kind of hospitals are those?" I asked my father.

He turned from the steering wheel and said, "They're apartments."

Next to him, my mother made no comment. In the back seat, my brother and sister showed no interest in the structures. Suddenly, the buildings vanished as we entered a tunnel and my father turned on the car's headlights.

In the city, the streets were strewn with newspapers. The wheels of our car kicked up the sheets of newsprint as we rolled.

"We never liked the city when we lived here," my father said. "That was years ago, before you kids were born."

"I could walk to my training program at a hospital," my mother said.

"They found the head of a person in one trash can," my father said, "and the body in another, right outside our apartment building."

*

We went through a fire door to get into the building where my father's friend Steve lived. We took a lever-operated elevator, then walked through a sliding metal door into a loft. The space had only a couple of pieces of furniture: a foldout couch, a glass coffee table and a bed. Clotheslines were strung from wall to wall. Most of the space was taken up by worktables with silkscreen presses on them.

In the bathroom, the toilet bowl was cracked, and the water tank for the toilet was near the ceiling. "Don't worry," Steve said. "It works like this." He made a sound in his throat of gurgling, rushing water, then of banging metal. "Just pull the handle."

"Whatever you do," my father said, "don't open the door for anyone."

Later, there was a knock at the door. Without asking who it was, my mother unlatched the lock and slid the metal slab open. A young woman was standing outside. She had straight brown hair pulled into a ponytail and appeared harmless. She turned out to be Steve's girlfriend, Pat.

*

In the loft, there wasn't much for my siblings and me to do except play with the resident cat. We threw a string out a window and let it dangle to the tar-covered rooftop below. A cat prowled on the lower surface. When it saw our string, it batted at the moving strand.

When my turn came, I cast the string out the window. I worked the line from side to side, jiggling it, until I felt resistance. "I got a strike!" I announced.

I "landed" the cat as I wound the string back up through the window. The cat jumped onto the sill and chased the end of the string into the room. "Got him!" I said.

"You're a good cat-fisherman," my brother said.

*

In the evening, Steve showed a black-and-white film. "It's called *The Bird*," he said. "It's been screened in art museums and galleries all over the world. These actors are stars in foreign cities."

In the movie, Pat was wearing a tutu, tights and ballet slippers. She ran over rooftops as a man in a bear suit chased her. A man in a clown suit chased the man in a bear suit.

"Those are our neighbors," Steve said, referring to the men in costume. "They do it all—art, teaching, acting."

When the bear and the clown got tired of running, they left the picture. In the end, Pat was alone on a tarpaper rooftop, next to a water tank, dancing.

"Look at this," Steve said. He brought out an issue of *Time* magazine and pointed at the cover. It showed a collection of posters under the headline "Happenings."

"See?" Steve added. "There it is!"

We all looked closely and saw a postage-stamp flyer for *The Bird*.

"That's great," my father said, "but I don't make popular art; I make real art."

*

At night, I slept on an air mattress on the floor, and the rest of my family slept on the foldout couch. My siblings were small, so there was room for both of them.

In the middle of the night, I saw Steve get up—no walls divided the space. Naked, he walked across the floor, under the clotheslines. Over his head, silkscreen prints hung from clothespins.

Once awake, I noticed that the air had gone out of my mattress: I was resting on the hard floor. I blew up the mattress, but I was too tired to inflate it completely. When morning came, I was again lying on the floor, with only a sheet of plastic between my body and the wood.

*

During the day, my family visited the city's main zoo. We walked through an aviary and past many animals in cages, then stopped in front of a rock garden that held gorillas. "They're so handsome," my mother said.

I looked at the male gorillas' protruding brows, huge shoulders, short legs and long arms. Their hair was matted. To me, they were ugly. When they looked at me, they seemed to know what I was thinking. They studied me with hatred.

"I want to take a picture," my mother said.

My father handed her a Brownie camera, and she held it in front of her waist to look through the viewfinder. She pressed the shutter button a couple of times.

"We didn't have gorillas where I grew up," she said. "We had pandas, in the bamboo forests, where tribes lived."

"Which tribes?" I asked.

"You'd call them aboriginal Chinese."

"We want to see the pandas!" my brother and sister said.

The zoo, as it turned out, had no pandas.

My sister picked up on a pop song she'd heard and sang it repeatedly for the rest of the day. She could carry a tune, but the sound of her voice hitting the same notes and phrasings soon became bothersome.

*

Back at Steve's place, my father looked into cabinets until he found some bottles of liquor. He drank from them and returned the nearly empty bottles to their places.

"A gorilla is not very smart," he said to my mother. "Why do you prefer a gorilla to me?"

"They are very handsome," my mother said.

"I don't need handsome," my father said, "and I don't need a family. That's my problem—a wife and kids."

When Steve came home, he opened cabinet doors and asked, "What happened to my liquor?"

"I drank it," my father said, "and now I'm going out to get more. I'm going to shake up this city."

At that moment, my father pitched forward. The bottom of his chin hit the edge of the glass coffee table. He twitched once or twice, then lay on the floor unconscious. A gash on his chin looked like a second mouth.

My mother took my father to a hospital emergency room. When they came back, my father was wearing a bandage. When Pat saw it, she asked, "What happened?"

"I cut myself shaving," my father said.

"The hospital was just like the one where I trained," my mother said.

*

On the way home, my sister was still singing the pop song she'd heard. The chorus went "It's a small world, after all ..." and because we were in a car, there was no way to avoid it.

My father was driving erratically. The bandage on his chin had been changed to a smaller one. Stitches were visible in his skin. At one point, I thought I saw a car coming the wrong way toward us on the interstate. I didn't know how it got into the wrong lane. Was it a police car, or a car with a drunk driver? I thought it might veer into our path, but it just passed by.

*

Later, when my parents got their photos developed, I looked through the stack until I found the shots of the gorillas. The look in their eyes was as baleful as ever. To me, their faces weren't handsome at all. Still, I sorted through the prints and gave the ones of the giant males to my mother.

Wild Birds

My father took my brother and sister and me to a town called Belleville. "It means 'beautiful place,'" he explained during the drive. "Amish people live in Belleville. They are plain people; plain is beautiful."

We saw horses and buggies on the highway as we neared the town. Actually, there was no town—just a two-lane road with farm fields on either side. My father pulled off the road next to a shed and parked. The shed had slatted walls and a corrugated-tin roof. Inside, the place was lit only by the sunlight that came through the windows. I saw clothes, shoes and boots displayed on shelves.

I walked through the aisles until I found the horse section. There were crops, buggy whips, bridles and bits. I wanted a horse paddle, even though I had no horse. I wanted one for my own use. But I had no money, and I wasn't about to smuggle the implement out of the store.

*

The next day, I went to the library and looked up "horse paddling." To my dismay, I learned that "paddling" was a manner of walking. It meant an animal was almost lame. A horse that paddled wouldn't be worth much on the market. The term had nothing to do with striking with a leather bat.

I didn't know what to do with this information.

*

When I got home from school, my father was there—presumably making artwork in his studio. My brother and sister were watching television in the living room. I didn't say anything, and when my father noticed my silence, he said, "He's sulking."

My sister picked up on his comment and asked, "What's wrong with him?"

"He's sulking," my brother answered.

When my father heard them, he said, "He's a sullen teenager. That's what they all do. They mope."

"How long will he do it?"

"Who knows? He needs his privacy, so he can sulk."

*

My mother came home from work carrying a large dead bird. She was wearing a long coat over her hospital uniform, and she was holding the limp animal in her arms. Its feathers were fanned out, creating an intricate brown-and-gray pattern.

"I don't know what kind of bird it is," she said.

When my father saw the bundle of feathers, he said, "It's a hen pheasant. The female can't be hunted; it's protected. But it should be good to eat. How did you kill it?"

"With my front bumper. I was driving and heard a bang."

"Good work," my father said. He spread newspapers on the kitchen table, placed the bird on the papers, and proceeded to pluck the feathers. He put the naked carcass in a bowl of vinegar and water. "It will marinate overnight," he said. "We'll have it for dinner tomorrow."

"Where I grew up," my mother said, "'wild pheasants' were streetwalkers. That's what we called them. They were outdoor geishas."

I pictured Asian women in glittery paint and feathers strolling the sidewalks in my mother's home city. They might not have been plentiful, but they must have been easy to spot.

*

My father was inebriated at dinner. "Can you lend me some money?" he asked my mother.

"Why do you need it?" she asked.

"Look," he said. "I'm not a money-grubber. I'm not like these people in their split-level houses. I want to live like the Amish. If they want to build a barn, they don't pay someone to do it. They get together and have a barn-raising."

"Drinking in a bar won't raise a barn."

"I drink only for medicinal purposes, just like the Amish."

"There's a Buddhist saying," my mother said. "'If you give up everything you have, you'll get everything you want.'"

"There's another saying," my father said. "'Woman with a wagging tongue is a stairway to disaster.'"

"We need a porch-raising," my mother said, referring to the crumbling wood platform around our house. "We need to fix the stairs."

"We'll have a porch-raising," my father said, "when these kids get off their keisters and do some work around here."

My mother handed him some dollar bills. He got up from the dinner table, pocketed the money and walked out the door.

*

I walked into my brother's room and saw that he had made drawings on the unfinished walls. The Sheetrock was not painted—our father had spread plaster and sanded it, but had stopped halfway. My brother had covered all of the blank areas with pencil sketches of comic-book figures.

The figures were life-sized, and they had claws and beaks, or at least the males did. The bird-men were wearing loincloths, and their muscles were well-defined. They were warriors of extraordinary strength. They carried swords and daggers in their hands and waistbands.

The female figures were clothed in bikinis. Their faces were human, and their hair was long and flowing. But they had claws instead of fingers. They were kneeling next to the bird-men.

The bird-men were resting their free hands on the bird-women's heads.

*

"We want to help our father," my sister said to me.

"How?" I asked.

"All we can do is make him more comfortable while he drinks. That way, he'll drink at home instead of at a bar."

"How will you do that?"

"We'll ask our mother to buy beer for him. She'll bring it home, and he won't have to leave to get it."

"She'll need a case of beer a day," I said.

*

Later, my father painted over the drawings of bird-people in my brother's room. He went over the walls with a coat of primer.

When my brother saw what had happened, he said, "That was my best artwork."

"We need to finish the room," my father said. "I'm going to paint the walls, and I'm going the preserve the original wainscoting."

"I can't make those drawings again," my brother said.

That night, my mother went into my brother's room and sat with him while he tried to sleep.

The next morning, my father asked her, "Why were you in his room? Were you coddling him?"

"No," my mother said.

"Were you fondling him?"

*

I walked to a farm on the edge of town. On my way, I picked apples from the ground. When I came to a shed in an overgrown field, I stopped. A couple of horses came to the half-door and stuck their heads through the opening. I fed the apples to the horses—they were the only animals on the farm. I held my hand out flat, and the horses kissed the fruits into their mouths. They bit down with great pressure, then chewed sideways.

I looked at the walls of the shed. There was a horse paddle hanging on a nail. I lifted it off the spike and took it home with me. I thought I could do some slapping with it.

*

I went to my room and pulled the shades. I looked at a book of my father's called *The Olympia Reader*. The collection contained descriptions of the libertine lifestyle. There were references to violence, criminality and blasphemy. The fantasies were not restricted by morality, religion or law. One story was about the paddling of a female student by a male teacher.

I was glad I owned a horse paddle but unhappy I had no use for it. I guessed I could practice on a horse, but that would give me no pleasure. My only choice was to paddle myself—an awkward operation.

While I was reading and sulking, I heard a hammering against a tree outside. It was the sound of a bird drilling a hole in the bark. The sound was so loud it had to be made by a large bird, maybe a pileated woodpecker. I had never seen that kind of bird, but I could picture it: a red crest, a long beak, and short wings that beat like crazy on takeoff.

I went outside and looked at the rotten cherry tree in our yard. It was only a trunk about twenty feet high. The bark was black and soft. No bird was in sight.

I kicked the trunk, and it splintered where my foot met it. I kicked again, and the old tree fell onto the grass. It lay there, all twenty feet of it.

When I looked closely, I saw a hole in the wood of the trunk, near the top. It was fresh and jagged—unmistakably the work of a large bird.

*

My father gathered bows and special arrows and told me were going to hunt for birds.

Before we left, my mother said, "Don't bring anything home." She made a circular motion with her arms. "All the feathers!"

I rode in my father's car to a place where a field met woods. When we got out, he handed me a recurve bow. "Watch me," he said.

He placed one tip of the bow against his foot. He bent the other end of the bow back with his arm and attached the string.

I had trouble stringing my own bow, so he did it for me. "When you get good at this," he said, "you won't be such a fairy."

He gave me a couple of bird arrows and gestured toward a tree. "Stand there," he said, "and when a duck comes by, shoot it."

He walked away to find his own place of concealment.

I studied my weapons. The arrows had large fletches for quick takeoffs and short flights. The bow had 45 pounds of draw weight held in check by a fiber string. I wanted to hit something. I wanted to see the metal tip sink in.

As I stood in the empty landscape, a medium-sized bird flew across my field of vision. I quickly identified it as a mourning dove. I pulled up and shot. The arrow buzzed and spun as it traveled. At the top of its arc, it stalled and headed straight down. The dove kept flying until it was out of sight.

New Friends

In the morning, I watched while my father took two bowls from a shelf and placed them on the floor. He spooned canned pet food into one bowl and poured milk into the other. Immediately, the family cat began to eat from the pet-food bowl.

The cat's meal was cut short by the arrival of our two dogs. They used their noses to push the cat away. Then they butted heads for sole possession of the food.

I didn't care which animal won, because I was more concerned with my own food—a bowl of cereal. I was lucky my brother and sister and I didn't have to fight for it. We didn't have to stick our noses in the bowl to see who could lap up the cereal the fastest.

I ate my breakfast with a spoon and watched the pets fight for the food on the floor. My father had left the room, and my mother had left the house for work. My brother and sister were still asleep. It was just the pets and me, eating in concert.

*

My father took my siblings and me to watch a hill-climbing race. During the event, stock cars roared up a closed road one a time, running against a clock. We were stationed at a curve in the road; we could hear the cars coming and could see them briefly as they rounded the turn. Between the screams of engines, there was relative calm—murmurs of spectators, wind in the trees, bird calls.

Presently, my brother got tired of standing. My father put an arm around his shoulders. My brother responded by putting an arm across my father's back. I had never seen my father embrace my brother before.

At one point, a car wiped out. It spun off the road and raised a cloud of dust on the shoulder. But it didn't flip over; it rolled on two wheels at an angle to the ground, then bounced down onto four wheels. After a few moments, it crawled back onto the road and continued toward the finish line.

*

Later, my father took me in his car to visit a boy who lived a few miles away. We parked at the side of a dirt road, then walked across a yard.

I heard a man call out, "Shithead!"

Presently, the boy we were visiting appeared.

"It's the only way I can get his attention," his father explained.

"Hey, buddy," he said to my father. "I brewed something."

The man led us to a small closet off the kitchen. On the floor were a couple of ceramic crocks covered with cheesecloth. The brewmaster lifted a corner of one of the coverings, and a sour smell filled the air. In the containers, wilted yellow flowers were floating on top of brown liquid. "It's dandelion wine," the man said.

"It smells bad," I said.

"I think it smells good," my father said. He bent toward the crocks to get a better whiff.

My father and his friend drank the hooch while I went outside with the boy. We stood in his back yard and looked at a pond in the neighboring field.

"I fell in there once," the boy said, "and I didn't know how to swim."

"What did you do?" I asked.

"I sank to the bottom, but I was carrying a baseball bat. I used it like a vaulting pole. I stuck it in the mud and pushed myself to the surface."

I pictured him planting the end of the bat and extending his arms, then shooting up through the water, feet-first.

After a while, the boy said, "I'm not a shithead; I'm a spy."

He went into the house. When he came out, he was wearing a suit and tie and carrying an attaché case. "Did you bring a weapon?" he asked.

"I have a compass," I said."

"What would you do with it?"

"Find my way home, I guess."

We hiked on the dirt road away from the boy's place until we came to the next house. Two red-haired girls were sitting on the steps of the front porch.

"They're twins," the boy told me.

I looked at my compass and said, "They're north of us."

Boldly, he approached the pair and said, "Hands up!" When they didn't respond, he reached into his pocket, pointed a finger, and said it again. Surprisingly, they raised their arms.

"All the way up," he said, and they stretched their arms overhead.

*

At home, my father told my mother about his new drinking friend. "He spent some time in Hollidaysburg," he said.

"How did he get there?" my mother asked.

"He went crazy," my father said. "It was either Hollidaysburg or jail. He chose the loony bin."

"How long was he in for?"

"I don't know. But he came out with a certificate of sanity. I saw the document. He's the only guy I know who can prove he's sane!"

"Did he do something wrong?"

"Listen. He said something that made a lot of sense: 'People wouldn't go crazy so often if they could only pay their bills.'"

"Where I grew up," my mother said, "the only people who went crazy were the ones who smoked opium. They were dreaming all the time. They dreamed so much they never woke up."

*

I rode my bicycle to my new friend's house. At the beginning of my trip, I took a road that passed through the local cemetery. The gravestones on one side of the road were smaller and more worn than the ones on the other side. On the ground between the newer stones were a couple of rectangles of newly turned earth.

Beyond the cemetery, there was a house with a sawmill next to it. I'd heard that the people who lived there poached deer at night. They didn't care if it was hunting season or not. They also didn't care if they were shooting at a deer or not. Fortunately, I didn't see anyone with a gun.

Presently, I came to the foot of the Ridge. The hill was too steep to climb by pedaling, so I got off my bike and walked. At the top, I could see the spine of the Ridge stretching in both directions. Across the divide, I flew like a bat around turns. I scraped gravel and raised dust. I raced against a clock in my head, setting a time that anyone after me would have to beat.

I turned left onto a farm lane and rolled past the redheaded twins' house. Again, the two girls were sitting on their front steps. I gestured with a wave as I went past.

*

In my new friend's living room, I saw the boy's father sitting in an upholstered chair. His eyes were open, but he didn't move or acknowledge my arrival.

As I walked past, he said, "If money is the root of all evil, shoot me the roots, Toots." I didn't know who he was talking to; then I saw his wife in a corner of the room.

"Don't call me Toots," she said.

In the boy's room, I saw a poster that said, "Loose lips sink ships." I took the warning seriously and tried not to say too much. But I told the boy I had seen the twins.

"What were they doing?" he asked.

"Sitting on their porch."

He took out his wallet, opened it, and withdrew a single-edged razor blade.

"What's that for?" I asked.

"In case I'm away from home when I have to do it."

"Do what?"

"Slit my wrists."

"Why would you do that?"

"I've been watching the twins. If neither one speaks to me, I'm going to end it. I'll have no choice. It's the only way."

On my way home on my bike, I looked for the twins but didn't see them.

*

My father showed me a charcoal image he'd made by rubbing a sheet of paper against a headstone in the nearby cemetery. The paper showed the outline of the stone, with the name Keturah Candy on it. The inscription said she'd lived to the age of 16 during the 1800s.

"I'm going to put this girl in my artwork," my father said. "I wrote a poem for her. It goes: 'Hello, lover! How is it down there? All stone and leather?'

"I have a silkscreen print to go with the poem," he added. "It shows the grave site, overgrown with weeds. Things were better when Keturah was alive."

*

In the morning, my father put out the pet-food dishes, and our cat arrived first. Shortly, our dogs got wind of the food and trotted into the room. They frightened the cat away and started to huff and chew. My brother and sister and I ate cereal at the kitchen table and watched the dogs.

"We're going out to the fields," my father announced, "and we're going to pick dandelions. There are acres of flowers. We're going to fill buckets with blossoms."

Soon, he was overseeing my brother and sister and me as we squatted in a field and pinched flowers off their stems. We picked until there were no more flowers in sight. When we were finished, we had filled a quart container.

Our father took our harvest and brought it into the house. "I'm going to start my own winery," he said. "I'm going to crush these flowers in a tub. I'm going to throw in some yeast, and I'm going to wait until the sugar turns to ethanol. Then I'm going to drink until I go blind."

*

Later, I noticed that one of our dogs was missing. I asked my brother and sister to help me search for him.

We found the dog's corpse between our yard and the neighbor's place. Someone had shot the animal with a small-bore rifle.

I walked to the house next door and saw a teenager sitting on the back steps.

"What happened to the dog?" I asked.

"I took him out," the boy said.

"Why?" I asked.

"He was running across my yard, so I picked up my .22 and plugged him."

*

That night, I looked out my window and saw a crescent moon. I saw a star not far from the crescent. The star was behind the curve, not between the points. I was expecting the star to sit in the concave space, between the moon's horns.

I looked out across a farm field and saw what I thought were animals sleeping on the ground. They might have been horses, cows or bales of hay. I couldn't tell.

It was the end of a lunar cycle. The moon would wax again.

Soon, the dandelion flowers we'd gathered would ferment, and a sour smell would fill the house. The flowers' sugar would turn into alcohol. My father would drink all of the potent juice.

Taking Hits

At school, I tried out for a class play. I read for the role of a king's son who doesn't get along with his father. The son is engaged to a young woman who has defied her uncle, the king. The son and his fiancée die by the end of the play, but not before they embrace and kiss.

I got the part, but didn't know what to do about the kiss. In a rehearsal, the rest of the cast watched while I put my arms around the female lead's waist and went for her lips with my lips. She was slightly taller than I was, which made the meeting of our lips awkward. I had to reach up, though I wanted to look down. We stood at the front of a classroom and went through our scene as the other actors sat silently at their desks, watching.

*

When I got home, my mother told me about an incident. "Your father hit your brother on the cheek," she said. "He cracked it."

I wanted to know where it happened, and she told me it was in the middle room, upstairs. That was a cold room, without a radiator for heat. I wondered why my father and brother had been in there. Had my father brought my brother there to yell at him and hit him? It seemed unlikely that my father could be so calculating. Would they have been doing something else in that room when my father went into a rage? There wasn't much to do, except look at frozen butterfly specimens stored in glass-topped boxes. Maybe they were doing some work, moving things around.

"They were crouching on the floor," my mother said, "and your father hit him without warning."

I could picture them crouching, and my father holding my brother at arm's length and shaking a finger in his face. There was no warning. How could my mother have known this? She wasn't there.

"Does he have to go to the hospital?" I asked.

"No," my mother said. "It's a bruise, but it might form a cyst."

When I saw my brother, I looked for evidence of a fractured cheek. I noticed reddening on his face, but no swelling. There might have been a bruise, and it might have gone to the bone. Eventually, I thought, the bruise might turn into a lump under the skin, and only a few people would know why it was there.

*

I went into the middle room to investigate and saw a set of shelves. The floor was bare, unfinished wood. I found a couple of my mineral collections on a shelf. I'd put the stones into display boxes, with cotton on the bottom. Some of the specimens looked like quartz. I didn't know what kind of minerals the others were.

On the same shelf, I found a geologist's pick. The head had a blunt end and a pointed end, and the metal handle ended in an inlaid-wood grip. My father had bought the tool and never used it.

I took the pick and walked up the hill behind town. I'd never seen any rocks worth noticing, but on this occasion I looked more carefully. I found slate that jutted from the ground and went to work with my pick. The pointed end of the hammer dug into the rock. I was looking for trilobite fossils, or the remnants of any extinct species. But what I ended up with was a pile of flat, sharp stones. They would have been perfect for skipping across water, if there had been any water around.

*

When I came home, my mother told me my father had taken a shot at my brother.

"What kind of a shot?" I asked.

"With a rifle," she said.

My father owned a deer rifle, a .30-.30. It was a serious firearm; it could power a slug straight through brush to kill a deer. A shot fired inside a house would be very loud and damaging.

"Where did it happen?" I asked.

"In the studio, next to the bookshelves. Your brother was heading for the stairs, and your father aimed at him from behind."

I looked around the space next to the bookshelves but saw no holes ripped in the floor or the walls. I didn't smell gunpowder smoke. Could a bullet have gone into a wall without leaving a hole? I didn't think so. I lifted some of my father's paintings off their hooks and looked for evidence of gunplay. I saw none.

I asked my sister if a shot was really fired.

"Yes," she said, but she wasn't paying attention to me. She was watching television. She looked comfortable on a chair with her legs folded under her.

*

After school, I took a bus to the house of the female star of our play. The place was her parents'; it stood in a prominent location on a back road. When I saw the actress, she was wearing suede pants that sat low on her waist. She had on some beads and turquoise jewelry. She looked like a hippie. She seemed mature, self-possessed. In that moment, I didn't know what to do.

We were going to rehearse lines, but her parents weren't home, so we ended up on a couch. There, we started making out. There was no problem with the height of our lips. I could easily find hers with mine. She obviously wanted this, but I couldn't figure out why. It didn't matter, because it was what I wanted, too. In fact, I wanted nothing more.

*

When I next came home, I sat in the kitchen and looked out onto the side porch through the screen door.

My father came in from the porch and at first didn't say anything. He bent over a counter and rolled a cigarette. Then he said, "You kids want nothing to do with me. You see me as 'the old man.' But there are other kids around. I can teach them, and they'll learn from me. They won't be like you. They'll listen when I speak."

I saw my brother climbing onto the cement of the porch from the dirt at the side of the street. My father lurched past me and banged through the door toward my brother. They met on the porch, and my father said something to him. For emphasis, he jabbed his finger toward him. At that point, my brother shoved my father. He flexed his arms and hit him in the chest with his hands. Our father fell onto his buttocks. There was a pool of rainwater on the porch floor, and he landed in it. My brother walked past him and came into the house.

"He won't touch me again," my brother said.

*

During the performance of our school play, I lay on the floor backstage with the female lead. We were next to each other, and we were holding hands. We didn't care what was happening on the stage—the king was giving his edict; his subjects were complying out of fear. We just wanted to talk to each other.

We spoke so loudly our voices could be heard over the action of the play. Soon, a teacher came backstage and told us to be quiet.

When our scene came up, we ran through it perfectly. We knew our lines; we expressed our deep feelings. My fiancée had been found guilty of defying the king, and I would voluntarily join her in death. Our kiss, however, was problematic. I put my arms around her waist and went in for her face, but I couldn't quite reach her lips.

After the performance, the teenager who'd played the king came up to me. "I was watching that last part," he said. "When you kissed her, it was the most embarrassing thing I've ever seen."

A little later, I heard similar comments from other audience members. I had to admit, their responses made sense. When I thought about the embrace, I felt the same way they did.

The Ore Hole

During a school day, a science teacher took my class on a field trip. We hiked to a patch of trees growing in a crater in the ground. "This was an ore hole," he explained. "Iron ore was dug here; then it was blasted in a furnace and shaped into pellets. That's what made this area rich."

All we could see were trees growing in a pit. In one place, people had dumped their garbage. Bottles, cans and other non-degradable items lay on the surface of the fill.

As we walked through the leaf cover, a girl announced that she saw a penis. "It's sticking up," she said.

"Where is it?" the teacher asked.

The girl pointed to a whitish, erect object on the ground. Around the base of the object was a dark-brown sheath.

"It's a mushroom," the teacher said, "It might be edible."

On closer inspection, the mushroom turned out to have an unpleasant smell. No one would touch it. We left it where it was.

*

In the evening, my parents started to argue about something—I couldn't tell what. I tried to watch television with my brother and sister and not listen to my father's voice.

"You've turned them all against me," my father said. "You're all against me, you and your chink children."

My brother and I didn't resemble our father. We looked more like my mother. My sister, though, looked more like my father. Her eyes were like a Caucasian person's eyes. Further, the irises of her eyes weren't brown, like my brother's and mine. Her irises were gray, like our father's.

But that wasn't what my father meant. He meant that none of us would put up with his behavior.

When I couldn't hear his voice anymore, I realized he'd left for the local bar.

*

In the morning, I got on the school bus and took a seat next to an empty one. When the bus reached the highway outside town, it stopped for a boy on the side of the road. He was standing in front of his house, a green-shingled shack with a tar-paper roof.

There were no open seats except for the one next to me, so the boy sat there. I knew him. He'd moved in not long before.

"I have a gun," he said to me.

"I know," I said. I remembered that I had visited the boy, and he'd shown me the gun. It was the biggest handgun I'd ever seen.

"A single-shot .222," he said.

"You only get one chance with that," I said.

When a seat opened up away from me, the boy moved.

*

I handed in a report about the penis my class had found in the woods. I wrote about how a girl had thought a fungus was a penis, and I believed it. That's what the thing looked like. Why wouldn't a penis be lying in the leaves in the woods?

When I got the paper back, I saw that the teacher had addressed me as "Flip."

"You might think you're funny, Flip," the teacher wrote, "but you're not. This is cruel, without humor."

I showed the paper to the girl who'd found the penis.

"I like it," she said. "I like all of the papers you write for class."

*

After dinner, my father took some aspirin with his beer. "I'm taking the whole bottle," he said. "If I take enough, I'll die."

I didn't want him to swallow the pills, but there was nothing I could do to stop him.

He went into his studio—a dark front room shaded by a porch roof—presumably so he could consume a lethal dose in privacy.

Presently, he came out and said, "I took the whole bottle." He waved the empty container to prove it.

I waited to see if he would die, but he didn't appear to be dying. He had lots of life in him. He energetically left the house and headed for the bar.

*

The next day, I walked outside and turned off the paved street. I followed a dirt lane until I got to the creek. Along the bank, I saw a clump of mushrooms growing from a dried pile of cow dung. They looked more like toadstools than mushrooms. I pushed one with my toe, and it broke off at the base. Its roots came out with it. This fungus, I decided, might belong to a psychedelic variety.

I took some specimens home with me. The thing was, I didn't know how to consume them. I thought about chopping them up, chewing them and swallowing them. But they didn't smell appetizing, probably because they'd been growing in dung.

So I decided to melt some chocolate. I threw a handful of chocolate chips, the kind meant for cookies, into a saucepan and turned on the heat. When the chocolate became liquid, I threw the mushrooms in whole and turned off the heat. I waited until the chocolate hardened into a slab of psychotropic candy.

*

My brother told me the boy from the tar-paper house had been taken away.

My brother was in the same grade as the boy. "He tried to shoot himself," my brother told me.

"What happened?" I asked.

"He was holding a gun to his head. When he saw the cops coming, he pulled the trigger ... and missed. He had only one shot in the gun."

"Where was he?" I asked.

"At the ore hole. He was sitting in the trees with the gun until they came look-ing for him. He said he wanted to go to the bottom of the pit. He said he was already there."

*

I ate the magic Hershey bar but couldn't tell if the drug was working. The mush-rooms, I thought, might not be psychedelic. They might be common cow-patty toad-stools.

I looked at the paintings in my father's studio to see if I was hallucinating. I knew one thing: I would never be able to forget the images. I would forever see in my mind's eye giant insects, biplanes, zeppelins, naked dolls, naked people, antique bottles, rusted tricycles and miners in gas masks. I had to get out of the studio. I had to find a place that was quiet, where nothing would assault my senses. I couldn't go to my room. It was lonely there. I found my brother and sister, but I couldn't tell them I was tripping on toadstools. I just sat with them while they watched television. But the dialogue, accompanied by canned laughs, was too much for me.

I got on my bike and started pedaling. Presently, I came to the ore hole. I sat in the trees and batted at gnats. The ore had been plentiful at one time. It had been dug, smelted, and made into steel. People got rich. Five steel-industry men from the nearby town became governor of the state. Now, the pit was a garbage dump. I kicked some leaves away from a pile of debris and found some antique bottles. One was for Lydia Pinkham's Liver Cure—the brand name was embossed on the side. I would take that bottle home for my father to use in a painting. I dug some more with my foot and found a child's doll, naked, with cracked plastic skin. I would also take that home for my father to examine.

Independent Study

I wanted to learn trigonometry just by reading the textbook. I didn't have time to sit for trigonometry lectures, so I thought I would study on my own and take the tests.

The trigonometry teacher discouraged me. "I don't think you can do it by your-self," he said, "but if you pass the tests, you'll get credit."

I started reading the book but quickly got lost in algorithm hell. I couldn't tell sines from cosines, or cosines from tangents, and I certainly didn't know how to use them to find angles, areas and distances.

I asked for help from a girl who did well in math.

"I can help you," she said, if you come to my house to study."

*

My father asked me to help him build a new frame for a door between rooms. He nailed wood trim around the frame and sank the nails into the wood. Then he applied paste to fill the holes. My job was to sand the paste after it hardened.

Instead of sanding, I wanted to measure the angles of the frame. I found a right-angled ruler and fit it into the corners. Then I took a protractor and laid it against the wood. I found one angle that was slightly less than 90 degrees, and one that was slightly more. Both, of course, added up to 180 degrees. My task was to bring each angle exactly to 90 degrees.

I took a block of wood and wrapped sandpaper around it, then rubbed at the wood strips. I went around the frame and thought I'd finished, so I stopped.

My father looked at my work and said, "You're not done. You have to do more. You have to use elbow grease." He took the wood block and worked on a filling to show me. He sanded so hard he made a groove in the board.

He gave me the sandpaper and told me get to work. I sanded until my arm turned numb.

*

I walked out of the house with my fishing gear hanging from me. On my way to the stream, I had to cross a barbed-wire fence. I pushed the bottom wire strand down with one hand while holding the top strand with my other hand. I bent a leg and eased my foot through, but the top strand dropped, catching my back. When I tried to free my shirt, the bottom strand snapped up and hit me in the crotch. I felt a wire barb pierce my skin. I kept moving and heard the tearing of clothes.

With rips in my shirt and jeans, I walked through a meadow until I reached the stream.

I spent a couple of hours in one place. In front of me, the pool was circular, carved out of limestone. It was a couple of feet across and a few feet deep. I slapped my fishing line into the water and noticed the point where the line bent as it broke the surface. I knew the effect was caused by the different densities of air and water. I could draw imaginary lines that showed how the light traveled through each medium. and how the angles of refraction changed. I didn't need a trigonometry book—or trigonometry at all—to understand the phenomenon.

*

As I was walking home. an old man stopped me. He lived in a decorated wood house on a corner of the lane leading from the stream.

"How did you do?" he asked.

"I caught one." I said.

"Let me see."

I pulled an average-sized trout from my creel and held it up.

"A lot of people don't know how to fish the crick." he said. "but you always catch something."

*

I went to the house of the girl who understood math. She spent some time going over trigonometry problems with me. but she seemed more interested in playing records. She had an album by the Nazz. "Listen to this." she said. "It's psychedelic."

She spun the record and brought out a small brown substance that looked like a deer dropping. "This will help." she said.

We fired up the brown chunk in a metal tube and inhaled the smoke. I realized. then. that there was a triangle between me. the girl and the Nazz. Of the sides joining us. which was longer? And which angles were sharper? One of those values would reveal the values of all of the other angles and lengths. All I had to do was use the right algorithms.

"I have to leave now." I said.

"You don't have to go." the girl said.

"I have to get going." I said.

*

I stopped reading the trigonometry book, and when it came time for the final exam, I was unprepared. I took the test and waited for the results.

When I picked up the exam, the teacher told me, "You got a D on the test and a C for the course. That's pretty good, considering you never came to class."

I told my parents about the results, and my mother said, "You have to memorize everything, the equations, the proofs. That's what I did. I learned everything by rote—the tables, the charts. I had an Eastern education."

My father said, "What do you need math for? To build bridges? I want to blow up bridges. That's the way to say something. That's the way to be heard."

He took a beer from a cardboard case he kept on the floor and opened the bottle.

I began to think that a C was all right, but my father added, "C's are not acceptable in this house. To blow up bridges, you need A's."

He drank his beer and rolled a cigarette, then leaned his head back and closed his eyes. I guessed he was picturing an exploding bridge.

*

Later, I saw some papers on my father's worktable. One of the sheets contained a hand-lettered poem, written by my father and printed by silkscreen. A line read: "Someday I will have a son who will transcend me." I wondered what that meant. 'Transcend' in what way?

I saw that my father had collected my own poems. They were typed and arranged in a short stack. I didn't recall typing them, and I barely recalled writing them. There was a poem about a field and a horse. The first line read: "In a field I saw a horse." The poem embarrassed me.

When I asked my father about the collection, he said, "What can I say? It's your writing. I don't know why it's so precious, but there it is."

*

During the night, I imagined I lived in a different place. Next to my bed was a window, and out the window was a walkway. On the ground was a bird I hadn't seen before. It had mottled feathers, and its wings were draped outward, brushing the ground. Its head had a red crest, which hung down. I couldn't make out its eyes.

The bird appeared to be resting. It wasn't able to leave, because wire mesh enclosed the walkway. It made a sound that was mournful, a long, low coo.

I could look at the creature as long as I wanted. Neither of us was going anywhere.

Making Progress

I didn't want to have my photo taken for my high school yearbook, but I didn't know how to get out of it. I let it slide. Then, one day, I was talking to a classmate. "I'd rather not have my picture in the graduation yearbook," I said.

"You can just draw your portrait," he said.

"Why would I do that?" I asked.

"That's what I'm going to do," he said.

Later, I told my father my plan.

"That's a good idea," he said. "You won't find ideas in schools. Schools are for sheep, who have no ideas."

He gave me a Rapidograph pen and a sheet of heavy paper. "Draw," he said.

I took the pen and paper and looked at my face in a mirror. I tried to sketch a likeness—I wanted to be precise. The problem was, the ink was black, and when I drew a shadow, it looked like hair. I produced an image in which I seemed to have a mustache. The finished portrait didn't look much like me, but it didn't look like my mother or father, either. It looked alien, like a creature with long hair, glasses and a mustache.

I brought the artwork to school and asked the yearbook supervisor if he would print it instead of a photo.

"Do you really want to show this?" he asked.

"I guess so," I said.

"If that's what you want," he said.

*

At home, I had a can of gunpowder that I'd taken from my father's workroom. The powder was supposed to be used to fill rifle cartridges. But I didn't care about reloading shells. What interested me was the powder itself—small cylindrical grains of saltpeter that were smooth, like seeds. What could I do with this stuff? I wanted to make fireworks and set them off on the roof outside my bedroom window.

I spooned the gunpowder into cardboard packages, mixed in blue coloring from my chemistry set, and made a wick by wrapping powder in a paper tube. I touched a match to the wick and watched the starter ignite. The first time, the flame fizzled out before it reached the main charge. The next time, the wick burned down and a small, satisfying explosion blasted through the side of the cardboard shell.

I brought my brother and sister into my room to see my experiment. "This is the scientific method," I said. "Exact replication."

They weren't impressed. "We'd rather watch television," one of them said.

"Yeah, let's go," said the other.

*

I was selected to speak on the topic of progress at my graduation ceremony. I put on a cap and gown over my regular clothes and went to the school auditorium. The gown hid my flannel shirt, but it didn't cover my jeans and sneakers.

I began my speech by asking. "What is progress?" I defined the word, then suggested that the opportunity for advancement was everywhere. I assured the audience—the graduating students and their parents—that we would make progress. We would go from where we were to someplace better. Some of us would arrive quickly, the rest would get there slowly—but we would get there.

At the end of my speech. I asked again. "What is progress?" and concluded that we were all prepared for it.

*

Later, my father said to me, "We were sitting next to one of your teachers during your speech."

"Did he say anything?" I asked.

"All he said was 'That's our jeans-and-sneakers boy.'"

I asked my mother, "Did the teacher say anything to you?"

"He didn't say anything," my mother said. "Maybe he was impressed, but I don't think so."

*

At home, my father called me to his workroom. I looked in and saw him sitting with a bottle of beer and a can of tobacco. Around him were paintings of landscapes and images of my sister. "You've got the jeans and sneakers," he said to me. "What are you going to do now?"

I shrugged my shoulders.

"I think you should make speeches," he said.

I stood there.

"I won't miss you when you leave," he continued. "Life will be better with one less sullen child around here."

*

I went to my bedroom and poured some gunpowder from the can. I didn't bother to pack it into fireworks. I just made a pile on the roof outside my window and set it off. The powder erupted like a volcano.

*

My mother came to talk to me. She crouched next to where I was sitting and said, "I was separated from my family when I was in high school. I was sent to the countryside because of the war. At the end of the school year, I had no way to get home. I walked onto a road and saw a truck coming toward me. People were riding on the flatbed. I rode with them to the city."

"Where was the truck going?" I asked.

"I don't know," she said. "Maybe it was taking refugees out of the country, on the road to Burma."

"They had a long way to go," I said.

"You have to do the best you can with what you have. Maybe Confucius said that. Maybe he didn't. I don't know."

*

When my high-school yearbook was published, I noticed that the classmate who said he was going to draw his picture hadn't actually done it. He'd had his photo taken, just like everyone else. My self-portrait stood out—there was no doubt it didn't belong with the photos of the rest of the students. Beneath the drawing was a personal quote. I wrote that I didn't need to swim the Hellespont, dance with the dervishes or sleep in a doss house. All I needed to do was to pay attention at the right time. I'd stolen the quote from Aldous Huxley.

I asked a couple of classmates to autograph my copy of the yearbook.

"I know you'll make progress," wrote one. "I just don't know which way you'll go."

"I'm only writing in this book because you placed it in front of me," wrote another. "I really don't know what to say."

"This is goodbye," wrote a third. "That means 'God be with ye,' unless you're an atheist, which you may be."

*

When I walked out of the school building, I saw the classmate who'd reneged on drawing his picture for the yearbook. He was sitting in a car, at the steering wheel. He opened the passenger door and motioned for me to get in. I slid into the shotgun seat.

He handed me a can of beer and opened one for himself. "At first," he said, "I didn't like beer. But now I've developed a taste for it. I can't get enough of it."

I pulled the tab off my beer can and sipped. I didn't like the bitter taste, but I drank some more.

"Are you hungry?" he asked.

He handed me a Baggie with a sandwich in it. The sandwich was a slice of white bread wrapped around a piece of meatloaf. I took a bite of the sandwich and drank the beer. The two offerings, taken together, were delicious.

Summer Session

My mother frequently complained about the fleas on our pets. "All these pets: all these fleas," she would say, throwing her hands up. "Where I grew up, monkeys had fleas."

I could see the fleas when I separated the pets' fur with my fingers. Next to the animal's skin, a dark speck would run for cover, toward the fur that was still in a clump. I could follow it with my fingers, but I didn't know what to do once I had exposed the insect. I could have taken it off the animal and thrown it away, but that wouldn't get rid of the flea. It would have been able to jump onto the next pet that walked by. I didn't know how to kill the fleas. Was I supposed to chop them in half with my fingernails? Was I supposed to eat them? If I ate them, wouldn't I be like a monkey grooming another monkey? Wasn't I high enough on the evolutionary ladder not to have to do that?

At one point, my father brought home a bag from a hardware store with some plastic nooses for the pets. He buckled the collars around their necks. The collars might have discouraged the fleas, but they didn't get rid of them. When I went through the pets' fur with my fingers, I could still see the fleas running away. But at least they were running away from the collar.

*

My father announced that he'd gotten a summer job at a college and would take the family with him. "I'm going to teach kids to make art," he said, "and I'm going to teach them more than that."

My father enrolled me in the art program. I was given a room in a college dorm—a step up for me, since I was just out of high school. The rest of my family stayed in a rented house with our pets.

In the dorm, I had to do my own laundry, but I had never done laundry before. I understood that the machines worked with coins, and that I had to pour in detergent during the wash cycle. I did a successful wash, but I neglected to use the dryer. I ended up with a pillowcase full of wet clothes, which I dumped in a corner of my room. I let the clothes air-dry, and I didn't fold them. They came out crumpled into balls. I picked the clothes off the floor as I needed them and put them on.

In my wrinkled clothes, I went to a workshop led by my father. First, he showed us how to attach a piece of silk to a wood frame with a staple gun and tape. Then he demonstrated the use of "tusche" to make a positive image. He laid the tusche on the screen with a brush. Then he covered the screen with glue, removed the tusche, and used a squeegee to force the ink through spaces made by the original drawing.

I was more interested in painting than in silk-screening. I took a small canvas to a stairway and sat on a step facing a window. I made an image of the dark stairs, the wood banister, and the window with sunlight coming through it. I tried to make my rendering as realistic as possible. I wanted to remember what I had seen.

*

After class, my father suggested a trip to a campus bar. He didn't make an announcement to the class. He selected a few students, maybe his favorites, and invited them. I went along.

In the bar, my father ordered a pitcher of beer.

"Don't drink from this," he said to the students at the table.

He poured the beer for himself, and the rest of us took sodas.

After he had finished a mug, he poured another. "I'm an artist," he said. "I have something to say. But I deserve better than I get. It's always been like that."

We sat and listened to him.

"I'm going to teach you about art," he went on. "Then I'm going to teach you about revolution. 'A revolution is not a garden party.' That's what Mao said. I follow Mao. It isn't hard. My wife is Chinese."

Shortly, an older man came into the bar. He looked around the table, at the students, but he didn't sit with us. He spoke to my father in a whisper and walked out.

*

My father brought one of the girl students and me to visit my family's house. My mother and siblings stayed behind.

The house was a couple hours' drive from the college. Maybe my father wanted to pick up something he had forgotten, or maybe he wanted the show the girl the place where we lived.

I was wearing items from my laundry on the floor: a wrinkled T-shirt and half-pants.

"Sometimes I hear lions at night," my father said during the drive. "No one else hears them. The lions come over the mountain from the empty valley, and they roar."

*

The house was quiet, abandoned; no one had taken it for the summer. The pets, of course, were gone.

When we walked into the living room, small creatures started jumping on our legs. They were fleas. Apparently, they had nowhere to live after the pets left for the summer. There was an area of the floor next to windows that was catching sunlight. The fleas seemed to like it there. They covered the floor like grains of black sand.

The girl and I received some bites. We brushed the insects off our legs, then left the house and stayed outside. We waited beside the car for my father.

"I like it there," he said as he started to drive back to the college. "Even though no one cares what I'm doing, people are good to me. If I need help, they come and give it. Someone will come in now, to exterminate."

*

I took a friend of mine to the house near the college where my family was staying. My father and my siblings were out—maybe my father had taken them to a bar. Only my mother was there. She stayed in the kitchen while my friend and I sat in the living room and listened to cassette tapes.

Much later, after my friend and I had left the house, my brother talked to me. "I heard you brought a girl home," he said.

"No, I didn't," I said.

"That's what Mom said. You brought a girl named Bonnie."

I realized that my mother had pronounced the name with a Chinese accent.

"That was my friend Barney, not Bonnie," I said.

"Barney?"

"Yes, Barney. He's a boy, not a girl."

"Oh," my brother said. "I thought it was Bonnie. I thought you were on a date. I heard 'Bonnie.'"

"No. It was Barney."

*

After a studio class, my father told me he wouldn't be running the workshop anymore. "Someone saw me with underage kids at a bar," he said. "He was a faculty member, and he ratted me out. I'll be able to finish this session, but that will be it."

*

After the summer session ended, I still had the painting I'd started in the stairway. It wasn't finished; there were blank spaces on the canvas. I had been finishing one area at a time. The steps and banister, and the ivy-framed window with sunlight coming through it, were clear. But the frame of the scene was missing. I could have been sitting in a void, or on another planet, when I was painting the scene. There was nothing between my viewpoint and the ground. I decided to leave the painting as it was. I wasn't going to finish it.

On the Way Out

My father went to a closet and took out what he called his "camel hair" jacket. I didn't know what the jacket was really made of, but I doubted it was camel hair. The jacket was a tan color—the color of a camel—but that didn't prove anything.

My father hardly ever wore the jacket; it was too formal for him. He usually wore a denim jacket, along with blue jeans. He spent a lot of time outdoors, working in his garden or hiking in farm fields.

"I didn't know I still had this," he said as he took the garment from its hanger.

He seemed disappointed. "Moths have eaten the fabric," he said.

I looked at the jacket and saw small holes in the cloth. There were too many to sew or repair. I didn't see any moths, but I saw some tiny cocoons, from which new wool-eaters would emerge.

*

My father went out to his garden. I put on my clodhoppers and went with him.

We bent down between the rows to thin the shoots. As we were pulling up small plants and throwing them away, we noticed a groundhog on the edge of the yard. It was sitting on its hind legs. "Quick," my father said. "Get the .22."

I stood up but couldn't move very fast in my boots. I found the light rifle in my father's workroom and ran outside with it, but when I got there, the game was gone. "Leave the gun here," my father said. "If it comes back, we'll be ready."

I propped the rifle against the tool shed, which used to be an outhouse. The rifle rested below a horseshoe nailed to the whitewashed wall.

*

My brother came outside wearing a football jersey. He was younger than I was, but he was bigger. When my father saw him, he said, "I'm not driving you to practice."

"I'll ride my bike," my brother said.

"If you want to be in a gang of thugs," my father said, "you go ahead. You'll become a better thug. That's what happened with the Nazis. Football is a gangster sport."

I walked away so I wouldn't have to listen, but when I turned around I saw my father and brother fighting over the .22 rifle. They both had hold of the loaded gun, and they were pushing and pulling on it. My brother wrenched the gun away from my father and beat it against the ground.

My father walked away, and I came over to my brother. I picked up the gun and saw that its barrel was slightly curved. I held the gun to my shoulder and tried to draw a bead, but the sights were out of whack.

"No one's going to be shooting this gun," I said.

"I'm leaving," my brother said. "I have to get to football practice."

*

My father left the house—he just disappeared. While he was gone, my mother showed me a photograph of a grave marker. "My brother went to our home city and took this picture," she said. "He sent it to me."

Most of the names on the stone were in Chinese characters, but a few names were in English. "Here's my father, Qi Xing," my mother said. "Below him are the names of the surviving family."

My father's name was there in English, and so was mine. Likewise, my brother's and sister's.

"There are so many people in the city," my mother explained, "there isn't much space for tombstones. Ancestors' ashes are all under one marker."

*

When my father came back, he called me to his workroom. "They're sending me to the hospital," he said.

I'm going to stop drinking," he continued. "Every time I take a drink, something comes up from my stomach. It's like I can't swallow."

I stood in the doorway and listened to him.

"I'm giving up silkscreen printing, too," he said. "All the ink fumes in the air, the acetone, the mineral spirits. I can't breathe without inhaling chemicals."

I thought about his clients, his source of income.

He went on: "I'm tired of printing logos on coffee cups and T-shirts. The businesspeople are exploiting me. They can find someone else. I'll sign the checks they write to me; that's it."

*

I wanted to see how badly the .22 rifle was damaged. I took the gun out to a field and set a cardboard box on the ground. I taped a protractor to the stock and rested the gun on the crossbar of a fence. I moved the barrel 10 degrees with each shot; I kept firing until I hit the target. I found the angle of a successful shot and recorded it on paper.

At home, I tried to use trigonometry to understand the ballistics. I should have had enough information to come up with an equation, but I couldn't find the right algorithm. Did I need a sine, a cosine or a tangent? Or did I need a tool other than a protractor? Maybe I needed a sextant or an astrolabe. Unfortunately, those tools weren't available for home use.

I asked my mother for help. She showed me how to look up the algorithms in the back of my trigonometry book.

When my father saw what we were doing. he said. "Instant success. That's all you care about. If you don't have instant success, you give up."

*

My father took a leather bag to the hospital with him. The bag was a nice piece of luggage, tan like the color of his camel hair jacket. I hadn't known he owned the bag. He normally carried a backpack for hiking and a creel for fishing.

He put some audio cassettes into the bag. I supposed he planned to listen to them in his hospital room. Would he actually have time to listen? Maybe his physical condition would preoccupy him. A couple of the albums were ones I'd played for him on vinyl. He'd gotten his own copies. He must have liked those bands.

He found a gray suit jacket to wear. It didn't match the color of the bag, but he seemed to think it was formal enough for a visit to the hospital.

*

When my family got into the car, my mother didn't want to sit in the back seat. "I might get sick if I sit there," she said.

She sat in the front, while I rode with my brother and sister in the back.

"That's what happened on our honeymoon," she said. "I had lobster Newberg, and then we got on a schooner for a ride on the ocean. I lost my dinner. I haven't had lobster Newberg since."

At the hospital, we learned that what my father had inside him was "not resettable." He was given some drugs to lessen the pain—those were his only option.

*

We came home without my father.

In the kitchen, my mother lit a stick of incense. "This is 'not too black' incense," she said. "That's what the wrapper says."

I looked and saw Chinese characters on the red-cellophane package. "What does that mean?" I asked.

"It means it's not too smoky," my mother said.

She held the burning stick up to the photograph of her parents' grave marker. "Here you are," she said. "Here's some incense for you."

She moved the stick up and down so the thin smoke made curlicues in the air.

Part 2

Crush

In college, I had a crush on a student who was smarter than I was. I knew she was smarter because she'd told me her standardized test scores, and I didn't think to question them. The purported scores were enough to convince me she was smarter, and all they did was make me crush on her harder.

I felt I had to do something to measure up, so I added her major course of study to my major. I was an art student, but I took on English literature as well. I wanted to show I could do twice as much schoolwork as I had been doing. I wanted to show I was worthy of a return crush.

I focused on my studies—I spent most of my free time in libraries and at my desk.

I didn't see her for several weeks; then I ran into her on a sidewalk on campus.

"I thought you'd dropped out," she said to me.

"No," I said. "I just changed my major."

*

In my dorm room, my roommate was lying face-down on his bed, reading a book. As he lay there, he made pelvic thrusts toward his mattress. When I stared at him, he said, "It's healthy."

A song came on the radio, and I asked, "What is the singer saying?"

"He's saying, 'I want to be erected.'"

I thought the lyrics were very explicit for radio. The singer was saying he wanted a boner. "Erected?" I asked.

"Yes, erected."

"He wants an erection?"

"That's what he wants." my roommate said as he continued to hump his mattress.

Later, I found out that the song was Alice Cooper's "I Want to Be Elected," about a political candidate

*

One day, I saw my classmate walking across a bridge. I caught up to her on the sidewalk next to a protective stone wall. I climbed onto the wall, which was about three feet high and a foot wide. On one side, cars passed. On the other, white water ran at the bottom of a gorge.

"Come up here with me," I said to her.

"No," she said. "People have fallen and died."

I walked on the wall until I got to the other side. Keeping my balance wasn't hard; I didn't even have to hold my arms out. I wasn't on a tightrope; I was on a stone wall. I stepped off lightly and easily.

*

One night, she came to my room. My roommate was sleeping in his bed, so I suggested that she and I go out to the hallway. We sat on the carpet and leaned against the corridor wall.

"Why don't I ever see you in class?" I asked.

"I changed my major to science," she said. "There's a scientist I want to see."

We didn't shift our positions until morning. We didn't even get up to go to the bathroom. I didn't know if she was expecting me to do anything, but in any case I didn't know what to do. At dawn, we stood up and looked out the window at the end of the hallway. That had been my goal, to stay awake until the sky got bright.

*

My roommate looked at himself in our mirror and combed his hair with his hands.

"I don't like it when the guy down the hall calls me Pretty Boy," he said.

He adjusted his jeans on his hips and carefully applied his contact lenses. "I mean," he said, "I don't call him Rat Face, so he shouldn't call me Pretty Boy."

Later that night, Rat Face picked the lock on our door and came over to my roommate's bed. He slid the bed around the floor—the bed was on casters—while repeating "Pretty Boy! Pretty Boy!" in a loud, high-pitched voice. Then he ran out of the room.

*

My crush didn't weaken. I changed my daily path so that I would have a chance of passing my classmate "by accident." But I didn't see her for months.

One day, I saw her coming toward me on a sidewalk. She saw me, too. She was eating something as she walked, some kind of fruit.

I wanted to say something as she passed, but she was chewing at that moment. She held up an apple with a bite taken out of it and waved it at me.

I nodded, and she nodded back, mimicking my motion. She winked at me. We didn't say anything. We just kept going in opposite directions.

*

My roommate told me he was joining a fraternity. It wasn't just any fraternity; it was the former home of the university's founder. "You can visit me once in a while," he said, "once in a very great while."

"Maybe I could join," I said.

""Maybe you could," he said, "but first, you'd have to wear a sign on your neck for two weeks. You'd have to wear it everywhere, even to class. The sign would say, 'I want to be selected.'"

"I think I'll move off campus," I said. "I'll get an apartment in town, at the bottom of the hill. I like walking."

*

After I'd moved to the bottom of the hill, I saw my classmate again. She was also living off campus, in a house near mine. We happened to be walking home at the same time, and she invited me in. I sat in the living room while she did something in her bedroom. I sat there so long I thought she'd forgotten me.

When she came out, she said, "Oh, you're still here."

"I was waiting," I said.

"I want you to give me some advice," she said. "I'm writing a letter to my boyfriend back home. All I've come up with is, 'The flower is wilting.' Do you think that's good?"

I didn't know what to say. "I guess so," I said. But I really didn't want to comment. Why would a guy without a flower of his own give advice to a flower that needed nourishment? Who was holding the watering can here, anyway? I got up and wasted no time leaving.

Sunshine

I was cooking in my off-campus apartment at the start of the fall semester. The weather was warm, so I'd left the front door open. My place was on a small, well-traveled street not far from the university.

Minutes into my food preparation, a man I'd never seen came through the door. "My name is Leo," he said, "but people call me Sunshine." He was blond, not tall, probably in his 20s. He spoke too loudly and gestured with his hands. "I'm going to be a student myself sometime," he said.

I didn't believe him, but we kept talking. When my hamburger mash was ready, I shared it with him. We ate on an unfolded card table in my bedroom. There was no space for a table in the kitchen.

That night, Sunshine stayed in my hallway. He lay on the carpet in his clothes and slept.

In the morning, I noticed he was wearing a pair of my socks.

"Did you take those socks from my drawer?" I asked.

"No," he said. "These are my socks."

"I don't think they are," I said.

"They're mine. I was wearing them yesterday."

When he walked out, I thought I'd never see him again, but he returned in the evening with two cardboard boxes filled with his clothes.

"Don't you have a place to live?" I asked.

"Sure, I live downtown," he said, "in a group home. But I'm leaving there. I have a new place; I'll show you the lease."

He pulled from his pocket a folded piece of paper that might have been a lease.

"Where is this place?" I asked.

"Right here, in town. It's not ready for me yet."

"You can't live here," I said.

"I just need a place to crash for the night," he said.

"Will you move into your new place after one night here?" I asked.

"Of course," he said. "Don't worry. I'll be around only when you're home."

When I headed for class the next day, I told him he would have to leave the apartment.

"I'll come with you," he said.

I took him to a lecture by a professor of astronomy. We sat at the back of the hall, and Sunshine brought out a bottle of wine. We drank from it and watched the professor, who frequently appeared on television talk shows. During his discussion of exobiology, he impersonated a space alien by flapping his bent arms and goose-stepping across the front of the auditorium. "They might look like insects," the professor said, "but they might save us from ourselves."

After the lecture, Sunshine said, "I liked that class, but the professor is a retard."

In the evening, Sunshine invited his girlfriend to my apartment. I greeted her, and she said hello. She explained that she was also from the group home downtown.

"What kind of a place is it?" I asked.

"It's for people who are between things," she said.

Sunshine sat next to her on my bedroom floor. I put music on my stereo and sat with them.

Presently, Sunshine proposed marriage to his girlfriend. He produced an engagement ring and tried to put it on her finger, but she jerked her hand away. "Come on," he said. "I've been saving this ring."

He grabbed her wrist and pulled her toward him, but she resisted. They wrestled for a while on the floor. Then he gave up, and she left the apartment.

I found some housing leads on a bulletin board and gave them to Sunshine. "You have to find your own place or go back to where you were living," I said.

"I'll get my own place soon," he said. "I have a lease."

A couple of weeks later, I realized he had no intention of leaving. He hadn't followed up on the leads I'd given, and he'd brought more boxes of his belongings. The hallway between my kitchen and bedroom was filled with his stuff.

One night, while he was out, I carried all of his boxes to the sidewalk and set them on the pavement. I came back in and locked my door. When I looked out in the morning, the boxes were gone. I decided I would not leave my door open to the street anymore, no matter how hot the weather became.

Great Leap Forward

When my activist classmates and I learned that the ex-premier of South Vietnam was scheduled to speak on campus, we made a coffin out of cardboard and carried it to the auditorium where he would appear. The prop stood for people who had been killed by troops enforcing his policies. I put a shoulder under one end of the gray-painted coffin and walked with my colleagues to the lecture hall. Inside, we set the coffin on the floor, next to the seating area.

Many protesters stood around the periphery of the room, holding placards. I saw one that read "Parasite Ky."

Nguyen Cao Ky began to talk but spoke for only a couple of minutes before being interrupted. "Did you profit from the heroin trade?" someone asked.

"I'm a politician, not a trafficker," he answered.

"Drug lord!" someone called out.

"Golden Triangle!" someone else shouted.

"In fact, I was an Air Force officer," the ex-premier said.

"How many coups did you lead?" someone yelled.

"How many kids did you kill?"

"I fought the Communists," Ky said.

"Capitalist tool!"

"Western puppet!"

We didn't hear an answer to the last challenge, because at that point the ex-premier walked off the stage and didn't return. We carried our cardboard coffin out of the auditorium in victory.

*

In my class on Chinese government, the professor said we would learn about the Communist revolution, the Hundred Flowers campaign and the Cultural Revolution. "We're going to talk about the initials MTS," he promised.

After class, I went to the library but couldn't find MTS anywhere.

In the next class meeting, I asked what MTS meant.

"It means machine tractor station," the professor said. "The MTS is the nexus of the communal system.

"In China," he added, "the government takes care of its farmers. It also takes care of people who aren't farmers by making them into farmers."

*

The next time I saw a tractor was at an art professor's house. My printmaking teacher was giving me yard work to help with my living expenses. When I arrived, he was mowing his lawn in the nude. He drove up to me on his small tractor, cut the engine and stood up. He was on a hill, and I could see the profile of his body against the sky. He looked like a classical statue, testicular basket and all, but more tanned and hairy than the ancient-Greek version.

"I understand you need some work," he said. "I'm cutting a maze through my field for a faculty party. I've marked the paths. You'll walk behind me with hand clippers. You'll trim the weeds after I go through."

I got into position as he swung back into the tractor seat and started the engine. He worked the pedals with his bare feet. I held the clippers at the ready as he rolled forward.

*

I went to the local welfare office to apply for food stamps. I didn't know if my application was legal or not, but I needed assistance—no doubt about it.

Soon after my interview with a social worker, I received an envelope in the mail. Inside was a booklet of food stamps in different denominations. The paper slips looked like Monopoly money.

I went to a grocery store and loaded up on items like eggs, bread, tuna and pasta. I even bought a steak. The problem was, I couldn't buy tobacco or alcohol with the stamps. I wasn't a big drinker, but I was a big smoker. I had to go to another store and use my own cash to buy unfiltered, fresh-packed, Virginia-blend smokes. I didn't mind spending the money; the cigarettes tasted great.

*

During the day, I attended my Chinese-language class. In it, my name was Mr. Gao. The word rhymed with the middle syllable of my last name, Rutkowski. The professor's name was McCoy, but we called him Professor Ma. Between classes, we practiced *tai chi* with an instructor named Holcomb; we called him Mr. Heh.

The language-lab instructor's last name was Fei, but we didn't give her an American name. We called her Fei *taitai*, which meant Mrs. Fei.

I befriended one of my classmates, whose name was Mr. Yu—his last name was Youlos. He would hang out with me and my off-and-on girlfriend after class. Usually, we sat on the mown lawn outside the arts hall.

Mr. Yu had a dog that knew one trick. When asked if it knew how to "speak Greek," the dog would bark one note. My girlfriend and I both found this hilarious.

*

I went away for a weekend, and when I returned, my off-and-on girlfriend said to me, "You know, sometimes you have to spread your wings."

Immediately, I knew she what she meant—she'd flown to someone else—so I asked, "Who was it?"

"Mr. Yu."

"Oh no!" I said. "Was his dog there?"

"Yes. The dog was speaking Greek. But that's not what I wanted to tell you. I wanted to say, his thing was really small."

That wasn't what I wanted to hear. I wanted to hear that the incident hadn't happened. It was just inconceivable. She didn't even know Mr. Yu. He must have had a lot of charm—a quality I'd never noticed in him.

She made a shape with her fingers. "It was the smallest thing I've ever seen," she said. "It was, like, an inch or two."

"Unbelievable," I said.

*

For some reason, I kept seeing my off-and-on girlfriend. I took her to the party thrown by the professor who'd cut a maze through his field. We walked the pathways and admired our host's ingenuity. At one point, we came to the naked professor himself. He was holding a drink and talking with a couple of other faculty members, with his toolbar and testes in full view.

Later, we went into the professor's house and watched a slide show presented by a visiting artist. His paintings contained brightly lit images surrounded by black areas. I could make out a hand, a bowl, and what looked like hair in the illuminated patches.

"I'm totally political," the artist explained. "I'm a Marxist, not a Maoist. I look for pure forms, visually and socially. I won't tolerate inequality."

My girlfriend didn't leave the party with me. When I was ready to go, I couldn't find her. I didn't know if she'd left or was hiding in some other part of the house, so I walked out alone.

*

In my spoken-Chinese class, Prof. Ma told me I had an aptitude for the language. "I gave a test to all of you at the beginning," he said, "and you got the highest score."

I guessed that was because my mother was Chinese. There must have been some kind of afterglow hardwired into my DNA, some remnant of radiation from the Middle Kingdom.

"After this class, you could take our full-year program," the professor said. "You could study Chinese all day, every day."

"Would I get financial aid?" I asked.

"We'd pay, of course."

*

I smoked some cigarettes and thought about my future. I decided that when I completed my Chinese studies, I would head to Asia. The Great Leap Forward might have failed, but I was ready to make a leap of my own. I had relatives in China, though I didn't know their names or where they lived.

I did know the name of their province and city. Yunnan and Kunming—the places where my mother grew up. I would just go there and poke around. People might not believe I knew their language, but I would grab them by the collar and yell, *"Wo shuo Zhongguo hua!"* I could speak Chinese! Sooner or later, I would find someone who would talk with me.

The Pauper of Wales

I wanted to visit a friend who attended a university a few hours' drive from my school, so I looked at a bulletin board for ride-share notices. I found some fellow students who were going to the same place during spring break. The price seemed reasonable, though I didn't have much cash. All I had to do was split the cost of gas with the other riders.

I was living on about $15 a week. That's how much I allowed myself to take out of my checking account, which held about $200 for the entire semester. Otherwise, I used food stamps. The coupons would buy any kind of food, but wouldn't cover cigarettes, which were more important than food. When I smoked, I could think.

I met my fellow students at the appointed time and place, and we headed out.

At the beginning of our trip, we followed a twisting road that was covered with snow. A young woman was driving, and I was riding in back. At one point, the driver went around a curve on the side of a mountain and lost control. The car started to spin as the wheels lost traction. I felt the chassis make a 360-degree turn beneath me and saw the edge of the road come toward us. I thought we were going to break through the guardrail and tumble down a cliff. I thought this was it—the end of the world as I knew it. I had a vision of my college roommates waiting in vain for my return. They wouldn't know what had happened—I'd been in a car that had wiped out on a snowy road and rolled down a cliff. The other riders must have been thinking the same thing, but no one said anything as the car skidded onto the icy gravel at the side of the road and came to rest.

Shortly, the young woman brought the car back onto the road and continued driving. After a while, one of the riders, possibly the woman's boyfriend, said, "You know, we're in no hurry."

After a leisurely remainder of the ride, I arrived at my friend's room. I told him I was hungry, and he said we could eat in the cafeteria in his residential college. He would use his pass card, and I would be his guest. We went to the cafeteria straight away and found it was closed for spring break.

"A college neighbor of mine has a sister here," I said. "We could find her, and she'll let us into her cafeteria."

We went to a different residential college but couldn't locate the sister. There was no directory of students' names, and since I'd never met the person, I had no contact information for her. I could picture the sister in my mind, and I could guess at her features, but I saw no one who fit the image. The cafeteria in that college was closed, anyway, except for the maintenance workers. The university had been abandoned for spring vacation.

"Maybe I could borrow some money from you," I said to my friend.

"I was going to ask you the same thing," he said. He pulled out the lining of his pocket, and nothing fell out. "I don't have a penny."

Banks were closed, and if I couldn't find a teller, I couldn't cash a check. "I guess we're broke," I said.

We came back to my friend's room to look for food. My friend had a fruitcake his parents had sent him in the mail, and he had some bags of mint tea. He boiled water on a hotplate, and we made a meal. We sliced the cake and put it on paper towels because we had no plates. We wolfed down the bread filled with candied fruits, nuts and spices—soaked in rum—and chased it with cups of hot, weak tea.

"I don't feel the rum," I said.

"Baking breaks down the alcohol," my friend explained.

Later, we went to a town bar and watched students drink. They were sitting at a large, round table and playing a game called Prince of Wales. One student would say something like "Prince of Wales lost his tails. Tails on *two*." Whoever was sitting two seats to the left of the speaker would have to immediately respond, "No," and the speaker would ask, "Who?" The second speaker would say something like "*Three*," and the person sitting in the third seat to the right of the second speaker would have to say, "No." If the person sitting two or three seats away didn't respond quickly enough (or was too intoxicated to count seats), that person would have to take a drink. Each swallow was accompanied by uproarious laughter. Whoever took a drink started the next round with "Prince of Wales lost his tails ..."

I had a hard time calculating who was sitting where, and I wasn't even drunk. I was just smoking my precious cigarettes, the ones that helped me think. I had a thought: I was not like the Prince of Wales; I was more like the Pauper of Wales.

When my friend and I got back to the campus, we discovered that the entry gate was locked. The whole school was shut down. There wasn't even a guard at the gate. Luckily, my friend's room was on the first floor. "We'll climb through the window," he said.

He shinnied up a stone wall and jumped to a ledge. He pried his leaded-glass window open from the outside and pulled himself in. I followed slowly, and he gave me a hand. No cops spotted us as we were breaking and entering.

Later, an Asian-American suite mate showed up. My friend asked him if he had any food, and he said he did. We followed him to his room, and he gave us two packages of instant noodles. He didn't say much; he just waved us away. Afterward, I asked my friend, "Was he wasted?"

"Of course," my friend said. "He studies really hard, and when he finishes his finals and papers, he blows it all out."

We cooked the noodles on the hotplate and ate them. "Do you think we'll still be doing this when we get older?" my friend asked.

"Maybe," I said. "I like ramen. Is that what you mean?"

"I mean we'll be doing some of the same things when we're older, we just don't know what. That's part of the continuity of life, the way some things change, while others stay the same. It's part of the mystery of existence. You think you can control things, when in fact your power is limited. For example, we'll probably still be friends, but we won't be eating instant noodles."

"I'm glad we found this ramen," I said.

The next morning, I met my fellow riders and left the university. The drive back was uneventful. People hardly spoke in the car. I didn't even know the riders' full names, and I didn't ask what they were.

When we reached my house, the woman driver's boyfriend told me I owed $10 for gas. "Can I pay you tomorrow?" I asked. "I'll find you on campus."

"No," he said, "you have to pay now."

It was a big university, and he obviously didn't think I'd take the time to find him.

"Can I write you a check?" I asked.

"No," he said. "It has to be cash."

I went in and asked my housemates if I could have $10 in cash. One of them asked, "How will you pay it back?"

"I'll write you a check."

"Will the check be good?"

"Yes, if I can postdate it."

"OK, but the date has to be soon."

I wrote the check, got the cash and paid the driver. I still had some cigarettes. With the smokes, I was ready to figure things out. As soon as I fired up, I started having thoughts. One was that even though I had some control over my actions, I had little power over money. How I would pay for things was a mystery, perhaps the biggest mystery—of my life, at least. My double major in fine arts and English wasn't going to help. I didn't foresee a future of prosperity for myself.

Brush-Offs

In my senior year of college, I was given my own art studio. It was a small room, with a worktable, a chair and a stool. Its best feature was an ivy-framed window that looked out on a grass-covered quadrangle.

I set up my easel on the paint-spattered floor and laid out my supplies on the pigment-crusted table. I had paint tubes, linseed oil, turpentine, canvas and wood stretchers. I also had a stash of small fireworks, for entertainment.

To begin, I prepared some canvases. I slid stretchers together, cut the cloth to size and pulled the fabric tight with pliers. I stapled the canvas with a spring-driven gun, folding the edges as I went. Then I applied a ground of rabbit-skin glue. When I was finished, I lined up the blank canvases on my worktable. The canvases stayed that way for days.

When my elderly independent-study professor came to visit, he looked around my studio and said, "You seem to have a talent for organization. Maybe you shouldn't be painting. Maybe you should be in the hotel school. We have an excellent hospitality program here. All you'll have to do is schmooze."

"I'd rather not work in a hotel," I said.

"Maybe the restaurant school," he said. "You could keep track of profits and losses. You could scout new locations. You could write menus."

*

In the morning. I stopped by my studio on my way to art history class. I removed the lid from a cup of coffee and poured whiskey into the cup. Then I replaced the lid and carried the coffee to the lecture. As Futurist images flashed on a screen, the professor said, "The theme here is movement, or as I call it, MVT. You can find the direction of the MVT in any Futurist painting. Below the MVT, you'll see the composition, or CMP. When you combine the MVT and CMP, you'll feel the overall impact, or IMP."

We examined the MVT. CMP and IMP in paintings by Boccioni, Russolo, Severini and others. The images glowed as I sat in the back of the auditorium, sipping my spiked coffee.

*

To further my independent study. I made a clay sculpture of a model. I tried to find the MVT in the model's pose, but there was no MVT. She was holding still. I could, however, give my sculpture some CMP. I hoped that when I was finished, my piece would have lots of IMP.

Using my fingers and a tiny spatula. I completed a clay likeness of the model's body, down to her fingers and toes. Later, I made a plaster cast. The clay version was destroyed in the process, but the plaster product was smooth and perfect.

*

I put the plaster figure on my studio's windowsill and set up a canvas on the easel. I used a knife to press paint onto the canvas. I smoothed out thick areas and defined edges with the blade. I was happy with the result: an image of a white figure against a dark. leafy background.

When my elderly professor came to give a critique, he pointed at the figure's legs. There was a space where the knees were bent. "What is that shape?" he asked. "A pair of lips?"

"No," I said. "They're legs, bent at the knee."

"I see lips," he said.

Later, I studied my painting's MVT and CMP. I could see that these elements weren't coming together for a satisfying IMP.

*

I took a large canvas, drew on it with pencil, then filled the areas with colors. I used house-painting brushes. When I was finished, the canvas showed an expansive field, a massive hill and an endless sky.

I hung the painting from a nail in a wall. The landscape filled my small studio; the image was overwhelming.

*

The sculpture model came to visit my studio. She was also an art student. She brought a young man who was wearing a suit and tie.

"This is Nilo," she said. "His family is in the clothing business."

The two of them sat on my two pieces of sitting furniture, the chair and the stool, while I stood.

"I see you made a still-life painting of that plaster cast," the model said. "What is that, a mouth with lips?"

"No," I said, "Those are legs. Yours."

"They look like lips," she said.

I picked up a hat from the table and put it on, then found my stash of fireworks. I tied a string to a bottle rocket and taped the other end of the string to my hat. I lit the fuse, and the rocket hissed out the ivy-framed window. The rocket ripped the hat off my head as it shot over the quad. When the warhead exploded, my hat tumbled from the sky and landed on the grass.

"Good shot!" Nilo said.

*

I visited the studio of a graduate student and saw that his walls were covered with self-portraits. In each of the portraits, the hair was dark and spiky. The chin was covered with a beard. One eye was open and the other was obscured—it was X'ed out. The facial expressions were intense.

"Why so many self-portraits?" I asked.

"This is what I see when I am here," he said.

*

I made some drawings of my own face. I set up a mirror on my worktable and looked into it as I sketched. I clipped part of my hair with a plastic holder and let the rest of my hair hang. I kept my glasses on and stepped away. Then I took my glasses off and got closer—I drew with my nose to the paper. I worked with pencil, charcoal and an eraser. I used my thumb and fingers to smear the carbon and graphite around.

I wondered if my features looked Asian or Caucasian. They could be either, depending on perspective.

*

I arranged my artworks in my studio for a final critique. I displayed landscapes and still lifes, along with self-portraits. I put up a couple dozen pieces. I left them there for my elderly professor to look at.

I thought I would get a good grade because there was a great variety.

I got a bad grade because, the professor said, I hadn't selected my best work. "In that painting of the model," he said, "I still see lips. I don't see legs. And who is the person in the drawings of faces? I can't tell if it's a boy or a girl."

"I can explain," I said.

"I read your written description of the work," he said. "What do you mean by MVT, CMP and IMP? Are you talking about motor vehicle transportation, a sleep-away camp, and a mischievous child? Did an imp get a driver's license and go to camp for the summer? Who is this imp, anyway?"

"I'm trying to show movement and composition," I said, "for maximum impact."

*

Before I put my works into storage, I hosted a party in my studio. I brought wine and set up a stereo. A couple of my classmates attended. There was the life model— without Nilo.

To my surprise, the elderly professor also came. He poured himself a glass of wine and said to me, "You know, wine is the drink of the gods, the Greek gods. You should make paintings of the gods. You know, the gods, gamboling on the grass, holding hands, totally nude. That's what I do. And my paintings sell."

The model signaled that she wanted to say something to me, and when I went to her, she said, "Don't ever think of touching me."

I turned the music louder. Later, I thought, I would light some fireworks. I had another hat. I would let a bottle rocket rip it off my head.

Absent Without Leave

Without warning, a friend of mine showed up at my door. I knew him from high school. His father had been a drinking buddy of my father's.

"Where did you come from?" I asked.

"South Carolina," he said. "That's where I'm stationed."

I remembered he'd been in college, but he'd dropped out to join the Marines. I was surprised he'd found my house. I didn't remember giving him my address. I was living in town with a couple of roommates for the year.

"How did you get here?" I asked.

"I hitchhiked. It took me a couple of days. I walked about twenty miles between rides."

"Are you on leave?"

"No, I'm AWOL."

"How long are you going to stay?" I asked.

"Until they come to arrest me, I guess."

*

I went to check my mail. I was waiting for a letter from my pen pal. I'd met her the previous summer, when she was in a program at the university. After the program, she'd moved back to the Midwest.

Luckily, I got a letter from her. Her stationery was irregular—it was torn and had doodles in the margins. She had enclosed a poem. As with most poems I'd read, I didn't understand the main thing she was talking about. But two lines from the poem struck me:

A scream is a yellow arrow.

A smile is shy violet.

The colors added to the expressions of emotion. Why not those colors with those feelings? I saw no reason why not. Some people associated colors with sound. The idea was alien to me, however.

I sat down immediately to reply to her. "I think we should see each other," I wrote. "I can get to where you are. I'll take the interstate. It'll cost me nothing, because I'll hitchhike. If it takes me more than a day, I'll put out my bedroll next to the road and spend the night there."

*

One of my roommates called me to her room. I didn't know her well; she was friends with other people in the house, not with me. She invited me to sit, and since there was no chair, I positioned myself on the floor. She also took a seat on the floor, with her back to a wall. Her nearly blond hair fell in strings past her shoulders. She looked at me sternly through her glasses.

"Your friend who's visiting," she said, "is he in ROTC?" She pronounced the abbreviation "Rotsee."

"No," I said, "he's an enlisted man, in the Marines."

"The Marines don't have a good record with women. They aren't feminists. I'm a radical feminist. I don't want a Marine in the house."

"Right," I said. "I'll ask him to leave."

In truth, I had no desire to evict my friend.

"I don't believe you," she said. "You just want to get out of this room. You've never wanted to talk to me."

"No," I said. "That's not it. I'm learning a lot about feminism, living here."

"I doubt it," she said. "You see women as sex objects."

"Not at all," I said. I meant I hadn't put women and sex together at all—I hadn't figured out how to do that in a real way—but I didn't explain myself.

"Do they even have female Marines?"

"If they don't, they should," I said.

"OK," she said, "you can go."

*

My friend told me about his life in the Marines. "Sometimes," he said, "we marched through a swamp at night. The water came up to our waist, and leeches grabbed onto our skin. The next day, we crawled on our backs while live bullets flew over us. If we stood up, we'd be dead. The sergeants called us Sweet Pea. They followed us and said, 'Move it, Sweet Pea.' If we weren't fast enough, or if we smiled at the nickname, the sergeants beat us."

"They just hauled off and hit you?" I asked.

"No, we had to stand at attention with our hands behind our head while they punched us in the stomach."

I could see why my friend had left his base without permission. "What are you going to do now?" I asked.

"I'm applying to become a conscientious objector. I already told my barracks leader."

"What did he say?"

"He told me I was as full of shit as a Christmas turkey."

*

I received a reply from my pen pal. Again, it was on unusual stationery: a white sheet with blue decorations, stapled to a plain yellow sheet. The handwriting went at an angle across the page. The words stopped at the bottom, then resumed in a smaller size in the margins. She had started writing the letter at home and finished it in a coffee shop.

I scanned the letter for a response to my offer to visit, and found it near the end. "You don't have to come all this way," my pal said. "After all, we're not getting married or anything."

*

I heard my feminist roommate call from the bathroom: "I smell body odor on my towel! Someone used my towel. Who was it?"

At first, I didn't know what she meant by "body odor." Which part of the body did she mean? Then I remembered my mother used to talk about "B.O." My mother said it stood for "bad odor," but I realized it could also mean "body odor." I knew the smell we were talking about.

My roommate confronted me with the towel in her hand. "Did you do this?" she asked, "or was it your friend from Rotsee?"

"He's not in ROTC," I said. "But I'll ask him."

Someone in the house was guilty of soiling the towel. It could have been my friend. It could have been me. I wasn't in the habit of identifying towels before I used them. I was a slob.

*

When I next saw him, my friend told me he'd visited the Army recruiting office on campus.

"Did you talk to anyone?" I asked.

"I found an officer, and he asked me, 'Are you in the service?' I said yes, and he brought me to his desk right away."

"What did he say?"

"He said that after 30 days of being absent without leave, I would be classified as a deserter."

"What does that mean?"

"Well, the penalty for desertion is court martial, possibly the firing squad."

"What did he say you should do?"

"Return to the Marines immediately."

*

I started out on a trip to see my pen pal in the Midwest. I had $10 in my pocket and a knapsack on my back. Between my town and the nearest interstate highway was a 30-mile stretch of road. I stood by the road and held out my thumb, then sat on my knapsack, then stood up and held out my thumb again. It took me about two hours to get 20 miles. At that point, I saw a county bus heading back to where I'd started. When it pulled over, I ran to its door and climbed in.

I wrote to my pen pal and told her I wouldn't be seeing her any time soon.

*

Weeks later, I heard from my friend in the Marines. He sent me a letter, saying he'd returned to his base soon enough not to be tried as a deserter. He was expelled from his training program, though. He'd been studying cryogenics—liquid-fuel systems for missiles—and was an A student. He'd been reassigned to a typing job on a Japanese island and was heading there soon. When his commitment was up, he would be discharged and banned from re-enlistment.

"I'm looking forward to Okinawa," he wrote. "I can learn some Japanese there, meet new people, try new foods. I just won't be able to leave for a year and a half."

Written in Blood

At the start of a painting class, I looked around the studio and saw someone I hadn't seen before. She was standing at an easel and glancing back and forth from her canvas to the male model. She was studying her work through granny glasses; her face was framed by a cloud of light-colored hair.

We laid paint on our canvases. The idea was to enjoy the way it seeped into the brush, then flowed onto the picture plane. I looked at the new arrival's work and could tell she knew how to paint. She had technique; she had excellent eye-hand motor control.

During a break, I talked to her. She was not in the art program, she said. She was attending the high school in town and taking classes before applying to college.

She asked what I was going to do with my art education.

I said, "Maybe I'll go into commercial design, make layouts, do paste-ups. If I get really good, I'll be graphic designer."

"I'm going to be an artist," she said, "a person who makes art—that's it."

"How will you do that?" I asked.

"I'll go to Yale. It's the best place to study."

"I don't know if you'll get in," I said.

"Why not?" she asked.

"Well, you're not even in college."

She looked hurt, as if she might cry, or swear at me.

Back at my easel, I became frustrated with my inability to duplicate the contours of the male model's body. All of the female students were doing a very good job of rendering his genitalia. In all of their images, the "junk" was really big.

I scraped the wet paint off my canvas with a palette knife. I washed the surface with a cloth soaked in linseed oil. When I was done, my painting looked like a smooth, blue-gray rectangle.

*

The new student took me to a park—she knew the place because she lived in town. Other than birds and insects, we were the only creatures there. I walked off the lawn and into a field. My new friend followed me. Suddenly, she ran out of the field. She didn't stop until she got to a paved parking lot.

I came up behind. "What's the matter?" I asked.

"I saw a snake."

"What kind?"

"I don't know. It was black or gray, with stripes."

"A garter snake," I said. "It was harmless."

I went back into the field, but she refused to follow me. I kicked at clumps of grass, hoping to dislodge a snake. I wanted to find a specimen to show her, but I couldn't scare up anything.

*

She came to the house I shared with other students. I brought her to my room, put on a record and turned up the volume. I had arranged my stereo so that one speaker was in my room and the other was in the adjacent room, where a housemate lived. My guest sat on the chair at my desk, and I sat on the bed. A cold draft blew through the windows.

"I can't wait to leave town," she said.

"There's a lot going on here," I said, "compared to where I grew up."

"I want to go to another country," she said. "I'll get a grant to live and make my art."

"You'll have other expenses," I said.

"The grant will also pay for travel."

My room grew steadily colder.

The next day, my housemate said, "I don't like listening to one stereo channel that I can't turn off. Please take your speaker out of my room."

*

At night, I walked to visit my friend. I carried a record that I thought we could listen to. I hiked up a hill to the college gate, crossed a quadrangle, and went over a footbridge that spanned a gorge. On the bridge, I looked over the railing at the white water below. The distance to the water was a couple of hundred feet. My stomach clenched.

My friend lived with her parents in the Heights, an affluent part of town. The house was dark when I got there. When she greeted me, she didn't turn on the lights. She led me through shadowy rooms to the basement. There, she turned on a dim lamp and put on the record I'd brought.

As we listened, I asked what her father did for a living.

"He runs a gas station," she said.

From the size and location of her house, I could tell that selling gasoline was a lucrative business.

She liked only one song on the album, the one where the singer gets a letter that makes him "mad, mad, mad." The words in the letter make him "sad, sad, sad."

She and I played the song repeatedly. We lifted the tonearm and set it back on the vinyl, then listened again. While we listened, we grabbed at each other and squeezed.

At the end of my visit, I was physically frustrated. There was a soreness in my groin. But I didn't complain. I hobbled to the door, did some more grabbing and hugging, and hit the street. I limped over the suspension bridge, across the campus, to my shared house.

*

Another day, I asked her to model for me. We were art students, after all. To my surprise, she agreed. She took off her clothes and sat on my bed. She looked pale, yet composed.

I sat on a chair and made some sketches with charcoal. My lines were jagged, spiky, almost out of control, but I managed to capture a likeness.

The thing was, I wanted to do more than sketch. But when I said, "I want to touch you," the drawing session ended. My model didn't say anything. She just slid off the bed, got dressed and left.

*

"What were you up to?" my housemate asked me later.

"I was doing some life drawing," I said.

"What's that?" he asked.

"Drawing from nature, from the natural body."

"That's good," he said, "but you've got to down to it."

"Down to what?"

"Down to the nitty-gritty."

"What do you mean?"

"You've got to get down to the roots, man." He made a pushing gesture with the heel of his hand to show what he meant.

*

I didn't see the new student again for a while. The semester was over and summer vacation had begun. I was living with my parents, so I took a bus to visit her. I brought the same record that I'd brought earlier.

Soon after I arrived, she told me she'd been accepted by Yale. "You didn't think I'd get in," she said.

"You're right," I said.

"That was your mistake."

"How so?"

"You didn't believe in me. You thought I shouldn't even try."

I started to feel sorry for myself, and she let me feel that way. Either that, or she had no idea how I was feeling. "Why don't we put on that song?" I asked. "The one that says, 'You don't have to go.'"

"I don't think so," she said.

I didn't say anything.

"What are you doing to do now?" she asked.

"I guess I'll leave," I said.

I went to the bus station, even though I knew it was the wrong thing to do. Still, I couldn't go back to her house. If I went back, I would be admitting I was wrong. I was too angry to do that. So I took the next ride out. But I forgot something essential: my pocketknife. I always carried it, and somehow I had left it in her house.

A week or so later, I received the knife in the mail, wrapped in a sheet of paper that had bloodstains on it. A note from my former friend said, "This belongs to you."

The stains were in the shape of lines, as if she'd used the blade to slice her hand, then pressed her hand against the paper. The blood looked real. Why would she try to fool me? I didn't think she had used paint that was the color of blood. I believed she had really cut herself.

*

I saw her again much later, when I was living in a city. She met me at my apartment, and the two of us walked to a park, where we sat on a bench.

"I got a Fulbright fellowship," she said. "I'm going away for a year."

"Where to?"

"Barcelona."

"I didn't know you could speak Spanish," I said.

"You underestimated me again," she said.

I walked her to a subway entrance and parted with her there. Then I returned to my basement apartment.

I didn't try to call her for a long time. The next time I tried, a man who spoke Spanish answered the phone. When I asked for my former friend by name, he pretended not to understand. I persisted, but he wouldn't let me speak to her.

Part 3

Pardon My French

When I arrived in Paris by train, I tried to place a call to a friend, someone I knew from my home city. Surprisingly, there was a phone service with a human attendant in the train station. I gave the phone woman the number I wanted to reach, and she dialed it.

Suddenly, she started yelling *"Occupé!"* at me. I thought she was telling me to get lost, so I started to walk away. She yelled more loudly and pointed at the phone. Slowly, I came to understand that *"Occupé"* meant "The line is busy." Presently, she put the call through.

*

My friend came in a car to pick me up. He had the car for his job; he ran errands for a commercial production company. As he drove, I watched green areas and monumental buildings swing through my field of vision.

Soon, we arrived at the commercial director's home: a converted storefront near the Bastille site. One of the perks of my friend's job was having this place to live. The apartment was large, with a spiral staircase connecting floors. I lugged my backpack up the metal steps and laid it in my friend's bedroom.

When I looked for food in the kitchen, I found a baguette and some pâté. The baguette was the thinnest bread stick I'd ever seen; its diameter was that of a U.S. quarter. Moreover, the pâté came in a very small tin—smaller than a cat food can. Undeterred, I popped the top and dug at the pâté with a spoon, then spread it on a disk of bread.

*

A young woman was staying in the same place. I didn't know what she was doing there. When I first saw her, she was watching a television show—the characters were college students who kept losing their pants and falling down.

One time, my friend played a game with the young woman. He lay on his back, held her hands and pushed against her stomach with his feet, so her body was balanced over him. Then he laid her on her back and knelt between her legs. He put his hands behind her knees and lifted her pelvis toward him. They stayed that way for a while, rocking.

*

I thought Paris was small, but actually only the amount of ground I covered was small. I would walk from one point to another and think that I'd gone from one side of the city to the other. The reality was, I'd passed only from one district to another.

The place I visited most often was the adult strip of the Rue Saint-Denis. The shops there showed films that played continuously. If you stayed past the end, the clip would loop back to the beginning. The effect was one of perpetual sexual activity.

I found an aggressive vignette featuring a black-haired woman wearing leather boots and a headband. I was convinced she was a Native American. I imagined that she'd been separated from her tribe. Off the reservation, she was confined to a small room, with only a sawhorse as furniture. This was not her lucky day.

The problem was, the film was only about ten minutes long, and the repetition soon grew tiresome. After the third loop, I couldn't watch another round of brutal behavior.

*

I went back to where I was staying. The baguette and pâté had been eaten, so my friend and I went to a restaurant. The thing was, we couldn't read the menu. We guessed at a selection and ended up with a plate of snails, which were not bad, not at all. They obviously had just been harvested from a damp lawn. I could taste the dew.

Later, we found a better place to eat: a cafeteria. The food there was plentiful, varied and cheap. In addition, the place was located near the Rue Saint-Denis—a big plus, in my opinion.

At one point, as we sat there, my friend asked me for some coins. "I need them to open the stall in the men's room," he explained. "There's some action back there."

"What do you mean by 'action'?" I asked.

"A man met my eyes with his eyes. You know what that means. Do you have any change?"

"How much?"

"Two francs."

That was about 50 cents. I gave him the coins. I didn't mind. I was off to the Rue Saint-Denis.

*

Another time, my friend and I were sitting in the apartment with the main tenant, the commercial director. The two of them were smoking a hashish-and-tobacco cigar and talking about someone they knew, Annie, whose name was pronounced Ah-NEE.

"I stayed the night with her," my friend said, "but she scraped me with her nails, and I got an infection."

"She's a bitch," the director said, grinning.

I helped them finish the hash cigar, and all of us meditated on Annie.

*

Later, my friend and I went to visit Annie in her apartment across the river. Her place was luxurious, with a polished-wood floor and a grand piano. Through the large windows, we could see a park with trees and the Eiffel Tower.

Annie wasn't unfriendly or friendly. She just sat there with us. "There are two kinds of people," she told me, "intellectuals, and those who follow their instincts.

"I'm the second," she continued. "I can meet someone on a train, get off at the next station, have sex with him, and get back on the train."

"I followed her here," my friend explained to me. "She's the reason I'm in Paris."

Shortly, I left the apartment, but my friend stayed. I hoped Annie would not scrape him again with her nails.

*

When I finally took the subway. I noticed that the trains ran quietly. They didn't shriek with the sound of metal against metal. My friend told me that was because the trains had rubber wheels, and I believed him. I imagined the tracks were flat, and wide enough for tires to pass over. I didn't look closely as a train went by to see if it had steel wheels—which, of course, it did.

I took one of the trains to meet a French couple I knew from New York. But when I got to the address they had given me, they were not home. Someone I didn't know was there, but he was hospitable. He served me a greenish-yellow liqueur. I disliked the taste but drank it anyway. Unable to converse, I sat in the small, unfamiliar apartment for a long while, sipping at my glass of chartreuse, nodding occasionally at my host.

The couple I knew never showed up. After a time, I took a quiet train back to where I was staying.

*

At the storefront apartment, I asked the young woman to sit while I drew her portrait.

Her face filled a page of my sketchbook. I thought it was a perfect face, but on second look, I could see its flaws. The mouth was too wide, the eyes too big. Those distortions, however, might have been due not to my model but to my own lack of skill.

At night, my friend brought out an envelope of drugs. "It's Paris-brand junk," he said. "It's stronger than what you get in New York."

I sniffed some of the powder and immediately felt sick. I ran to the WC, but by the time I got there, the wave of nausea had passed. I returned to my friend's room, sniffed some more, and lay down. Again, I felt sick, so I got up and returned to the WC. I repeated this pattern for most of the night.

*

In the daytime, I went out walking. I still believed I could get anywhere I wanted on foot. I walked to the cathedral in the middle of the river. The structure had flying buttresses and craning gargoyles. The animals' heads stuck out on long necks, ready to spew boiling oil on anyone who approached.

I wanted to go into the cathedral, but a private event was being held. It was my last day in the city. I walked around the outside of the structure, looking at the buttresses and gargoyles, enjoying the flow of the river and my freedom from Paris-brand junk.

*

The next day, I had to take a train to another city. The train ran all night, and there were no seats, so I slept standing up. I leaned against a wall and dozed until my knees buckled. Before I fell over, I woke up. Then I leaned back and dozed again.

In a waking dream, I saw two women behind the glass door of a nearby compartment. They were sitting on opposite sides of a fold-out table. One of them was holding a carrot with a Band-Aid wrapped around its middle. She pointed at the bandaged root, and her companion looked at it closely. The carrot was large and well wrapped. The companion gestured in turn at the erect carrot, and both women started to laugh uncontrollably. The first woman held the carrot over her head and waved it while both women covered their mouths with their hands.

As the train proceeded, the names of towns changed. Mulhouse became Mül-hausen, Bale became Basel, and La Suisse became Schweiz. At first, I thought I was really getting somewhere. I thought I was entering a different country. But soon enough, I realized I was still in France.

On Gobble Street

When the train arrived at its last station, I got off and looked for a local connection. To my disappointment, I learned there would be no more trains for several hours. I called the Swiss friend I wanted to meet, but he wasn't home. I remembered he'd written to say he would be on vacation. I didn't know where he'd gone or if he was still wherever he was.

I had two choices: I could go back to where I'd started, or I could continue on to my friend's town. I had no place to stay where I'd started, so I decided to keep traveling. The problem was, it was midnight and the next commuter train left at 6 a.m. I sat on a bench and waited. The station was empty and quiet. Using my bedroll as a pillow, I tried to sleep.

I caught the first train out at dawn. When I got to my friend's village, I called him again. Miraculously, he answered. "I just got back from vacation," he explained. "I knew you were coming, but I forgot which day."

He gave me some directions on the phone, but he had to spell the name of his street. "It begins with a G," he said, "as in 'gobble.'"

I found Gobble Street and met my friend. In his apartment, he had three food items, which he offered freely. There was a loaf of hard bread on a wooden board, a collection of cheeses on a second board, and a bowl filled with tangerines.

"I don't eat *Fleisch*," he explained.

I sliced the bread with a serrated knife and examined the cheeses. One looked like a cheddar, another seemed to be a Swiss, and a third was unidentifiable but stinky. We ate some bread and cheese, then peeled tangerines. My friend sniffled and snorted as he sat with me. At one point, he sprayed medicine into his nostrils. "I have polyps," he explained.

"You mean cancer?" I asked.

"No, the stage before that."

My friend's apartment was in the top half of a house. The owner lived below. To take a shower, I had to go outside and around the back.

When I emerged from the shower stall, a middle-aged woman approached me. She questioned me, but I didn't understand what she was saying. She reached toward me, then said something that contained the phrase "*Haar waschen*." She mussed my wet hair with her hand.

I nodded yes and ran away from her.

My friend worked as a carpenter. In college, he and I had been art majors. "None of my college credits would transfer to Switzerland," he explained, "except for my credits in German literature. So I became an apprentice. I climb onto house roofs and use ten-inch nails to fasten the beams."

My friend rode a motorcycle to get to work but offered his scooter to me for local transportation. The two-wheeler was clunky, and it had a high center of gravity. When I sat on it, I felt top-heavy. "Too bad it's kind of slow," my friend said. "My bike goes off like a shot."

After I watched my friend launch himself down the road, I got on the scooter and followed a railroad track that led into town. I opened the throttle, and the scooter cruised at about 40 kilometers per hour.

When I hit a patch of gravel, the bike slid out from under me. The wipeout seemed to happen in slow motion. The bike leaned to the side, and I went down with it. I jumped away as the machine hit the dirt. Uninjured, I picked up the bike. It weighed a ton, but I managed to right it. I got on and rode to a bar located next to the train track. When I walked in, I saw that the ceiling had chairs nailed to it—upside down. The place was called Balance, which was pronounced Ba-LAHNCE.

A few men were sitting at a table. Boldly, I sat with them. They tried to engage me in conversation, but when they found I couldn't speak *Switzerdeutsch*, they ignored me. I moved to a different table and sat by myself.

A tough-looking man came over and started speaking to me in my language. "I hate your president," he said. "But I don't want to assassinate him. I want to start small, with a county executive, to send a message to the higher-ups. If the warning doesn't work, I'll knock off a governor. Then I'll rub out the vice president. We'll see if the president gets the message."

I went into the restroom, and while I was standing there, a guy came in and threw up next to me. I wanted to ask him if he was OK, but I didn't know how to ask.

Shortly, I left Balance, rode the scooter home and decided not to ride it anymore.

I spent about a week at my friend's place. During the day, I walked up to the woods that covered the surrounding hills. Sometimes, I gathered twigs and sticks and built an open fire on the ground. Even in daylight, the flames were filled with energy. Passing hikers noticed the fire, but no one told me to put it out.

When I told my friend about my fire, he said, "That's a 500-franc fine, if you get caught."

One evening, my friend took me to a bar and ordered a couple of *grossis*, or large beers. A young man came up to my friend and asked if I was his *bruder*.

"He's not my *bruder*," my friend said.

"He looks like your *bruder*," the man said.

"Don't try to insult me, you fucker," my friend said.

At night, I slept in the same room as my friend. The room had an extra bed the size of a cot. I unrolled my sleeping bag and laid it out on the narrow mattress.

"You seem unhappy," my friend said. "Are you thinking about that girl you met in college?"

"The one in our art program?" I asked.

"Yes. The one who was going to be an artist."

I remembered her. My mistake was not taking her seriously. As it turned out, she became an artist. She won prizes. She traveled while I stayed home. But I was traveling now. "No, I'm not really thinking about her," I said.

During the night, I could hear my friend inhaling and exhaling. He sounded like he was taking his last breaths. His huffing and puffing kept me awake, then woke me after I'd fallen asleep.

My friend left the house early for work. I went to the back of the house for a shower, and when I emerged the landlady was waiting for me. She put out her hand and touched my hair. She said something that included the phrase "*Haar waschen.*"

I nodded at her and ran.

I went upstairs and ate. At the table, I made a sketch of the still life in front of me. There was the loaf of hard bread, a serrated knife, cheeses on a board, tangerines in a bowl. In the background was a wooden cabinet where the food was stored. I drew lines to represent the edges of cabinet doors, handles and hinges. I put the sketch away in a notebook.

I let the main door lock itself and started my hike along Gobble Street to the train station.

Mentorship

A woman I knew slightly invited me to her place for a party. It was quite a place—a duplex loft in an artists' community, for which she paid very little because she was a professional artist. When I saw the layout, I thought I should apply for a unit myself, but I suspected I wasn't a professional artist. You had to make your living from your artwork to qualify for these places, and I made only a few dollars from selling the booklets I carried around. That was no living, even if I somehow wouldn't have to pay rent. I still had to eat. I'd starve in my artist's loft if I had to live from sales of my booklets, which were worth basically nothing. (That wasn't entirely true. I'd seen one of my booklets on sale in the bargain bin of a used bookstore for 50 cents. The joke was, the book was originally free.)

Maybe my host was interested in me; maybe she liked me; maybe that's why she'd invited me. We'd had a date, though it might not have been a date. For me, it certainly wasn't. It was a meeting of friends, or of two people who might become friends. Saying our connection was "just friends," however, might have insulted my companion. So I didn't say it. I just thought it, and I kept my thoughts to myself.

What I said (on our date) was, "How did you become an artist?" It was a mystery to me how one could earn a living from one's art. I thought this woman might become my mentor.

But my potential mentor wasn't forthcoming. "You know," she said, "I really don't know."

She didn't want to talk about art. She wanted to know how much money I made. "What does a publishing assistant make?" she asked, referring to the job I worked to pay my rent.

"Well, I've been saving up," I said. "I might have enough for a car."

"A Jaguar?" she asked.

I was familiar with the model. It might cost as much as a small house where I grew up. I hadn't saved that much money. In fact, I'd saved only enough for a used car, a clunker—probably a junker. But I didn't say that. Such a statement might have seemed unappealing to someone who thought she was on a date.

At her party, I was lost in a crowd. My potential mentor had lots of friends of her own. Apparently, it was her birthday.

There I was, among the well-wishers. They were all strangers to me. I didn't mingle. Instead, I looked at the birthday woman's paintings, which hung in pools of light on the walls. They were huge, pink-and-yellow nonobjective works, full of gesture. It must have taken a long time to complete them—hours of painstaking work.

I liked the paintings. I could see in them a high level of achievement. I'd once had an art teacher who told me, "There are two ways of painting. One is tight, and the other is loose." I'd tried my hand at painting, but my style was too tight. Then I'd switched to writing, but my booklets were too condensed. My potential mentor, on the other hand, was loose, but not too loose. She was just loose enough to succeed.

I looked up from where I was not mingling and saw her on the second-floor landing. She was the queen of her subsidized realm. I approached her and said, "Nice place you have here."

"I'm happy with it," she said, "but my daughter isn't. She thinks she grew up poor. She thinks she was a waif. A waif!"

At that point, I noticed her daughter, who didn't look like a waif. In fact, she looked well clothed and fed. She also looked like she had a boyfriend. A young man always seemed to be standing between her and any other man at the party. He just slid in and stood there. He was a master of the quick maneuver, the fast break.

When people wished the host a happy birthday, I found out she was 17 years older than I was. That seemed like a big gap. I didn't know how I was supposed to relate. Was I supposed to be a perpetual mentee, always hiking the path to creative realization? Was I supposed to be the provider for her artistic activities, once I found a way to buy a Jaguar? Or was I supposed to be a guy who'd met her a couple of times and disappeared?

Perversely, I could see myself relating to her daughter. But would it have been polite to speak to her? I was a guest of the mother. I'd had a one-to-one meeting with her—not a date, more of an exploration of friendship, at least in my eyes. But who knew how the mother had seen it?

A plan presented itself to me. I could adopt the daughter, if I married her mother. I would be closer to the daughter that way. But if I had feelings for her, the situation would be incestuous. Wasn't that what making art was all about, being incestuous? Wasn't incest best? If I adopted the daughter, I'd get her boyfriend in the bargain. That would make me jealous. Since I wouldn't be able to get rid of the boyfriend, I would feel left out. Worse, the mother would become upset because I was paying attention to her daughter, not to her. As a result, she wouldn't teach me anything about making art. The creative process would remain a mystery to me.

I had some of my worthless booklets with me. I held them in my hand to see if anyone noticed, but no one did. I spread them out on a table, hoping that someone would take a look, but no one paused to examine them.

On the Move

I was invited to a party in New Jersey. After a train ride from the city, I arrived at a house where several graduate students lived. I met the host, then went into the kitchen. As I stood there, I saw a young man crawling on his hands and knees. When I asked what he was doing, he said he was counting the linoleum tiles. He was going from one wall to the other, keeping track in his mind.

Presently, I met a student who seemed interested in speaking to me. When I told him where I lived, he said, "I'm moving to New York soon."

He told me he'd "busted out" of graduate school. "I was majoring in history," he said, "but I was interested in only one thing: Druids. I used my teaching fellowship for Druid research, and I failed my comprehensive exams."

"What are you going to do now?"

"I'm going to use my computer skills to make lots of money."

*

In the city, my new friend asked me to meet him for lunch at a university club. The place had a dress code, so I put on a necktie. My friend was wearing a suit.

"I see we both have our monkey costumes on," he said. "I'm a systems architect now; I dress this way every day."

During lunch, he said he'd been seeing a therapist. "I've discovered something," he said. "I'm bisexual.

"I've had girlfriends," he went on, "but I've always noticed that when I'm in a men's room, I get embarrassed. It's all the penises, you know."

After the meal, I thought about what he'd said. I knew that no one was one hundred percent, but he wasn't even fifty percent.

*

My off-and-on girlfriend took me to a gathering of science-fiction fans. She was a fan herself. She'd read many books in the genre and knew many authors.

At the conference, I met a writer who was famous for his space-age jungle series. I was glad he was talking to me, but his attention wandered. He noticed a woman with large breasts and pointed her (and them) out to me. "Those could choke a horse," he said.

Later, he invited my girlfriend and me to his home in Queens. He lived on a hill, in an old two-story. Inside, the house looked like a museum. Shelves were filled with hardcover books by authors like H.P. Lovecraft and August Derleth.

My girlfriend took me upstairs and showed me a room called "the dungeon." I saw torture instruments hanging on the walls, but I didn't believe the home owner actually used them. "These are decorations, right?" I said.

"No," my girlfriend said. "He once put thumb cuffs on a girlfriend of mine. Then he hit her on the thigh with a flail."

"What did she do?" I asked.

"She couldn't do much. Her thumbs were cuffed."

Before I left, the author said to me, "I like boys, too. I often have sessions with young ones. A session lasts about an hour.

"Take this," he added, and gave me his business card.

*

My systems-architect friend invited me to his house in New England. "I built this when I was an undergraduate," he said. "Now, I rent it to a couple of professors here."

The professors, who were married, were leaving the house when we arrived. The two of them looked alike, with wire-framed glasses and bushy, light-colored hair.

"They were friends of mine before they were tenants," my friend said. "I got them naked once."

When I went upstairs, I noticed that the platform bed had eyebolts screwed into its corners. The metal loops obviously were anchors for ropes. I wondered which member of the couple did the staking out, and which one got staked, or whether they took turns.

When I pointed out the eyebolts to my friend, he said, "So that's what they're into."

During the day, my friend brought me to a clear, cold stream. The two of us took off our clothes and waded in. As I stood with water rushing past my waist, my friend snapped pictures of me.

*

The next time I visited him, he projected the photos onto his white wall. I'd forgotten he'd taken them. There I was, standing in a stream, looking like a nudist.

"I often lie in bed and click through these pictures," he said.

"I want you to move in with me," he continued. "I'll build a room for you. Your rent would be very low. This is a great neighborhood."

Through his windows, we could clearly see the World Trade Center. The lights in the twin buildings sparkled. The towers were almost in our faces.

*

Shortly after I moved in, my roommate told me he was leaving for the West Coast. "I've met someone," he said, "and he wants to move there."

"Who is he?" I asked.

"He's a dental student."

I remembered a young man who'd brought a plant as a gift. The plant was some kind of tree, maybe a fig tree; it was as tall as he was.

"When I leave, you'll have to move out," my roommate said. "But I want you to do me a favor."

"What's that?"

"I want you to take my fig tree and care for it."

*

I moved to an apartment in a different borough. It was a dark basement flat, but there was a garden in the back. My landlords were a Chinese couple with children who lived down the street.

I set up the fig tree in the one spot of indoor sunlight and planted a few marijuana seeds in the garden. In a couple of weeks, the seeds grew into six-inch plants.

At one point, one of my landlords—the wife—came over. She looked at the garden and asked me, "Are those marijuana plants?"

"Someone upstairs must have thrown seeds out the window," I said. "The seeds must have sprouted when I wasn't looking."

After she left, I pulled up the plants.

*

One night, as I was walking home through the nearby park, I noticed a man walking a dog behind me. Another man was coming toward me. No one else was in sight.

As I reached the man walking toward me, he stood in my path, blocking my way. He opened his jacket and showed me a small, nickel-plated revolver. The man with the dog was now standing behind me, blocking my escape.

"We're taking your money," the man with the gun announced.

I gave him nine dollars.

He tore off my glasses and stepped on them. "Now," he said, "run."

I started walking away.

"Run, or I'll shoot!"

I ran.

When I got back to my apartment, I decided to report the incident. I would call the local precinct. After the cops made their visit, I would move to a different apartment, probably in a different borough.

'Crazy Man on Bicycle!'

When I was a child, I wanted to play polo, but I had no pony. All I had was a bicycle. It was an English bicycle, and therefore I thought it could substitute for a pony. Weren't English ponies the kind used for polo? Polo was the sport of kings, and England had a king. I didn't have a king, but I thought I could ride my bike in tight patterns and knock a ball around with a mallet. But I had no polo mallet—all I could find was a croquet mallet, and a wooden ball. The croquet mallet was too short to reach a ball on the ground from a bicycle seat, but I figured I would just lean over.

Then there was the problem of teammates, not to mention opponents. Who would I play with, and who would I play against? I knew a few other kids who rode bikes. My brother was a serious rider—he rode his bike to football practice. But would anyone want to pick up a mallet and ride in tight patterns to hit a wooden ball into a goal? I doubted it.

So I practiced by myself. I went to the nearest mown-grass field, at the local school. But the field had an uneven pitch. It slanted downward. I rode in anyway, and I gained speed as I rolled downhill. When I leaned over to hit the croquet ball with my mallet, my bicycle hit a bump and I went flying over the handlebars. I flew straight ahead as my front wheel froze and my rear wheel rose into the air. I landed on the grass without injury, save for the loss of faith in my ability to play polo on a bicycle.

*

When I moved to a city as an adult, my brother gave me one of his bicycles. It was a good one, used for racing. I rode it as often as I could. I rode it in the rain, wind and snow. I rode it when the streets were wet and drops of mud flew up from the rear wheel and splattered against the seat of my pants. I rode it when water neutralized the hand brakes and I could not stop when I wanted. I rode it when the temperature was almost zero and I had to wear layers of clothing to keep moving.

One day I chained the bike outside a grocery store, and when I came out it was gone. All that was left were a couple of broken chain links on the ground. I reported the theft to my brother, who seemed to think it was my fault. "You can't leave a bike on the street in the city!" he said.

The next bike I got was one that had already been stolen. It was spray-painted black. Even the handlebars and wheel rims were black. It was a "stealth" bicycle, hard to see, impossible to track. I bought it at a flea market, from a vendor hidden in a corner.

Soon enough, the stealth bicycle was stolen, too. It vanished from a pole where it had been cable-locked outside a bar. The cable wire had been cut. I thought I saw the stealth bike one more time—I saw a man riding an all-black bicycle in circles on the street. But I didn't approach him. I just didn't think he'd give the bicycle back.

After that, I bought a lock with very thick metal parts. The device was called the Fuggedaboutit. If my bike were stolen while secured, the maker of the Fuggedaboutit would replace the bike. After I started using the heavy device, only my bicycle seat was stolen. I came out of a building one night and found a bare support rod where the seat had been. I had to Fuggedabout the seat, at least until I got a new one.

*

When I had a working bike, my routine was to ride from the Lower East Side to midtown west. I was single, and I rode the route to find my kicks. I went to the stores around Times Square, to places with big neon signs and names like XXX Video.

I didn't want to see any friends during my rides. Friends might wonder what I was doing in that neighborhood, and I might wonder the same about them. Were we both looking for thrills? We probably were, but not for the same kind of thrills. Thrills were very specific. I had to locate the right aisle, in the right store, and zero in on the right genre. If I were lucky, I would find dozens, maybe hundreds, of items that contained my favorite fetish. I could spend the next hour or two sorting through the selections to find the perfect one, the most compelling one, the one I would revisit again and again. Or I might fail to find that one and have to go to another store, where I would spend the next hour or two searching the aisles, racks and titles.

If I happened to see anyone I knew on these trips, I would ride the other way. I didn't want to confront them. I didn't want them to ask me, "What are you doing here?" and I didn't want to ask them the same thing.

*

I started to keep my bike in the courtyard of the building where I lived. It wasn't really a courtyard; it was a basement without a roof. I chained my bike to a communal railing. When rain fell, the stored bicycles were unprotected. In a matter of months, my bike's frame was covered with rust.

In time, some of the moving parts of the bicycle stopped working. The back brake wouldn't open, so I removed it. The front brake was enough. Then the gear changer stopped shifting, so I rode in one gear. It was a high gear.

Despite the rust, the chain transmission continued to engage, and the wheels continued to spin. I could get where I wanted to go, and I was determined to ride as long as the bicycle would roll.

*

One night, I chained my bike to a tree, and when I came out the bike was lying on its side. I picked it up and started to ride, then noticed that one of the tires was flat. I was in front of an apartment building. Maybe someone had objected to my parking the bicycle there. Maybe that person thought I had harmed the tree with the chain. Maybe someone had slashed the tire out of revenge.

I took the bike a repair shop, where a man asked me to wait. He put the bike on a rack and tried to turn the pedals with his hand. The pedals quickly became locked, so he sprayed oil onto the rear cogs. The pedals went around a couple of times, then froze. "This bike is junk," he said.

"I bought it new," I said, "but I've been keeping it outside."

"If the wheels turn," he said, "I guess you can ride it."

"Can you fix the seat?" I ask. "I've tried but can't."

The seat was frozen in its post. "If you can move this seat," the man said, "you might have a job here."

*

I rode my bike from the Lower East Side to midtown west. I wasn't looking for kicks; I was going a restaurant to meet a friend. I looked at flowers as I rolled past a park. I spotted daffodils, crocuses and tulips. I wondered why no one had cut any of the flowers off at their base and taken them home. It would have been easy; all one would need was a knife and the nerve. I had neither.

I parked outside the restaurant, and when I told my friend I'd ridden there, he seemed surprised. Maybe he thought the streets were too crowded to navigate. Maybe he thought I was too frail to make the trip. Maybe he expected the bike to be missing when we came out of the restaurant. But when we were finished, the bike was still where I'd left it.

On my way home, I entered a cross street and was squeezed to the side by traffic. There was a truck next to me, and cars behind. I didn't care that the vehicles were crowding me. I could ride in tight patterns, learned from playing bicycle polo as a child. I could thread my way toward a goal while flying downhill.

Next to the curb, I ran over a pylon. It wasn't a traffic cone; it was a tall obstacle that said, "Bus Lane Only." I hit it, and it went over. I wavered for a half-second, then kept riding, and as I rolled, I heard a man on the sidewalk call out, "Crazy man on bicycle!"

An Urban Weapon

I brought a gun from my mother's house to my apartment in the city. The gun had been stored in her house since my father died. No one used it for hunting or target shooting anymore. It had been taken away briefly by my sister's husband, who looted the place after my father's passing. He'd piled some guns into a pickup truck and driven cross-country with them. My sister went along for the ride. She'd taken one of my father's paintings—it showed a silver zeppelin floating over a cornfield. Halfway across the country, my sister and her husband had an argument. My sister got out of the truck and took a bus the rest of the way. Her husband drove on with the guns and the rest of the loot.

My sister's husband didn't have the guns for long. My mother took a plane to retrieve them. She had to get the state police involved to get the guns back. She showed a photo to prove she owned the guns, and the authorities shipped them to her. My mother picked up the guns at her local state police barracks. My sister and her husband kept the canvas showing the huge silver zeppelin.

On one of my visits to my mother's house, I found the gun my father had given me for a birthday. It was in its canvas case, propped in a corner of a closet. I unzipped the case and saw that the metal was blue and free of rust, and that the stock was unscratched. The gun looked as good as new. I picked up the case by its leather handle and brought the gun home. I was in a car, so the cops didn't see me. No one stopped me.

*

I wondered if I needed a permit or license to keep the gun in the city. I looked up the laws. The city I lived in had the toughest restrictions in the nation. Handguns were illegal, as were assault rifles, semiautomatic weapons and portable bombs. Any gun that could be concealed or could hold more than five rounds of ammunition was banned.

My firearm couldn't be concealed—it was about four feet long. One of its barrels was threaded—that was the rifle barrel. Below the rifle barrel was a shotgun barrel. This model was an "over-and-under," a sporting gun perfect for shooting wild turkeys. The shotgun could bring down a turkey crashing through the trees above, while the rifle could drop a turkey standing a hundred yards away.

The gun didn't have a detachable magazine or a collapsible stock. It couldn't hold more than five rounds of ammunition—it could hold only two. It was not a semiautomatic weapon; you had to cock the hammer before firing. It couldn't be used to launch grenades. It was less illegal than a switchblade or a "throwing star"—the razor-edged disc Bruce Lee tossed in movies.

I requested a gun registration form. I didn't want to break the law. But when the form arrived, I decided not to fill it out. Even though I had a right to own the gun, the registration fee was steep. I kept the firearm out of sight, propped in its case in a corner of a closet.

*

One night, my neighbor's place was robbed. He'd walked upstairs to talk to me, and he'd locked his door, but he hadn't shut the window leading to the fire escape. When he returned, he saw that the screen was torn and a stereo amplifier was missing.

He came back to my place to tell me what happened. I thought we should act fast. I owned a deadly weapon. If we saw someone with an amplifier under his arm, I would have the upper hand. I would have the choice of firing the gun or just holding it in a threatening manner. "Drop the amp," I would say, "and step away. No one gets hurt."

But my neighbor thought that approach was overkill. "We don't need a gun," he said.

I picked up a hammer. I had never bludgeoned anyone, but I was ready to start. The invasion of our building had put me in high dudgeon.

My neighbor and I walked out to the street. There, we saw another neighbor. "I was worried," the other neighbor said, "when I saw a guy on the fire escape throwing something down to a guy on the street."

"What did it look like?" we asked.

"A stereo amplifier."

I hefted the hammer. It would do great damage if wielded like a club. "Where'd they go?" we asked.

"They vanished into the crowd," the other neighbor said.

There were a number of pedestrians on the sidewalk and street. None of them were carrying an amplifier.

*

The son of a woman friend of mine stayed with me for an afternoon. He was 11 years old, and I was his sitter. I thought the gun would amuse him, so I brought it out of its hiding place. I tried to explain how it worked. "It's an over-and-under," I said, "with a rifle on top and a shotgun on the bottom. If you see a turkey, you get one chance with the shotgun. Then, if the bird flies away and lands, you can try again with the rifle."

The boy picked up the gun and put it over his shoulder. He marched around the room, swinging his free arm and lifting his legs high. He looked like a soldier. He knew the drill. He would pass inspection.

"No, no," I said. "You cradle the gun in your arms as you hike through the woods."

I took the gun and cradled it, then walked around the room stealthily. I lived in a large, loftlike space, so I had plenty of ground to cover. "You kick the brush to scare up game," I said as I made sideways motions with a foot.

When I came to the couch, my cat ran out of hiding. "There goes one," I said and raised the gun to my shoulder. The end of the barrel covered the animal. The cat didn't realize the danger—it had no experience with weapons.

I didn't pull the trigger. The gun wasn't loaded, anyway. The cat was safe.

"I don't want to hunt for animals," the boy said. "I want to be in the Army."

"You don't want to be in the Army," I said. "You might get killed."

"I want to see the movie *Dead Bang*, with Don Johnson. That movie has some shooting in it."

When the boy's mother came to pick him up, she found out what we'd been doing. She got angry but tried not to show it. She just trembled and said, "I don't want my son in any home where there's a gun."

*

I went to visit my brother. One night, he brought out his collection of handguns. He had several semiautomatics. All were loaded and ready to fire. He picked one up, removed the clip and worked the top action to make sure a cartridge wasn't in the chamber.

"Sight down the barrel," he said as he offered one of the guns to me.

I held the gun at arm's length and pointed it at a window. I lined up the bead with the rear notch. Any living thing in that pinpoint would be dead.

He picked another gun. "This one could start a war," he said.

He popped the clip out of the handle. "It holds fifteen rounds," he added. He showed me how the cartridges were staggered in the wider magazine. He took the cartridges out, then reinserted them carefully. He slipped the clip back into the gun. He cradled the gun in his palm.

I didn't ask if he had a permit or license to own the guns. I figured he could do what he wanted. He seemed to place great value on having the weapons. They were things that gave him a feeling of confidence, made him happy.

*

Later, a friend of mine came to visit me, and I told him about the gun I was keeping. "It's a hunting gun," I said.

"I'd like to take it out sometime," he said.

"You have nothing against guns?" I asked.

"I'm a Communist," he said. "I never know when I'll need a gun. The revolution could start anytime."

I brought out the gun, and we broke it down. We held up the barrels and looked through them from the back. We looked out through the front, the way bullets or pellets would travel. The shotgun barrel was smooth, and the rifle barrel had a clear spiral thread.

"Did you have to take a course to learn how to shoot?" my friend asked.

"Yes," I said. "The instructor set up a cabbage and told us, 'This has the consistency of a man's head.' Then he pointed a shotgun at it and pulled the trigger."

"My god," my friend said.

"Just showed what could happen," I said.

*

I remembered the last time I'd used the gun. I was a teenager, and I was hunting with my father. "Why don't you shoot?" he'd asked me. "What are you, gun-shy? The sound of a gun won't hurt you."

To prove his point, he fired his shotgun next to me. I tried to cover my ears, but I wasn't fast enough. The sound was the worst I'd ever heard.

Later, we were walking through some low pine trees, and I heard a grouse take off. I barely saw the bird—I only heard the drumming of its wings—but I lifted the heavy gun and swung the barrel along the bird's flight path. I "led" the invisible bird by a couple of feet and pulled the trigger. The blast was deafening.

I went to where I thought the bird might have fallen, but saw nothing but torn pine needles on the ground.

I stopped using the gun then. It was too heavy to lug around. I started to carry a lighter gun. After I moved out of my parents' house, I didn't hunt again.

*

I didn't know why I was keeping the gun. I wasn't going to stop robbers with it. I wasn't going to hunt with it, and I wasn't going use it to shoot at targets. I'd never shot a clay pigeon in my life. I wasn't a gun nut.

After storing the firearm for a while, I got rid of it. I took it back to my mother's house and left it there. I urged her to sell it—I didn't want her to give it to my sister and her husband. They weren't hunters; they were looters. They still had my father's zeppelin painting. It was hanging on their wall.

Loft Living

My landlord invited me to a party in his loft. His place was in a fashionable neighborhood, and it was bigger than I'd expected. It had two floors and covered about 3,000 square feet. When I arrived, I stared at the fixtures and exposed wood. The appliances were shiny, and the railing around the balcony looked like it was made of oak.

During the party, my host pretty much ignored me, but when he noticed me, he took me aside. "You know," he said, "your rent is nothing, compared to what I pay."

I was the host's subtenant. I lived in a building that had been abandoned, then sold to a group of artist-entrepreneurs. It was a de facto co-op. "I'd like to have a permanent lease," I said.

"Don't worry," he said. "We're going to fix your place up; then we'll sell it to you."

"An option to renew my lease would be enough," I said.

He slapped me on the shoulder. "Buddy," he said, "you could be a friend of mine, except you're my tenant."

At the end of his party, he released dozens of balloons that had been held in a net near the ceiling. As the balloons bounced, he said to me, "I'll say one thing for New York. It's the easiest place to get laid."

*

I invited a young woman I'd met at the party to my loft. She didn't seem to mind the fact that I had no furniture. After all, I had a big space.

She and I sat at a table made of two-by-fours and particleboard. Under the table, a split in the floorboards revealed a slice of the downstairs apartment. Below us, the couple in residence was yelling at their dog. First the woman, then the man, would shout, "Klaus, no!" We could see them as they passed beneath the hole in the floor.

"You remember the party where we met?" my guest asked.

"Yes, of course," I said.

"It had a theme."

"It did."

"The theme was 'Say yes to love.'"

"I remember."

From below, I heard the woman, then the man, yell, "Klaus, no!" but when I looked through the crack, I couldn't see the people or their dog. I didn't know what Klaus was doing wrong.

"It was a nice party," I said, but I didn't really think so. I'd come there with a couple, and by the end of the party, they'd broken up. The man had met another woman and ignored his date.

"You have to say yes," my guest said. "You have to say yes to love."

Downstairs, my neighbors said "No" again.

Later, I walked my guest out to the street and helped her hail a cab. I must have been nervous, because when I shut the car door for her, the metal frame hit me in the face.

*

My landlord sent a man named Olaf to install a new wood floor in my place. Olaf had a routine: He would align a plank, then sink a nail into it with one blow of a hammer. He repeated this action hundreds of times. In two days, he was half finished with the job.

I noticed that the floor wasn't level. It swelled where the old subflooring was higher, and it dipped where the former floor had settled. I pointed this out to Olaf. "The floor is curved," I said. "You have to level it by using shims. You have to shim it up. Do you know how to shim?"

I couldn't tell if Olaf understood, because he didn't say anything.

I tapped the floor with my foot. "You call this a shim?" I asked.

Olaf left then and never came back. The floor remained as it was. Half of it was new, and half was the old, rotting wood.

*

At one point, I noticed that cockroaches were infesting my place. I sprayed the surfaces with insecticide, but it didn't make much difference. So I called a phone number I'd found in a classified ad for extermination services.

Two women came to my place. They called themselves the Lady Killers. They blasted white powder from squeeze bottles into every crack and seam. "It's boric acid cut with baby powder," they explained.

At first, there was no change, except that the roaches ran around covered with white dust.

After a while, I saw fewer insects, but the powder stuck to everything. Whenever I picked up a glass, dish or utensil, I had to clean off a residue of roach dust.

*

The tenants in my building formed a group to fight against our landlords. None of us had renewable leases or predictable rent increases. We retained a lawyer, who advised us to put our rent into a bank account. The money would remain there and would show that we were able to pay, if we wanted to. We just didn't want to.

I was appointed treasurer for the group. I set up an escrow account, collected rent from all of the tenants and deposited the money. I kept a record of the amounts on paper.

*

One night, a couple of other building residents came to visit. We sat at my particleboard table and played cards. Now and then, the gas heater mounted in a nearby window kicked on with a bang.

"My heater doesn't do that," one of the residents said.

"Don't worry about it," I said. "When it restarts, it always explodes"

People seemed startled every time the gas ignited.

Presently, we heard a knock on the door. I opened it and saw a young man standing in the hallway. I thought he was a friend of one of the other residents. "Do you want to come in?" I asked.

He handed me a paper document. When I asked what it was, he said, "Just read it."

I brought the document inside. It was a summons to appear in court. We had been subpoenaed.

*

One of my neighbors came back from a deposition. "I listened to the statement of one of the owners," he said. "She kept saying she was an artist."

He imitated her: "'I am AH-tist! Give my space back!'"

The owner was Asian and spoke English with an accent.

"What are we?" my neighbor said. "We're artists, too. We're AH-tists. Artists don't pay rent."

*

I started working with a couple of guys to rehabilitate an abandoned building nearby. We planned to clean it up and occupy it. We were going to move in and take ownership.

There was a secret door to get to the stairs—it was a piece of sheetrock nailed to a frame. The three of us pried the board off the frame and went through the opening.

As I walked through the empty apartments, I saw rooms with different-colored walls. There were pink rooms, blue rooms, yellow rooms. I saw shelves with dishes still stacked on them, and floors covered with papers, clothes and plasterboard shards.

Using a broom and a shovel, I scooped up as much trash as I could—I worked hard.

After a few days, the three of us had made no dent in the piles of debris.

I called our housing lawyer—the one guiding the dispute with our landlords—to discuss the situation. "Maybe we could live in this abandoned building," I said. "We would move in and just refuse to move out."

"Who owns the building?" the lawyer asked.

"The city."

"You don't own it?"

"No."

"Do you have a lease or any sort of contract?"

"No."

"What you're doing is tantamount to walking into a bank and saying, 'We're going to take some money, but it's for a good cause. We're going to give it to the poor.'"

*

Our landlords made us an offer: a four-year lease, or no lease at all. If we moved out immediately, we could keep the rent we'd saved in the bank.

Most of my neighbors chose to move out right away. I withdrew money from the escrow account and gave them their portions. One person, however, claimed I owed her for one month more than I had recorded. "You have to give me another two thousand," she said.

"I don't see it on my record sheet," I said.

"I'm not leaving until I get it."

I should have told her to sue me, that I wouldn't hand over the money without a fight, but I didn't. I didn't have the time to argue. I gave her the extra amount.

*

I chose the four-year lease. I knew I'd never be able to afford a place as spacious as the one I had. I decided to live with the unfinished floor and the exploding gas heater and enjoy the loft for as long as I could. Klaus and his owners were moving out. I could still look through the floorboards to the apartment downstairs. Who knew what I would see? It didn't matter. If a dog didn't move in, things would be quieter over the next four years.

Bad Matches

When I came home, I found my live-in girlfriend lounging with a couple of her friends from the building. Two of them were sitting on chairs, and my girlfriend was lying on the couch. Her bare feet were propped on an upholstered arm.

When I asked what they were doing, they said they were tripping. "We each took a hit," one said.

"Of what?" I asked.

"Ecstasy," said another. "We were going to give you one, but there are none left."

"You're in an altered state all the time anyway," my girlfriend said.

I sat there and watched them smoke cigarettes. They had incredible stamina for staying in one place. I tried putting on music, but they told me to turn it off.

"You really are insensitive," said one.

They turned on the television to *The Phil Donahue Show*.

I baby-sat them for a couple of hours. When the drug wore off, the ones who didn't live with me went home.

*

Later, my girlfriend spent the night with a man she'd met through one of the women from our building.

"What's his name?" I asked.

"Scott."

"Scott?"

"Well, his real name is Maynard, but Maynard sounds like 'mallard.' A mallard is a duck, and a duck lives on the water. *The Great Gatsby* takes place on the water, and that book was written by F. Scott Fitzgerald. So we call him Scott."

"Did you actually sleep with him?"

"Of course."

"What the heck!"

"Don't worry," she said. "I'm moving out soon. I'm getting my own place with half of your money."

*

I called a woman I'd met at work. I hadn't seen her in years, but even so, she seemed happy to hear from me. She invited me to her place. I went to the edge of Manhattan, then walked into an apartment complex built on a landfill. She lived on a high floor of a tower.

Inside, every line was straight, every surface smooth. The lines where the walls met the floor were sharp and clean. There were no nail holes anywhere. I felt my compulsion meter rise. I wanted to mess things up.

"My sister is away," she said.

"I didn't know you had a sister," I said.

"She's a real estate agent. Nice place, huh?"

She turned on a stereo. I sat on the edge of a couch next to a low glass table. "Listen to the lyrics," she said.

I concentrated on the words and heard something like "I'm not your Weed Whacker. I'm just a strong black man."

"You know," she said, "I used to work as an exotic dancer."

"Where?" I asked.

"A truck stop on Long Island. The kind of place where you can get anything you want."

She tore a match from a book. "Here's a trick I learned," she said.

She split the cardboard stick partway, unbuttoned her shirt and placed the two pieces of cardboard around a nipple. The match stuck like tweezers. She took another match and lit it, then used it to light the unlit tip. We both watched as the match head flared.

The smell of burnt sulfur and the sound of rap music filled the air.

"What if your sister comes home?" I asked.

"I'll invite her to join us for tea and match tricks."

*

When I opened my apartment door, I could hear small paws running toward me. The cat that my girlfriend hadn't taken wanted food, so I opened a can and spooned out some of the mush.

I smoked a fake cigarette. The object looked like a real cigarette, with a white-paper barrel and a tan filter, but was made of plastic. I took a few empty tokes to steady my breathing. I thought it would make me calmer, but it didn't. I needed something else. I picked up a racket and a tennis ball and slapped the ball around the apartment. I kept going for minutes without missing.

I still wasn't satisfied, so I chewed a stick of gum. I chewed for a long while, until the gum disintegrated in my mouth. The wad became granular, no longer taffy-like. I had to spit it out.

At night, the cat came and slept on my bed. Its nearness was a comfort.

*

My former girlfriend invited me for dinner. She was staying with a friend of hers, a woman she'd met at one of her brief jobs.

When I came into the kitchen, I could see that she'd used many utensils to prepare our meal. Pots and pans were everywhere. She'd always been good at cooking, but the cleanup (my job) had always been a big operation.

"Thanks for the food," I said. "It's very good."

"I followed what that person said on *Donahue*—you know, the cooking expert."

After dinner, we had sex the way we used to, except there were no props in the apartment. I had to borrow some of her silk scarves, and they worked fine.

She told me she loved me, and I said the same to her. But she didn't ask me to visit again, and I didn't invite her to return to my place, either.

*

Later, one of the women who lived in my building knocked on my door. I knew she wasn't looking for my former girlfriend, because she knew she'd moved out.

"I left some Ecstasy here," she said. "It's in your freezer."

Sure enough, there was a frosted plastic bag in the ice compartment. I took it out and handed it to her. The bag contained one big pill.

"I'm giving it to Scott," she said.

She looked at me as if to say, "I hope you've learned your lesson, now that you have no girlfriend," but she didn't say anything as she left.

Kehena Beach

I went to an artists' retreat and was given a room in a large, airy house. My room had a bed and a small desk. In the window frames were screens, not glass panes. The screens didn't keep out mosquitoes. I could hear them whining around my head at night. They were louder than the coqui frogs that chirped from all directions.

In the shared kitchen I found lizards living behind the appliances. They were geckos of some sort. They clung to the walls when I made coffee. Maybe they liked the heat radiating from the stove coils, or maybe they just liked clinging to walls.

*

While I was in the common room, I heard what sounded like a bird flapping in the hallway. I went to look and saw it was an insect, huge by my standards. It resembled a large cockroach; maybe it was a water bug.

I'd seen a movie about cockroaches that grew to the size of people and lived in subway tunnels. These were evil insects, intent on killing people. To disguise themselves, they wore trench coats and top hats, and stood in the shadows of subway platforms. When unsuspecting riders approached, the mutant roaches threw off their costumes and attacked.

I wondered if I would have the same experience. I might walk past a closet, unaware that a six-foot insect was standing on its hind legs inside, wearing human clothes. As I passed, it would jump me.

*

During the day, I visited the pool, where the dress code was "top optional." There weren't many people next to the water—just me, a young man, and a topless young woman. I watched while the young man picked a coconut from the ground and split it with a machete. He broke through the husk and shell with one blow.

Gently, he offered the coconut to the woman. She held it and drank the milk straight, then discarded the rest of the coconut.

*

After dark, the pool was "clothing optional."

I went there at night and saw a couple of naked men heading for a hot tub, but I didn't follow them. I did, however, strip to my birthday suit. As I sat on a chair in my natural state, I saw what might have been a large bug strolling across the cement. But I wasn't wearing my glasses, so I couldn't tell. I couldn't even determine its size. It might have been two inches long or two feet long. It might have been a mutant bug, intent on stealing my discarded clothes to disguise itself as a human.

*

During the night, I could hear rain hitting the roof of my temporary home. I imagined that the water encouraged growth, especially among insects. Mud helped, too. The mutants were frolicking in the mud, getting ready to emerge as human-sized bugs. The exo-plates on their heads would look like human faces. When the insects were wearing clothes, I wouldn't be able to distinguish them from people.

*

I went to a black-sand beach. People were swimming, but they were on another part of the beach, a short distance from me.

I waded into the surf, and when I reached the deeper water, I noticed I couldn't swim in the direction I wanted. The current was pulling me out to the open ocean. I looked toward the beach and saw people there. I waved my arms and called for help.

The people saw me but didn't respond. Maybe they didn't understand, or maybe they didn't know how to take action.

I had a last thought, or what could have been a last thought: The people who knew me would be without me. That's how they would be for the rest of their lives.

Suddenly a man appeared beside me and shoved me toward the shore; then he swam away. I paddled and floated, and soon became tired. I almost gave up. Then a teenager arrived on a boogie board. "Don't stop yet," he said.

I kept paddling and reached the shore. I steadied myself, then found the teenager and thanked him.

"I tried to swim out there once," he said, "but it was like swimming in a washing machine."

*

I went to a kava bar for a drink. The place was a thatched stand with a couple of large containers in the middle. I had one bowl of muddy water and didn't feel anything, so I had another. I noticed a tingling in my fingertips and a rush of energy to my brain.

"Where are you staying?" the bartender asked.

I told him about the artists' retreat. "It's called Harmony," I said.

"We call it Harmony *Iki*," he said. "That means Harmony the Pit. It's built over our burial grounds. We want to tear it down."

I started another bowl of kava, but the taste was so unpleasant I couldn't finish it.

"I almost drowned today," I told the kava man.

"Where?" he asked.

"Kehena Beach."

"Kehena Beach!" he said. "A couple of tourists went there once and jumped into the ocean. They were never seen again."

*

As I lay in bed, I thought I hadn't made it back. My spirit, I believed, had returned to visit. I could see myself in the room that was temporarily mine.

I got up, or saw myself get up, and went to the closet. I expected to see a human-sized insect standing there, but saw nothing but clothes. The articles were damp.

Sounds of partying came from outside. A stereo was playing in a cabin decorated with colored lights.

I walked outside, or saw myself walk outside, and noticed a pink glow in the sky. The red fire of lava was reflecting off the mist. Was it a good sign to see that? A bad sign? I didn't know what the fire glow meant, in terms of good or bad magic.

*

Warts and All

When she called, I thought she was making a date. That's what I wanted—a date—because I hadn't seen her in a while. Before the lapse, I'd seen her every day for months. We'd met at an artists' retreat, and we had chemistry there. We were simpatico. We'd grabbed at each other and held on tightly—in odd places, like the side of the road. We'd had a good time, I thought, despite our disagreements. I thought that situation was ideal. I thought I had it made.

After all, we didn't disagree every day. But when we did, she would start to tremble. Then she would shake as if she were about to explode, and she would say something like, "What is this, a cross-examination?"

I was no attorney, but my lousy job had something to do with our situation. I didn't have the time or the mind-set to discuss things calmly. I got up, went to work, came home, visited her, crashed, and did it again the next day. She would have liked me to stay around and do something of value, like weatherproofing the windows in her apartment. But I left when I had to, and our differences remained unresolved.

So when she called, hope rose. I thought we could do things differently, more harmoniously. But what she said was, "You should see a doctor."

"Why?" I asked.

"You need to be checked."

"For what?"

"Genital warts."

"Why would I have them?"

"Because I have them," she said.

"How did you get them?"

"I don't know. Maybe from you."

I thought back to when we were seeing each other. Neither of us had warts then. Why did one of us have warts now? Or did both of us have warts now? Maybe she was right, and I didn't know I had them. I made an appointment with a doctor.

After I'd explained the reason for my visit, the doctor said, "Well, it's easy to tell if you have warts."

"How?" I asked.

"They look like warts."

We both looked to see if I had any cauliflower-shaped lesions on my private parts. I did not.

Suddenly, I realized that if I hadn't given the warts to my friend, someone else must have. She must have been intimate with someone other than me. There must have been skin-to-skin contact. I hadn't known about her other encounter or encounters, and the new knowledge made me angry.

I tried to tell her how I was feeling, but I couldn't get through on the phone.

When she finally answered, I told her I had no warts.

"I must have gotten them from a towel," she said.

"Whose towel?" I asked.

"From Vibeke's towel." She meant the towel that belonged to the Finnish au pair who lived with her and her children.

"Why would Vibeke put warts on her towel?"

"How should I know?"

I could sense that something like a timer was ticking inside her. I heard the rumbling that preceded an explosion, then a click that signaled a hang-up.

Vibeke seemed so young, so innocent. All she did was take care of my former girlfriend's children. She wasn't much older than a child herself. Apparently, that meant nothing. I had noticed that she called men "meat." That must have been what women called men in Finland. That country was home to a lot of fresh meat.

Vibeke might have decided to check out the meat market in our city. There was even an area called the meatpacking district. She must have gone there, to a place called The Cooler. Located below street level, The Cooler had a cement floor and industrial-sized weighing scales. She could have hooked up with a nice slab there. Satisfied with the grade, she might have showered after her expedition, then shared her towel with my erstwhile partner.

But that wasn't what happened. One of my friends told me about my ex's dating activities. "She went out with a friend of mine," he said.

Suddenly, everything became clear to me. My ex-partner was hungry for her own kind of meat. I even knew the guy. He looked like Graham Nash. Who had more animal protein than a guy who looked like Graham Nash? Certainly not me. Obviously, she had chowed down and come up with the skin virus.

What made things worse was the fact that I'd gone back to a previous girlfriend—the one just before my most recent partner—and told her about the warts. At first, she didn't respond, or at least she didn't respond negatively. Soon, though, she got back to me. "I'm covered with warts!" she shouted through the phone.

"Are you sure?" I asked.

"Well, I haven't seen a doctor yet."

"Then maybe you don't really have them." Hope rose momentarily.

Then she lost control. "That's it!" she screamed. "It's over!"

That, I knew, was that. Even so, I called her later, just to learn her diagnosis. She admitted she'd raised a false alarm. She was wart-free. She still didn't want to talk to me, though.

Where did that leave me? All I had was a tenuous connection to the children of my most recent girlfriend, the one who'd really had warts. But since I didn't see her children anymore, I sent them books and short notes. Along with one title, I wrote: "I hope you like this story. It's called *Pete's a Pizza*. It's about a boy whose father puts pepperoni on him, then bakes him in an oven. This boy Pete, see, is a pizza!"

I didn't hear back from the kids, maybe because they didn't want to answer, or maybe because their mother didn't want them to answer. After a while, I stopped sending books and notes.

Later, at a gathering of colleagues, I ran into my former girlfriend, the one who'd had the warts, and she gave me her business card. It said she was a designer of instructional materials for children. I guessed she would be good at that, because her background was in education. She also had some knowledge of psychology. She knew when to cut her losses, how to stop things before they got worse.

I saved her card, but I didn't call the phone number on it.

*

Part 4

Riding the Rails

I'm waiting to take the subway. Before the train arrives, a musician on the platform tells me a story about where he used to live. I don't know where that was—which borough of the city—but he had a wife then, he says.

Robbers lived upstairs from their apartment. The robbers stole everything they could get their hands on. Once, he saw them rolling a safe on a dolly along the street. Another time, they robbed the Big Apple Circus and brought home a small monkey. They couldn't sell the animal, so they gave it to the musician's wife.

The monkey wore a red hat, and whenever anyone approached, it would hold out the hat and look at the person with wide eyes, as if asking for money. "The monkey would make a few coins that way," the musician says, "enough to get food for its owner."

The musician's own hat is on the platform, brim up, open for donations. I drop 30 cents into it. It's not much, but the musician seems to appreciate it.

"What color was the monkey?" I ask.

"It was an old monkey," the musician says. "It was turning gray."

The musician's own hair is totally gray. It's curly and falls past his shoulders. He could have been a hippie once.

"That was the only thing the monkey could do," the musician says. He holds his hand out and looks upward with hopeful eyes. "Just like that," he adds. "People would give him money."

*

I take the subway uptown. The ride lasts a long time, more than an hour, so I take a seat and read a book. My reading is interrupted by a man delivering a rant. "Sorry for bothering you," he says to the train riders. "I'm not a criminal. I love Jesus. Can you spare a dollar or a sandwich?"

I avoid eye contact with the man, but as he moves through the car, a larger man says something to him.

The smaller man says, "I love Jesus" and "I'm not a violent man," but it is clear he is a violent man—he has violent emotions—and all he needs is a push to go over the edge. The larger man shoves him and wraps his fingers around his throat, then releases him.

"Are you laying hands on me?" the smaller man asks. "Are you mentally ill?"

"Just get out of my face," the larger man says.

"Move on!" a woman yells.

The smaller man walks away, then comes back. "Are you a violent man?" he asks the larger man.

"Back off, or I will lay hands on you."

I get off the train. I walk to the middle car and say to the conductor through his window, "There are two men fighting on the train."

I look into the car where I've been riding, just to make sure, and see they aren't there anymore.

Suddenly, the smaller man appears next to me. "Are you saying there's a fight on the train?" he asks. "Are you saying there's a violent man on the train?"

As I leave the station, I see that the violent man has gotten into a fight with another man. They are in a clinch, scuffling next to the bars that separate the token area from the platform. A woman is reaching through the bars and grabbing at them. She is screaming, "Stop it!" but they are ignoring her. How can she stop them, I wonder, when she is on the other side of the bars? And if there were no bars separating her from the fighters, what would she do then? Would she take hold of the men and try to overpower them?

*

Later, I see the musician whose wife owned the monkey. "Does your wife still have the monkey?" I ask.

"Not anymore," he says. "The monkey's gone, and my wife died a long time ago."

"I'm sorry to hear that," I say.

"She had a terminal illness when we were married. The doctors gave her four years, but she lasted eighteen."

I can't imagine having a spouse who is going to pass away. But I don't say anything. The musician seems happy enough. "That monkey was clever," he says. "He would look at you until you gave him money."

The musician goes on to tell me about a secret passageway between subway tracks. I know the place he's talking about—it's where I get on in the morning—but I never noticed a passageway. "I thought you had to get out and go across the street, then pay again if you wanted to switch trains," I say.

"There's a way across, on the inside," he says. "Some guys told me about it."

I can picture the guys he's talking about—guys who probably lived in the passageway. "Are those guys still there?" I ask.

"No, they were evicted for starting fires on the tracks."

I drop some coins into his upturned hat. We give each other a thumbs-up as the next train approaches.

*

At the last stop, everyone is supposed to exit. But I don't hear the announcement and stay on. With me are a couple of homeless men, sleeping on the seats. They have lots of room—they can stretch out.

I stand at the front of the first car and look out the window at the signal lights. I watch them change from red to yellow to green. I look for signs of life in the tunnel: old clothes, cardboard boxes, garbage. I see all of these things, and, fortunately, none of the flammable items are burning. The tunnel is clear of smoke. We are passing under a building, beyond the last stop. Surprisingly, there are skylights in the tunnel, made of milky leaded glass. These windows seem to be from an earlier era. The panes form an Art Deco pattern. The train makes a U-turn, and the next platform comes into view. People are standing closer to the edge than they should.

I get out and climb to the street. I'm in the area of a former disaster. The streets were once filled with rubble—I remember seeing piles of concrete and dust here.

Instead of emerging between tall buildings, I am walking next to pools of water—ponds in vacant lots. The pools are man-made—apparently dug with backhoes.

I want to investigate these ponds. I want to go from one to another and look into the water.

Odd Wedding

We're in the bed of my childhood—a bed I never shared with anyone. Somehow, she is in the bed with me. We move past foreplay. But my father interrupts us by coming to the door. I know he's there, but I can't see him.

She leaves the bed to take a shower. This is surprising because there was no shower in my childhood home. There was only a bathtub—an old-fashioned one with legs. I want her to come back to my bed, but she is taking a long shower. After she's done, I understand, she'll return to her home, not to my bed.

*

I see the double bed, the dresser and a night table in the spots I remember from my childhood bedroom. I don't know what I'm doing here. I've just awakened. I'm going to a wedding on this day, and I have to get ready. Downstairs, my father is dressed and ready to go.

My father never comes into sight, but I know he is wearing formal clothes, an outfit suitable for a wedding, something like a tuxedo.

He wants me to hurry up, and I want to comply, but I can't. I'm too involved with what I'm doing, with my preparations.

*

I'm on my way to my own wedding. The person I'm marrying is someone I've known for years, yet when I see her, she looks like no one I've ever seen before.

The wedding takes place just before I have to be at work, so I'm in a hurry.

During the party, I see some old friends. Then I realize I'm already married, and I don't need to get married again. But I like the person I'm marrying. She's almost the same as the person I'm married to.

The repeat wedding is held at a small college, a place where I would like to work but where I will never be employed. The college president, a woman, speaks at the ceremony. She is lively, and she sways as she speaks.

*

I don't want to be seen, so I put my fingers over my face. My bride's mother says, "When you walk into the room, I can smell you."

I don't question her judgment. If she finds me disagreeable, then I must be.

I'll have to stay somewhere else for the night and leave my bride with her mother. But I don't know where to stay; I haven't planned on being away.

*

I take a subway I've never taken before. Some of the passageways have ceilings that are so low I have to stoop. The signs are in another language. I arrive at an ornate, domed platform and look for a connecting train, but I can't find one. The subway line I'm on goes across town, and I need to go downtown. I don't know how to get a regular train.

I have to walk across a long, low bridge to get to my room. I know which building it's in, but I don't know the room number. I figure I'll use my key to find the room, but the key opens every room. The first door I try reveals a young man and two empty sleeping bags. "You can stay here," he says to me.

*

I want a cigarette. Even though I've quit, I think it will be OK to smoke one. I want one made of loose tobacco, the light-brown, stringy leaf. My father smoked this kind of tobacco—he rolled it in thin, small papers.

I acquire the ingredients I need and start to roll, but the cigarette paper is as big as a sheet of typing paper. I don't have enough tobacco to make a giant cigarette. My cigarette is all paper, and the paper gets thicker as I roll. I never light the cigarette.

*

Some other force is controlling my bed. I'm the only one on the mattress—my wife is staying with her mother. The force takes the form of spiders around my pillow. These creatures are not alive; they are mechanical. I can't sleep until the outside energy allows me to. I can't even pull up the one thin blanket on my own. I spend a lot of time lying awake as the night goes on.

I walk around the bedroom; I'm having trouble breathing. I want to say something, but I can't make a sound. All I can hear are my labored breaths. When I do make a sound, I'm not walking anymore. I'm sitting on a couch. I let out two loud moans that would frighten anyone who happens to be listening.

*

I'm looking for something, but I'm not sure where to start, and I'm not sure how to recognize it when I find it. And when I am in its presence, when it is before me, what will I do? Will I keep it secret, away from prying eyes? Or will I come out with it, wear it on a chain looped through a soft part of my flesh, make it jingle as a tease, follow as my partner pulls a string attached to it, then hang it from my partner's skin so we can take turns fetishizing? Why don't we just get matching rings and put them on our fingers?

All I have is my secret fetish, to which I'm deeply devoted.

*

My door buzzer sounds as I'm getting ready for bed.

The visitor turns out to be the woman I'm married to. I remember the ceremony in a carriage house, with a Jewish cantor and a jazz band. I rushed to meet her as she walked into the crowded room. While friends and family members listened, we recited the vows we wrote. With my foot, I broke a glass wrapped in a towel. My bride's mother was happy for us. We danced a swing step while the saxophone-led band played. Afterward, we traveled to an ancient place.

I push the intercom button to let her in.

When she sees me, she says, "I was walking by and thought I'd ring your buzzer."

I'm a little embarrassed, sitting there in my underwear. "I'm in my skivvies," I say.

"I don't have to stay," she says.

"I want you to stay," I say.

In the Reich

I went to Berlin so I could participate in a free event in an art gallery. It was a long way to go for no pay. Fortunately, I was able to take my wife and our small daughter with me. My wife had friends in the city—a couple who also had a small child—and they offered us a place to stay.

We arrived at an apartment that was not occupied—the friends hadn't moved in yet. Like many new European apartments, this one came with no furniture or fixtures. For light, there was one fluorescent desk lamp. The kitchen had only a sink, no stove or refrigerator. For sleeping, there were two air mattresses and a child's wood-frame bed. Thankfully, the water closet contained a tub and commode.

Our child had no complaints about the accommodations. She was a little over one year old. She didn't know many words, and she didn't know how to walk. All she could do was stand up by holding onto some kind of support. She would crawl from wall to wall, then grab onto a shelf or door frame and pull herself to her feet. She would stand there, smiling.

In the apartment, our child found a toy phone that played notes when she pushed its buttons. The toy belonged to the tenants' child. Our daughter spent a lot of time experimenting with the phone. She managed to turn it on in such a way that it wouldn't turn off. It just kept playing notes. We had to put it outside the apartment, in the hallway, so it wouldn't keep us awake at night.

*

At bedtime, I started out sleeping on a soft air mattress, but when I woke, I was resting on the wood floor. Half-conscious, I blew up the mattress, but in the morning I found myself sleeping on a flat sheet of plastic again.

At dawn, I walked quite a distance to find a place that sold food. I didn't know where I was going. No street led to any store. After a while, I came to a large, empty plaza, where there was a cafeteria. Inside, a few people stood in line. I watched as a young woman bought a single hard-boiled egg. The egg didn't seem like enough food for one person, but that was all she took.

I pointed to some croissants and managed to ask for coffee, then brought the food back to the apartment.

*

Before my wife, daughter and I went out for the day, we talked to our friends on the regular land phone. The father had some advice for me. "Watch out for *die Bullen*," he said.

"Who are *die Bullen?*" I asked.

"The cops."

*

At a subway entrance, we put our child—in her stroller—on an escalator. At the bottom of the ramp, a man started yelling at us. Obviously, we'd broken a rule, but which rule? A rule against riding an escalator with a baby in a stroller? Would the buggy's wheels get caught in the moving stairs? Would my fingers be severed when I tried to free the wheels? Would the child tumble from the stroller and bounce on her head to the bottom of the metal steps? All of these outcomes were possibilities.

On the subway platform, we didn't buy entry tickets because we couldn't read the instructions on the machine. Sure enough, at the next stop we were caught by *die Bullen*.

"Papers," one of them said to me. "Passport."

I had no papers or passport. "You should be helping us," I said, "not harassing us."

"Arrest!" *der Bulle* said. "Station house! Interrogation!"

"Why don't you just show us how to buy tickets?" I asked.

"OK," *der Bulle* said. "Sixty dollars each."

I paid for our freedom.

*

Our friends met us at the gallery where my event would be. The wife said she had an art piece, a video. She wanted to show it during the opening.

The main exhibit was made up of photographs of roadside memorials. There was a paper map on a wall. Pushpins had been stuck where fatal car accidents had occurred. The room was filled with the sound of rain playing through speakers.

The wife's installation consisted of a TV screen and a silent video loop that showed cars rolling along city streets. The cars moved slowly; they were caught in a traffic jam. None of them hit another. There were no fatal accidents. At one point, however, a car knocked a grocery bag from the arms of a person crossing the street. The pedestrian went through the motions of yelling at the driver while picking up the items. The only sound was that of rain.

When I read my material aloud, no one in the audience responded. One reason could have been that few people in the audience understood English. Another reason might have been that the material wasn't interesting.

After the reading, my wife and daughter returned to our apartment, and I went with some people to a bar. The man who'd invited me to read said, "Welcome to the Reich."

"The Third Reich?" I asked.

"Of course not," he said. "The Reich. Do you hear? *Ach tung!*"

"We were stopped by *die Bullen* today," I said.

"*Haut die Bullen, platt wie Stullen!*" he said. 'Hit the cops, make 'em drop!'"

"This isn't Auschwitz," someone else said.

*

I walked many blocks to get back to the apartment. I went from one district to another. On my way, I passed a number of women who looked like they were going to a costume party. Some were wearing ruffled dresses that reached the ground. Others were wearing leather accessories—halters, skirts and boots. But I didn't see any festivities; I didn't know where the women were going. They seemed to be wandering aimlessly.

*

At the apartment, our daughter could not find the toy phone she'd been playing with. Other than crawling around and pulling herself into a standing position, she had nothing to do. However, she seemed happy to lean against a wall.

I stopped trying to inflate my air mattress. I slept directly on the floor. Fortunately, my wife's air mattress worked fine—for her—and the small, wood-frame bed seemed comfortable for our child.

*

Our friends invited us to their apartment for an evening. As we sat on soft furniture, the father served me absinthe. The bottle came from a place called the Absinthe Depot.

"They have seminars at the Depot," he explained, "where you learn the ritual. You learn to use wormwood to reach enlightenment. Many people attend. No one leaves unchanged."

My host poured a shot of absinthe into a glass. Then he cooked sugar in a spoon over a candle flame. He held the spoon over the glass and let the burnt sugar fall in. He filled the remainder of the glass with orange juice.

He and I drank and waited to see what would happen.

I held my hand in front of my face, fingers splayed. I looked at my hand and saw that only the tips of my fingers were visible. Either I was hallucinating or I was getting a migraine. Through a window I could see the globe of the Television Tower. It seemed to be rotating. Either that, or it really was rotating.

"Was there a costume party on the *Sofienstrasse* last night?" I asked the father.

"*Sofienstrasse?*" he said. "No parties there."

"I saw women dressed up, in Victorian gowns and leather."

"Those were professional dominants. You were on the prostitute block."

Later, he took the toy phone out of his pocket. "I had to bring it back for our kid," he said. "You can have it again now." He punched a few buttons to make some musical notes. Our daughter smiled.

"You know," I said, "we never learned how to pay for the subway." I took a handful of uncanceled tickets from my pocket. "Can you use these?"

"Did you put them through the machine at the end of your trip?" our host asked.

"Never did," I said.

"We'll take them."

*

My wife and daughter and I rode the subway toward where we were staying. The train stopped one station before the one we wanted. It wouldn't go any farther. An announcement came over the public-address system, but we couldn't understand it. We got off and watched as the train reversed direction and went back the way it came. The next train did the same thing.

We thought about walking, but we didn't have a street map. "Walking will take a long time," I said. "We might get lost."

We studied the trains. The one on the opposite track—leading away from where we wanted to go—was also stopping, then reversing direction. If we got on and rode the wrong way, we could stay aboard until it went backward and brought us the right way. We crossed the platform and waited for the next wrong train.

*

We were leaving the next day. During the night, as before, the toy phone made notes without stopping, so we had to leave it in the hallway, where it played rudimentary music until morning.

*

Make It Funky

I have our child with me. We are crossing a street, on the east side of our city's main park, and someone says something to me, or gets in our way while we are walking. Maybe he says, "You should move out of the intersection."

Instead of thanking him, I threaten him. I don't say anything; I walk up to him and stare in his face. He walks to the other side of the street, turns, and makes a gesture at me. He lifts his arms away from his sides and curls them, like a muscleman taking a pose. I know what he means; he means I am acting like a tough guy. The odd thing is, I am nothing like a tough guy. I am just protective.

"Fight?" our child asks.

"No," I say. "We're just crossing the street."

*

I go to a gym to work out. I feel I should get in shape, get cut. But my regular gym has closed. A sign on its door directs me to a new place.

I go to the new place, where the setup is unfamiliar. No one is manning the front desk, so I walk into the main area and put my jacket and backpack on the floor. I unroll a yoga mat and lie on it.

I look at an exercise machine. It combines equipment into one stack. First, I face the center and pull a bar down in front of my stomach. Next, I sit on one side and pull the bar down toward my head, then switch to the other side and pull handles in toward my chest.

On my way out, a man at the front desk sees me leaving. "How long have you been here?" he asks.

"About half an hour," I say. "I have papers."

I show him the receipt from my former gym, the one that closed. "There was a sign in the window," I say. "It said you'd honor the time remaining on my contract."

"They did bad business there," the man said. "That's why they closed. We have no connection to them. We'll give you your time, but there are stipulations."

"What are the stipulations?" I ask.

"First, you have to join and pay the membership fee. After that, we'll give you your remaining time."

"I'll think about that," I say and walk out.

*

At home, our child tries to imitate us, her parents. She sees us lighting matches, so she decides to light matches herself. She holds a book of matches in one hand, pinches off a stick with the other, and strikes the head against the sandpaper strip. She doesn't press hard enough, and the match doesn't light. Unwisely, I show her how to hold the match head between the cardboard cover and the phosphorus strip. She does so, pulls the match out fast, and the end flares up.

The thing is, she doesn't light a candle, as we would before sitting down to dinner. She just holds the burning match. She shakes it, as she has seen us doing, but it doesn't go out. When the flame gets close to her fingers, she throws the match away.

I'm concerned that, at some point, she will toss a lit match and it will land on curtains or upholstery, and the whole place will go up in flames. Quickly, I take the matches away from her, but I know it will do no good. If she wants them, she will find them. If she wants to light them, she will. If she wants to destroy the place, she will.

*

I take the subway a short distance to a bar because I'm upset. Here, I know one of the bartenders. I find out, however, that he's not working on this day.

I greet a man at the bar—someone I don't know. After I start on my drink, he says, "You look happier now."

"How do you know?" I ask.

"You look happier than me."

"Why?"

"I used to work at an airport," he says. "It was a good job. But they decided I was redundant. That was five years ago."

"Do you get a pension?"

"I'm supposed to, but I don't."

"Social security?"

"I paid into it, but I don't get it."

"Why not?"

"Ask them," he says. "Ask the government."

"What are you living on now?" I ask.

"Nothing."

I can tell this man is not going to buy me a drink, so I buy him one.

*

On my way home, the sound of bass and percussion draws me to a band playing on the subway platform. They are a three-piece band, with an electronic beat box, two bass players and a soprano-saxophone player. A woman is dancing a short distance from them; she has an easy way to her movements. She's wearing a winter coat over black jeans and sneakers. She's looking at the sax player, a tall black man who carries the tune.

At a break in the music, someone calls from the platform across the tracks: "Make it funky."

All of the musicians in the band chant, "Make it funky." Their voices find a rhythm: "Make it funky! Make it funky!"

The next song starts, and the sax player comes forward to dance with the woman. Her blond hair covers her face. When she looks toward me, I see she is grinning. She becomes more animated in her dance—she claps her hands on accented notes—and the sax player, when he doesn't have to play with both hands, puts his free arm around her. They continue to dance as the next train arrives. I get on and notice that the woman doesn't take the train. She stays with the band. As the train car pulls away, I see her dancing with the sax player.

*

I take an escalator to exit the subway station. Between levels, I see a platform I haven't seen before. It's halfway between levels; it's a metal ledge, with steps leading off to the sides. Where do the steps go? There is an elevator next to the ledge, but the elevator doesn't open onto the platform. The door looks permanently sealed. No one can get off there.

Maybe you could open the elevator door, if you had a key. You might have to do that in a special circumstance, on the occasion of a bomb attack, say. To escape the smoke on the subway platform, you could walk into the elevator, turn the key, and choose the secret floor. You would get out there, along with everyone else who was able to fit in the elevator, and find the secret door, the one that leads to the outside. Only the people in the elevator car would be saved.

*

The next day, I want our child to go out with me. I think she should take a walk, get some air. But I can see she doesn't want to leave, so I keep saying, "I'm going out, and you're coming with me. I'm going through the door. I'll wait for you in the hallway."

I turn to my wife for help, but she says, "It's up to her."

"Come talk to me in the house," the child says. She has made a house around the living-area couch. She has set the cushions on end for walls and has used the fold-out mattress for a floor.

I walk over to the couch. "Let's go," I say.

"You're not in the house," she says. She points to the rest of the apartment. "That's not the house."

"I'm not climbing into the house," I say.

"Watch," she says. She drops a toy dog down a couple of cushions aligned end to end, one of them at a steep angle. "He can go down the sliding board without falling."

She's wrong: the dog falls onto its head on the floor.

I start to walk out.

"Wait," she screams from inside her house.

"Put on your socks and shoes," I say.

"Get my pink boots," she says.

"What?" I ask.

"Get my pink boots!" She means the funky ones, the ones that look like go-go boots.

I fetch them, and we both hit the street.

Soon enough, as we are walking along, we see the band that makes things funky. The musicians are there, but not the woman who was dancing with the sax player. My daughter and I stop and listen for a few minutes. Then I think I see the same blond woman walking toward the band. She is starting to dance under her winter coat.

*

Good Eggs

When I left our apartment, everything was more or less normal. But when I returned, I saw the turtle tank—it had arrived while I was away. Along with the tank came a turtle—a mature red-eared slider. My wife had bought the tank while I was on a short trip. Maybe she'd waited until I was traveling so I wouldn't stop her.

I was surprised by the sight of the aquarium, with its sun lamp shining and its air pump bubbling. In it was the turtle, treading water. It was a big animal, for its species; its carapace measured about eight inches front to back, and six inches across.

My wife and daughter had gotten the reptile free of charge because someone had abandoned it at a pet store.

We knew our seven-year-old daughter needed a pet, but I'd put my foot down about a cat. Our place was too small for a cat, I believed. Our daughter named the turtle Mystic.

I didn't think our relationship with this new pet would be mystical. The idea of having an alien creature, a reptile, in our home for an indefinite time was unsettling. Mystic wasn't cuddly or strokable, and her face conveyed little expression beyond wakefulness. Her line dated from the late Triassic period, about 200 million years ago, and included short periods of gigantism. Red-eared sliders were tough—they had become the most common house turtle, and now were listed as one of the world's most invasive species. Would our apartment be big enough for all of us? I didn't know, but I had no choice but to accept our new housemate.

Of course, no one except Mystic had any use for the tank. She swam in it, ate in it and slept in it, until she had to lay eggs. When that time came, she would climb out of the tank and fall to the floor with a loud thud. It was a long way down—at least four feet—and I worried that she would crack her shell. But I was never able to catch her, she fell so fast.

If she were unlucky, she would land on her back. If that happened, she would wave her legs until she got some sort of traction, and she would right herself. Then she would run as fast as she could across the flooring strips. It took her a few seconds to cross the room. I would walk to her, and when she saw me she would retract her neck and head so that only her nose showed. If I got too close, she would hiss at me.

After I walked away, Mystic would look for a soft place, maybe among dropped clothes, where she could dig a shallow pit for her eggs. She would scratch and knead with her hind feet. But the floor was hard, and no amount of scraping would dent it. Giving up, she would try to leave through a window. She knew where the windows were, but she wasn't able to climb to them. All she could do was scrape at the wall beneath a window with her front claws. She would raise her lower shell an inch or two off the floor and then fall back, repeatedly.

The idea at this point was not to push her with my foot, that is, not to kick her. The temptation was there, because she was low to the ground. I didn't want her in my clothes, or in our bedroom for that matter, so I wanted to nudge her out of the bedroom with my toe, then shut the door. But if I were caught by my wife and daughter while I was pushing with my foot, I would hear some screaming—some accusations of animal abuse. "You stepped on her head!" our daughter might yell.

So I would bend down and pick her up by the sides of her shell. If my moves were sudden or rough, she would panic and scratch me with her back claws, which were sharp, for digging.

It would take a week or two of her escaping the tank before she found an egg-laying place. Usually, it was not a good place. It was the hardwood floor, or the ceramic tiles in the bathroom. She would deposit eight to ten eggs there. Some of the eggs would remain whole and perfect. Others she would step on and smash.

The first person to discover the clutch would let out an "Oh, no!" and the rest of us would come quickly to look.

The eggs would not hatch, because there was no male turtle around. We saved a couple of the undamaged eggs, as souvenirs, in our freezer. We cleaned up the rest with a broom, dustpan and sponge. Once, four whole eggs disappeared when we weren't looking. "There were four eggs," my wife said on that occasion, "and then they were gone. She had white stuff on her mouth."

Mystic had no delicacy when it came to eating. She was a predator in her own right. She loved to eat goldfish. I'd thought the feeder fish would live for a while after we put them in the tank, that we'd have a turtle and a couple of fish swimming around for a few days. But the fish lasted about five minutes. She snapped them up with the speed of a striking snake. The activity was so violent it was banned in our home after the first feeding.

The tank stayed where it was, on top of a cabinet in the living room, until it was replaced by a bigger tank—one Mystic might not be able to climb out of. But as it turned out, she could get out of the larger tank when she wanted to—or when she needed to. She quit the tank whenever it was time to lay eggs. Precisely when that time would come was the question, one that required mystical knowledge to answer.

For the most part, Mystic was a healthy reptile. One day, however, I came home to find my wife and daughter on the couch, weeping. They were staring at the aquarium, where Mystic was floating listlessly. "She looks sick," my wife said, pointing.

"Is she going to die?" our daughter asked.

"I don't think so," I said. "Sliders can live 30 years."

"We have to take her to the vet," my wife said.

My wife and our daughter carried Mystic to the reptile clinic in a cardboard box. When they returned, I asked after her.

"She got a shot of vitamins," my wife said. "She'll be OK."

We fed Mystic larger doses of the food sticks called ReptoMin, and she recovered quickly. The following days, weeks and months were uneventful (in turtle terms), but we were waiting for the egg-laying to begin.

While we waited, we played music. Sitting on the simulated-stone ledge above the water, Mystic seemed to listen intently to the sounds of pop or rock filling the room. As she listened, she studied the leaves of a hanging plant and, if they were low enough, ate them. If she couldn't reach the leaves, she extended her neck and struck at specks of dust in the air. Or were they specks of dust? Perhaps they were dust mites, too small for us to see.

"You should read to her," our daughter suggested.

"I don't think she'll like that," I said.

"Why not?" our daughter said. "She listens to music and watches television."

As far as I could tell, Mystic never had much on her mind. Her brain, after all, wasn't much larger than the head of a pin. Still, this pinhead knew all she needed to know. Whenever I came close to the tank, she knew something was up. I would stand there looking at her, and she would start to beat the water with her forelimbs. She would splash like a mad turtle until I fed her something—grapes were best—or until I took her out of the tank and set her (gently) on the floor.

*

It's been a long time since Mystic has tried to get out of her tank to lay eggs. Maybe she has stopped laying eggs—we don't know. But if she starts again, we will put pillows on the floor to cushion her fall.

Over time, I've become Mystic's main grape provider. One by one, I put grapes on the end of a plastic fork and feed them to her. I once tried spearing the grapes with a ballpoint pen and offering them that way, but the action brought a quick correction. "Don't feed her with a pen!" our daughter said. "The ink is bad for her."

I switched to the plastic fork (easier on the beak) and stayed with it for the feeding ritual.

Each night, Mystic sees me across the room and starts splashing with her forelegs. We make eye contact, and I reach for the grapes. I remove the stems and choose ones that aren't too large. I don't want her to choke.

Family Life

When it's time for our daughter to go to bed, I ask, "Do you want me to read to you?"

"No," she says. "I can't recognize your voice. I can recognize only Mommy's"

"What about when she's away? Can I read to you then?"

Her mother isn't away often, though. And when she is, everyone's routine is upset.

"Why don't you read to the turtle?" our daughter asks me. She means the pet reptile named Mystic that lives in a tank in our living room. The turtle sleeps, mainly underwater, and I suppose it needs to relax before it closes its eyelids. "I don't think the turtle would understand," I say.

"She would. She understands music and television."

I guess I could pull a chair up to the aquarium and read aloud to the turtle. But the animal's brain seems quite small, sitting as it does between close-set eyes. I don't believe this is a thinking man's turtle. A person with fins and gills—someone like Aquaman or the creature from the Black Lagoon—might have something to say to Mystic. Yes, a merman and Mystic would be able to communicate with each other. But I have no fins or gills. All I have is a snorkel mask and a breathing tube, stored for occasional use. Mystic might accept me in this getup, if we were both in a big tank.

But I'd rather not read to the turtle. I'd rather read to our daughter. I don't think I'll get a chance, though, as long as my voice doesn't sound like Mommy's.

*

We take our daughter with us to a party. On the walk there, I say, "We're going to Broome Street."

"Does a witch live there?" she asks.

"Maybe," I say, "but this Broome is spelled with an E. A witch rides on a broom without an E."

"There's a lot of garbage around here," she says. "Rats live here. She's probably a real witch."

She's right. We're walking through a trashy area. We come to an industrial building, with an unmarked door. Inside, we climb a straight flight of steps between cement walls.

"Are we in a basement?" she asks.

"No, we're in a hallway," I say.

When we meet our host, it turns out our daughter wasn't far off. The host is not a well person, though her infirmity may just be due to age. She tries her best to accommodate us. She leads us out to a grille on a deck in a hollow between buildings. She gives me a bag of charcoal. "Can you start the fire?" she asks.

I get the fire going and look around. There are twisted-metal sculptures lying on the deck. On a table and on ledges, there are many unlit candles, burned partway before rain put them out. The day is ending, and the deck has no artificial light.

In turn, the guests read poetry incantations from paper copies in the gathering gloom. Our daughter listens while I read, then runs among the metal sculptures with her mother.

On our way home, while walking through a maze of trash, she says, "She was a real witch."

*

"I know you're the tooth fairy," she says to me. She picks up the dollar coin left under her pillow. "It's change from your MetroCard!"

She means from the MetroCard machine, where I bought a subway pass earlier in the day and received a silver dollar in change.

My concern was that I hadn't left her enough money, that a dollar wasn't enough for a lost molar. I didn't think I'd be exposed for who I was (a daily subway rider) and who I was not (the tooth fairy).

Without my powers, will I be able to convince her, when her sock is filled at Christmas, that Santa has visited? For that matter, when Halloween rolls around, will the jack o' lantern—complete with glowing leer—lose its frightening aspect? During Hanukkah, will the candles of the Maccabees fail to remind her of the one-day oil that burned for eight days? And in the spring, will the bowl of colored Easter eggs no longer summon the bunny?

No doubt those sleights of mind won't go over anymore. But the spirit will remain. We'll tack up the socks, carve the pumpkin, light the candles and dye the eggs. We'll even leave a contribution from the tooth fairy, though not in MetroCard change. We'll channel the magic that we don't understand with the primitive tools that we have.

*

She likes boxes—shoeboxes, candy boxes, mailing boxes. She likes to put things in the boxes: sleeping dolls, sleeping artificial pets, sleeping space aliens. For the sleeping beings, there are soft blankets made of silk and wool scarves.

One candy box holds three small nests or shells made from clay. Along with the three nests or shells, there's an eraser. In the world of boxes, the nests serve a purpose. They hold clay eggs, provide a safe place for incubation. But what about the eraser? It must have a use other than rubbing surfaces clean. Maybe it is a pillow, or a park bench for the birds that live in the nests.

There's also a frame made of painted Popsicle sticks. It could be a sandbox or a swimming pool—or a living room in the box house.

Of course, these boxes are in my way. I can't walk around the floor without stepping on someone's home. So I stack the boxes willy-nilly on a coffee table. The table then looks more like a palace or a village. It's a community of homes, without yards or streets. It's more like an inner city of boxes, a neighborhood like our own.

I notice a small green coil in a purple plastic lid. It must be the power supply for the village. I don't want to cut off the power and leave the inhabitants of this town without heat or light. They need their electronic devices. So I leave the energy coil where it is.

Over time, the town grows. Layers of buildings rise on the original foundation. Soon, the coffee table will become an archeologist's dream.

*

When she walks in, she tells me to turn off the radio, and I comply. I know she doesn't like the sound because it distracts her.

There's silence for a few minutes; then I hear some staccato, high-pitched notes, repeated in a pattern of two at a time. "You've got to stop that whistling," I say.

"Why?"

"Because it's noise," I say.

"But it's happy noise," her mother says from another room.

The whistling goes on. "Is there a bird in here?" her mother asks.

I want to say, 'It's no bird,'" but I don't say anything. I can't say anything, because I bought her a bird whistle as a gift. It emits a piercing shriek, but I have to admit, it sounds a lot like a bird calling into my ear, a bird that's happy to be alive.

*

"Would you be happy if I wasn't a job?" she asks.

"Yes," I say, but I misunderstand her. I think she means, would I be happy if she weren't working a job? I picture her in a textile factory, sewing, or in a cotton field, picking. There are laws against child labor, at least in this country. Compelling children to work would be inhumane. (Compelling them to do schoolwork, however, is acceptable.) Anyway, she wouldn't make much money as a small-handed laborer. We need pots of dough, and she'd bring in only pennies.

"There's no need for you to work," I say.

"No," she says, "if I weren't a job for you. Like if I weren't here, you wouldn't have the job of keeping me."

I understand that she is referring to her very existence as work (for me), and I start to think of all the things I could do, all the things *her mother and I could do*, if we didn't have the task of caring for her. We could listen to dance music in a hookah bar until the late hours and come home smelling like smoke. We could listen to stand-up comedians and get insulted from the stage when we are spotted laughing. We could walk down the street and just go into a place because we are beguiled by the looks of it. Yeah, I think, those are the things I used to do! Those are the things I want to do! Those are the things I cannot do!

"Are you happier when I'm gone for a play date?" she asks, and I see a hypothetical empty night stretched out before me, *before us.* I can imagine a feeling that can only be called relief. I see the enormous task of child care theoretically falling away.

"No," I say, "of course not. I like having you around."

"Good," she says. "Let's play a game."

It's time to lay the cards on the table, then.

*

When a young man delivers food to our door, I give him a tip of a couple of dollars. It's less than 10 percent of the cost of the food, but I'm feeling light on cash. I say goodnight to him, but as he turns away, he says, "Fuck you." Or at least that's what I hear.

When I repeat what I heard, our daughter says, "Maybe he said, 'Thank you.'"

"I doubt it," I say. "I think he was upset."

Perhaps he saw that I was a person of color. He himself was probably South Asian, since our order came from an Indian restaurant. I hadn't lived up to his expectations of a fellow of color, and that was why he swore at me in the worst way.

"Maybe," I say aloud, "I should go after him and give him another dollar. If I can't find him, I'll go to the restaurant and leave money for him there."

"Don't do that," my wife says. "He was the one who was rude."

But I think that, since I'm a secret Asian man myself, I somehow deserved to be cursed. I didn't tip the guy like a brother of his would have done.

At the dinner table, I eat my Madras dish in a dark mood. My wife and daughter, though, are in good spirits.

"Did he say it clearly?" our daughter asks, "or did he mumble?"

"He mumbled," I say.

"In that case, he said, 'Fuck you.'"

Toasted

When I leave our apartment, I can't remember if I've turned off the toaster oven. The appliance doesn't go off automatically. If it is on, you have to turn the knob to the left or unplug the whole gadget. I have a picture in my mind of the heating elements glowing red, and the food crumbs catching fire inside. I know this can happen because I've seen it. I'll be toasting something, and I'll see a flickering yellow light through the oven's small window. If I do nothing, the fire will continue unabated. If I open the oven door, the inflow of air will feed the flames.

The fire inside the appliance could spread to the plasterboard wall. The cardboard layer is flammable; a high temperature will set it off. A painting of mine hangs near the toaster. It's a harmless still life on canvas stretched over wood. Are there any better materials than canvas, wood and Sheetrock to fuel a fire? Maybe the painting deserves to be burned. But even if it does, I don't want the entire apartment turned to ash.

On the street, I smell smoke, either from my burning apartment, or from a vehicle's exhaust pipe. I can't tell. In any case, the sensation puts me on alert. I know what can happen. The smoke will turn into flame.

What should I do? Return and check the toaster-oven knobs, or continue on my way? If I keep going, maybe something else will grab my attention and I'll forget about the toaster. Maybe I'll arrive at my workplace and discover that an email I was supposed to send hasn't been sent. When I realize what has happened, it will be too late. Someone else was supposed to take the email and reformat it. That person needed me to send the raw material. I remember making some revisions. I remember seeing the file name on my computer screen. I remember attaching a document, something about a proposal, a proposed law, new coverage. But I don't remember highlighting the recipient's name and clicking the Send button.

Maybe the work problem will take my mind off my burning apartment. Maybe I'll realize what's done is done—there's nothing else I can do. Either I've set fire to my building or I haven't. Anyway, it doesn't matter, because if I don't start the fire, someone else will. Many of my neighbors have appliances with electric heating elements, and, as I see it, they don't care as much about safety as I do.

One time, when I was living alone, I was awakened by the smell of smoke. The source was somewhere outside my apartment. I opened my entrance door and saw that the hallway was filled with smoke. I went back in and looked out my window. On the street, a firefighter shouted through a bullhorn, "Don't leave your apartments! Stay inside and keep your doors shut!"

I opened my door again and saw a woman run out of the apartment next to mine. She had nothing but the clothes she was wearing and her cat, in a carrier. She ran down the stairs, through the spray of the sprinklers, and onto the street. I looked out my window and saw her on the sidewalk. She and her cat were soaked, but they were safe. I followed instructions and stayed inside.

From where I was, I could hear firefighters walking on the stairs. As they arrived at each apartment door, they pounded. If no one answered, they broke open the doors with their axes. I could hear the sound of metal against metal. When they got to my place, I opened the door before they struck. "Good," one of them said. "We won't have to pop your lock."

The next day, I learned that my first-floor neighbor had turned on an electric heater and let some bath towels fall over it. Then she went to sleep, and the towels started to smolder. Her place became a bath-towel furnace, and the building turned into a smoky sauna. No one was harmed, but I coughed up smoke particles for the next few days. I imagined that my neighbors and their pets were similarly afflicted.

Bottom line: If my neighbors don't set a fire, our child will. Our daughter doesn't know how to work the "Toast" and "Heat" buttons on the toaster oven. She thinks that once the timer stops ticking, the oven is off. But if the control knob is still turned to high heat, the oven is on. I picture the toaster switched off while the oven is set to 450 degrees. That's hot enough to ignite anything burnable.

A solution, of course, would be to clean the toaster oven and move it away from the wall. That way, there would be nothing to burn. But these steps are beyond me, mainly because I never think of them while I'm in the apartment. I think of them only as I walk away from the building that will shortly become a cinder.

Now, as I walk away from home, I could call someone who is still inside to see if the appliance is off. I could use my cell phone—my question is urgent. But I don't think anyone is home. Even if anyone were there, all they would tell me is that the place is engulfed in flames.

I make the call. Someone answers, but I don't know who it is. "This is Daddy," I say.

"Daddy?"

"No, not Daddy," I say.

"This is not your daughter," my wife says.

"Can you do me a favor?" I ask. "Can you check to see if the toaster oven is off?"

"Hold on."

I hold, and as I hold, I imagine my wife batting at the flames that are licking the walls.

*

Asia Lite

Before we travel to Asia, I worry about getting dengue fever—I'm afraid of contracting the disease from a mosquito. I've read that millions of people are infected every year, and thousands die. There is no vaccine; the only prevention is to avoid being bitten.

"Don't worry," my wife says, "we won't see any mosquitoes."

When we arrive in Hong Kong, we take a train from the airport to the center of the city. Not too surprisingly, the train is full of mosquitoes. They are trapped inside the car. We don't know if they are *Aedes aegypti*, the dangerous kind—all we can tell is they're of the small, brown variety. We bat them away, but there is no escape. We can't leave the train. We have to stay on and share our space with the tiny whiners.

As we check in at our hotel, I ask a young man at the counter, "Do you think we'll get dengue fever? We were bitten by mosquitoes on the train."

"Don't worry," he says. "If you're strong, you won't get sick."

*

At night, I walk into an alley that's filled with activity. There are many smells of cooking, some fresh, others rotten. As I walk through a dark section, I see a small Buddhist shrine on the pavement next to a building. Incense sticks in a brass holder send off wisps of smoke. The shrine is illuminated by two electric bulbs.

A young man beckons to me from a food cubicle and speaks in words I can't understand.

I say, "I'm looking for food."

He says, "English! I wondered what language!"

I ask myself, what language did he think I spoke? Chinese, Japanese, Tagalog, French?

The young man motions me into his shop. Inside, I study pictures of various dishes and point to something that looks like bacon strips wrapped around leek stalks. Energized, he cooks the food on a grille. Smoke pours out the front window.

I notice he is eating something out of a Styrofoam container. "Where did you get that?" I ask.

He gestures vaguely down the street. "Another place," he says.

I bring the cooked food back to where my wife is waiting and our child is sleeping. "There are no utensils," my wife says.

I give her my penknife and go at the food with my fingers.

*

I speak Chinese to a staffer at our hotel. "How are you?" I ask in Mandarin.

He nods his head.

"We are well," I continue in Mandarin. "All of us are well." I indicate my wife and daughter.

"Your Chinese is very good," he says in English.

Encouraged, I keep going. "My mother is Chinese," I say. "My father was American. We are American."

He smiles, as if to say, "Go on. Get out of here."

"Goodbye," I say.

"Are you leaving for good?" he asks.

"No," I say. "We're coming back later."

He smiles again, as if to say, "Get out of this city."

*

On the street, a pair of women approach me. One of them hands me a business card and asks, "Do you need a haircut?"

I wonder if my hair is too long for this part of the world. I look around and don't see many men with long hair, or even longish hair. Perhaps I look like a rapscallion, someone up to no good.

The card seems legit. It has the name of a hair stylist and a street address. But the price for a cut, translated into U.S. money, is $38. That's more than I pay back home.

Later, I ask my Asian host what to make of the solicitation.

"It's unusual to be stopped on the street," she says.

"Maybe I'm having trouble communicating," I say.

"It's easy to communicate here," she says. "This is Asia Lite. If you call the post office, they answer in English."

"Do I look like I need a haircut?" I ask.

"Here, 'haircut' doesn't mean 'haircut,'" she says. "It's code for something else."

*

A person suggests a restaurant that we might like. It's called American China. To get there, we walk along a street once popular with sailors. Many of the old entertainment spots are still open. One, with a neon likeness of Popeye the Sailor above the door, is called Cockeye the Sailor. Outside each establishment, young women in hot pants and tank tops linger. They are a preview of what's inside. They aren't much older than our daughter. In fact, the only difference between them and our daughter is their lack of clothing.

"We don't want to be on this street," my wife and daughter say.

"We're almost there," I say.

Inside American China, we point to our daughter and take out a sheet of paper. On it is a sentence in Chinese characters: "She is allergic to peanuts."

During the meal, we watch for signs of an allergic reaction: hives, difficulty breathing, uncontrolled shaking. We are ready to jump up and run to the nearest hospital emergency room.

I enjoy the food, but our daughter eats nothing.

*

We spend our free time walking around the city. At one point, as we pass a cement crater where water has collected, we notice a sign warning us about mosquitoes. "If you see an infestation," the sign says in English, "tell the authorities. Don't hesitate."

We see one or two mosquitoes, nowhere near an infestation.

We walk past a hardware store and see a product with a "Sale" sign on it. The product is a couple of feet high and a foot wide. It's made of plastic and metal, and it has knobs and vents at the top. A hand-lettered label identifies the machine as "The Dehumanizer." Apparently, if you turn on this machine in your muggy apartment, you will be dehumanized. You will no longer be human. Mosquitoes won't bother you then.

Next to the street, we see another sign. This one reads, "Vehicle waiting will be prosecuted without warning." Luckily, we are not driving.

*

We travel for half a day to see a giant statue of the Buddha. In the temple courtyard, large incense sticks are smoldering. The sticks are bigger than baseball bats. We climb many stairs to the foot of the statue, but we don't bow when we get there.

When I go into a men's room, I see a metal trough that runs around the perimeter. Other than that, there are holes in the floor. Each hole has a plastic rim. I hear from my wife and daughter that the facilities for women are similar, minus the metal trough. These facilities might be sufficient for the monks, but they are freaky for us.

I buy some incense as a gift and ask an attendant what kind of incense I'm getting. It is "not too black" incense, she says.

"What does that mean?" I ask.

"It's not too smoky."

That's the kind of incense my mother used to burn. I buy three packages of sticks wrapped in red cellophane.

*

We visit an exhibit of live butterflies. The display is in a greenhouse. The air in the glass-covered room is thick. Shortly, our daughter has an allergic reaction. She breaks out in hives and gasps when she breathes.

"We have to go to a hospital," my wife says.

We find the nearest hospital. It's a modern, steel-and-glass structure. Unfortunately, our health coverage does not apply here, and the charge will be high. In addition, there is a long wait. We talk to an attendant. We explain we were at a butterfly exhibit when our daughter was struck.

"They feed the butterflies peanut butter," the attendant says.

While we wait, our daughter recovers. The hives disappear, and her breathing becomes normal. We leave the hospital without seeing a doctor.

*

I go to a small theater in the Central District for my event—the reason I've come to this city. In the lobby is a photo gallery. On this night, there's a "gallery crawl," and many people are passing through the gallery to look at photos. Few people, however, go into the theater itself.

On the stage, the lights are bright. A camera crew is present, and for a moment I think they are going to film me, but they are here to film my co-presenter. When I meet her, she tells me she has been taking public-speaking lessons. A table at the entrance is filled with stacks of her books. A few of my books sit on a corner of the table.

I wait while the moderator makes her speech. When it is my turn, I say, "My mother was born and raised in China, but I haven't been here until now. I can't believe it's taken me this long to get here."

The program goes smoothly. I explain that my books aren't self-published, even though they might appear to be. Afterward, my co-presenter's books sell like hotcakes.

Someone tells me to take the historic trolley back to my hotel, and I do, but when I come to a crossroads that points to "Hollywood," I don't know which way to go. I get off the trolley car and walk the rest of the way.

One Degree of Separation

At the entrance to the Kam Shan Country Park in Hong Kong, a sign told us that if we followed the trail, we would almost certainly see wild monkeys. The sign was printed in Chinese and English. Sure enough, a hundred yards in, we ran into a band of lesser primates. I was walking in front, and I stopped at the sight of long-tailed macaques sitting in pensive poses. I put out my arms like a school-crossing guard and signaled back to my wife and daughter that there were monkeys ahead.

We might have been afraid of the monkeys, but they weren't afraid of us. They just wanted to know if we were carrying food. I had a banana in my backpack, but I didn't take out the fruit. It would be recognized immediately. What then? The monkeys might charge at me, shrieking and baring their teeth, clawing at me until I gave them the banana. I didn't want to give up the banana. I didn't want to fight over it, especially with a monkey. I wanted to eat it myself or give it to our daughter.

As a result, we didn't have much to communicate about, we and the monkeys, even though more than 90 percent of our DNA was the same. We just eyed each other in a human/simian standoff.

We walked past the macaques uphill, toward the top of Monkey Mountain—the local name for the reservoir area in Kowloon. Oddly, there were no monkeys on the mountain. There were, however, plenty of mosquitoes. I remembered that the sign at the park entrance had warned of mosquitoes—they could be carriers of dengue fever. We batted at the insects, but batting did no good.

We rested at the side of a brook as giant butterflies flapped around us. These were Mormons, with dark wings and erratic flight patterns; they were nothing like the Mormons in Utah. The trail we were on stretched out in shadow, through the jungle. The mosquitoes didn't let up. They buzzed around our ears and landed on our faces, arms and hands. More often than not, they drew blood. They made it impossible to appreciate the brook and the butterflies. So we decided to head back to where we'd started.

We had a peaceful hike on the way down. That is, until I walked under a tree that belonged to a monkey. I heard a snarl, a hiss, and looked up to see a lesser primate baring his teeth at me. He was only a few feet away. I didn't want a monkey on my neck, or on my back, and I considered taking out the butter knife I'd brought to defend myself. (It was the only knife I could find in our hotel.) I could have flashed the utensil at the aggressor in an attempt to frighten him away. There was no way the blunt end would have pierced his hide. This specimen had arms the size of my legs. So I just stepped back from the menacing display.

Shortly after, I heard my wife call my name. "I'm scared!" she shouted. I walked quickly toward her and saw a healthy male—with pink buttocks—circling her. He looked at me as if to say, "What is she screaming about? My buttocks aren't blushing. I'm just hungry."

Soon, we were surrounded by monkeys. They were swinging through trees, dropping into a lake beside the road, then emerging on our side, where they shot from the water to swing through more trees. They swam like dogs—not gracefully, but well. When they came out of the water, they blocked our path. They sat on the flag-stones in meditative protest over not being fed. I recalled that the sign at the entrance said not to feed the creatures; they were known to attack.

Luckily, we were carrying no nuts—nuts would have driven them crazy. I'd read in a guidebook that some unwary travelers had been attacked—and injured—over a bag of nuts. We had only the banana, and I was hanging onto it at the risk of my life. We approached the macaque mothers with children. They seemed fairly sane. They were just walking around—the smaller one clinging to the underside of the larger one, the smaller one's face mirroring the features of the larger one's—in a quiet hunt for food.

We walked along the monkey road as the lesser primates passed watchfully in the opposite direction. We didn't run, and they didn't run, either. We walked past each other calmly—they on four limbs, we on two. They were less threatening that way, walking on their feet and hands. If they didn't stand up, they couldn't grab my butter knife and use it against me.

As we waited for the bus that would take us out of the park, we were alone with the macaques. There were no services, no concessions, just a footbridge over the highway and a pull-off area for the bus. The monkeys joined us. Dozens of them occupied the footbridge and balanced on the railings. They sat on the steps leading down to the highway. One of them pulled a weed from the ground with its hand and ate the root. Another flicked at a cricket on the pavement with its fingers, playing with the snack. Still another combed the fur of its offspring, looking for edible parasites.

A Chinese woman showed up and fed some of the creatures. She had something in a bag that she rationed out. When the monkeys came too close, she pointed at them and hissed some words. They turned and ran a short distance, then came back. I guessed they were planning to outflank her, then close in for a final assault on the food.

When the city bus arrived, the kids inside looked out the windows and pointed at the animals. The monkeys showed no interest in the passengers.

We got onto the bus, found seats on the upper deck and rode away, in the direction of downtown Kowloon. I still had the banana; I took it out and gave it to our daughter.

Appointments

I'm running late for a dentist's appointment, set for 8 p.m. It's an unusual hour for an appointment, but I'm glad I have the time slot. It's now 7:45, and I'm walking to the West Side.

On my way, I stop at a bar where someone I work with is having a drink. I plan to just say hello, so I go in and take a seat. When I head out of the bar, I look at my watch and see it's 9:15. I don't know how I lost track of time. Maybe the dentist will still be in his office and I can see him anyway. If not, I wonder if I'll have to pay for the appointment. I probably will.

I keep walking, but I cut across an avenue too far uptown and find myself next to a canal. The street I'm on has no bridge over the water. I'll have to backtrack to the east, head south and turn again to the west as soon as I find a street that crosses the canal. There's no way I'll make it to the dentist's office before a very late hour.

*

On the subway, a homeless man asks me for money. He's standing next to me, but I'm reading a book and can hide my face behind the pages. His voice is soft enough that I don't have to listen to what he says. I move my foot and touch his heel, and he falls to the floor. I'm surprised he lost his balance. Did he fall on purpose to get my attention?

I step away from him and look back. He has a bag, a cup and a cane; he's blind. And he's young—in his 30s? his 40s? I return to him and put my hand under his arm. His body feels warm through his jacket, as warm as my hand. He's dead weight; I can't lift him. But he rises slowly on his own.

After I leave the train, I remember the warmth of his arm.

*

Someone is giving me shoes. I'm in a place with lots of shoes—a shoe store or a sidewalk display. But all of the shoes are green. "I don't want green shoes," I say, and I give all of the shoes back. I make a pile of them.

I do take a pair of boots, because it's raining. I'll have good, protective footwear for the weather. But when I get into the rain, I see that the boots have no toes. There's an open space at the front. The shoe leather comes up from the sole in a simple wrap. These boots won't keep my feet dry at all.

But I'm stuck with them. These boots come with a no-exchange policy.

*

At my workplace, a staffer creates a history of our company in the form of a graphic novel. I have to proofread the book, and I see there's a frame or two about me in it. The drawings of my face are recognizable. But I don't like what's said about me. In a dialogue balloon, a supervisor says, "I've heard he's old."

I don't like my quote, either. In my cartoon frame, I'm saying, "I been here for so long I can't count the years."

So I complain to a woman in the graphics department, but she ignores me. I want to complain to a higher-up, but I can't find one. Soon, a higher-up finds me. "Who is this woman?" he asks.

The woman he's talking about is in my section of the graphic novel. I don't know who she is, but I see she's a fictional character based on a real person who needs companionship.

I go back to the graphics woman and say, "I want to change my quote to this: 'The boss isn't going to make it out of his dip-shit job, either.'"

*

On a subway platform, I hear the sounds of a flute, then see the player: a man with long white hair and wire-rimmed glasses. He's blowing into a wooden instrument, larger than a recorder. There is a carving on the barrel, maybe a dragon's head. He's just improvising; the style could be Tibetan. The piece sounds like music that Buddhist monks would make to accompany prayer.

I've seen this musician before. I've talked to him, but I don't really know him. I don't know his name.

I doubt he has any formal training. I should know, because I took music lessons for years as a kid. I can hear the notes with a discerning ear.

I pass the flute player on the crowded platform, but presently I feel compelled to return. I say to him, "I was going to walk away, but the music brought me back."

"That's the best compliment I could ever hear," he says.

I give him a MetroCard to ride the trains. "It's unlimited," I say, "but it expires at the end of today."

"Thank you," he says. "I'll have to think of where to go with it."

*

In our apartment, I hear my wife and daughter arriving. Our daughter opens the door with her mother's keys, then shuts the door. Outside, her mother knocks to be let in. The child twists the knob, but her mother opens the door too quickly and a metal part of the lock hits the child on her lip and tooth.

I hear wailing.

"You broke my tooth!" the child screams.

"I'm sorry!" her mother says.

The cries and apologies continue for a long while as we, the parents, examine the tooth. It is indeed damaged, but what has happened below the surface can't be determined. Gradually, our daughter stops sobbing.

We get on the phone and make an appointment for her, at the earliest possible time.

*

I'm on time for my next dental appointment. In the clinic, I take a seat in the operating chair. I lean back and wait. This time, the dentist is running late. I don't mind, because our daughter got off easy. Her accident caused no cracking or loosening; her front tooth has been remodeled by an expert.

When my dentist shows up, he has one hand behind his back—I know he's hiding a syringe.

"I'm not sure what's going on in your jaw," he says. "but it could spread. It could reach your brain."

"What would that feel like?" I ask.

"Fever. Chills. Dementia."

"What are you going to do?"

"I'm going to go in and look around. Have you got the pills I prescribed? The antibiotics? The narcotics?"

"You know," I say. "I'm feeling no pain. In fact, I'm feeling fine."

He leans against a wall, with one hand still behind his back. "Then let's not do it," he says. "It was probably a sinus cold. Come back when you have a real problem."

"Are you sure?" I ask.

"Yes. When I looked at the X-rays, I couldn't see anything. I have only your word to go on."

When I walk out of the dentist's office, I can't believe my good fortune. Everything is great. No matter what anyone says to me, nothing will bring me down. I'm so happy I head back to work, to my office, to finish out the day.

The Stupidest Thing I've Ever Done

The moment after I fall, I think I can't get up. I see the headlights of a car a few feet away. The car is waiting to cross an intersection, but I'm lying in its way. One leg of my jeans is wet from sliding through water. My backpack is still wrapped around my shoulders. The pavement is icy beneath me.

Somehow, I get up and walk out of the intersection. I know something is wrong with my arm, but I don't know what it is. A guy coming toward me on the sidewalk says, "You've got to break your fall, man!"

At the door to our building, I notice that I can take my keys from my pocket, but I can't reach the lock. It's too high. I switch my keys to my other hand and open the door.

Inside, I say to my wife, "I fell and hurt my arm."

At night, I have trouble sleeping. When I try to raise my injured arm, it won't go. So I leave it at my side. The position doesn't help the pain, though.

*

I visit the office of my regular doctor and see the nurse practitioner. She asks me to raise my arm, and I raise it an inch or two. "That's all you can do?" she asks.

"That's it," I say.

She runs out of the exam room and calls back to me: "Falling is dangerous!"

She sends me for an X-ray.

As I stand in front of the machine, technicians sit at a computer screen in an adjoining room. I hear them saying, "Fracture" to each other.

Several hours later, I see the report, which states that the humerus has been split. The break is an impacted fracture of the greater tuberosity. There is a probable extension into the surgical neck, a widening of the distance between the humeral head and the joint. There is a suspicion of effusion. My shoulder is royally messed up.

I find an orthopedist, someone in Chinatown. I have the idea I will feel sibling-hood with an Asian doctor. Plus, she takes my insurance.

When I get to her office, I learn that my health insurance will not cover another X-ray so soon after the previous one. I return to the hospital where I got my original X-ray, receive a compact disc with the pictures and return to the orthopedist.

We look at the images together. "Not a big deal," she says. "You'll have internal bleeding, and the bruise will go past your elbow. We'll give you a sling."

An assistant brings a lightweight black sling. "That's a nice sling," the doctor says to the assistant. "Did we just get these?"

I learn to wrap the sling around my right arm and pull the strap behind my neck.

"Do you have someone at home who can take care of you?" the doctor asks.

I'm thinking that my daughter is not a good candidate, because I have to take care of her. Maybe my wife can take care of me. Maybe not. I don't think I'll need much care, anyway.

*

While waiting with my daughter for the subway, I put on my sling, then pull my coat over my bent arm. The coat drapes down from my injured shoulder, so one sleeve is empty. My daughter is sitting on a bench, and my briefcase is on the seat beside her. I start to pick up my briefcase so I can sit, but as I'm doing so, a man with a guitar starts to put his instrument down on the same seat. He motions with his hand that it's OK for my stuff to be there. "I'd just like to sit here," I say.

"Are you being sarcastic?" he asks.

"No," I say. "My arm is broken. I'd like to have a seat."

"You're talking like an asshole," he says.

"What do you mean?" I ask.

"I mean, you're talking like an asshole."

"Do you want to take it outside?" I ask. I mean, does he want to take it upstairs, onto the sidewalk next to the subway station. I'm guessing he wouldn't assault someone with a broken arm, but if he did, I could sue him for injuring me.

"Stop it," my daughter says, jumping up next to me.

"I don't want to take it anywhere," the man says. He carries his guitar to a spot a few feet away.

I wonder if there was something in my tone that made the man angry. Was I not speaking to him with respect? I stare at him, but he doesn't walk back to me. I keep looking at him until the train arrives.

*

At my checkup, the doctor asks how I'm doing.

"Mediocre," I say, "so-so."

"Why is that?" she asks.

"I'm having trouble sleeping. My arm hurts at night and wakes me up."

"Some people with an injured shoulder sleep in a reclining chair," the doctor says.

"Here's my pattern," I say. "I take a pill, then go to sleep on my regular bed. The pill wears off in about three hours. I sit up, on the edge of the loft bed, and climb down the ladder to the couch, where the cushions are softer. I sleep for another couple of hours, then get up and sit for a while. The arm likes it when I sit. I take a couple more pills, but weaker ones, not the narcotics, then climb back to my regular bed, where I sleep for a couple of hours. I get up for good way before dawn. I'm tired all the time."

"I want you to stop taking the narcotics," the doctor says.

"What should I do when I wake up in the night?" I ask.

"Exercise the arm. Lie on the floor on your back. Lift the arm over your head with your other hand. Then push it to the side with a stick. Stand up and pull it up behind your back with a strap."

I try this for the next few nights. The first time I wake up, I do the exercises. The next couple of times, I'm too foggy to do the exercises. Every motion is too painful to repeat. I miss the narcotics.

*

While I lie on a table, a physical therapist calls me Honey, then starts torturing my arm. She holds my wrist and tries to move my arm over my head, then tries to pull it out to the side, but it won't extend very far.

"It's nobody's fault but my own," I say, grasping my nose with my free fingers and wincing.

She hands me a cane and shows me how to use my good arm to raise my bad arm to its limit—and hold it there.

"Falling was the stupidest thing I've ever done."

"Honey," she says, "keep going. Give me twenty."

"Have you ever thought about joining the Army?" I ask.

"I don't know whether to take that as a compliment or not," she says.

She bends my arm at the elbow and pulls the whole limb to the side. "One more," she says.

"Geez," I say. "I can't do this."

She notices where I am on the table—I've shifted to the side. "Where are you going?" she asks. "Come back to me."

I slide toward her so she can continue beating my arm. When she is done, I notice that her hair has come loose from its bun. "Why is your hair down?" I ask.

"Were we wrestling?" she asks.

*

In an airport. I'm stopped at the detection machine. A man comes to check me more carefully. "Can you move your arm?" he asks.

"In what direction?" I ask.

"Away from your body."

I understand the space between my elbow and my ribs would be a perfect place to hide contraband, or explosives. I lift my elbow away from my side, and the man pats my arm and my ribs. "OK," he says, "go ahead."

Later, another official asks me, "Do you want a wheelchair?"

I don't think I heard him correctly. I'm walking, after all. "What did you say?" I ask.

"Do you need a wheelchair?"

There's an adult stroller handy. I see it folded there. "No, thanks" I say, and I walk away. I try to put a spring in my step to show I'm still spry, I'm not disabled, but I don't succeed. I just shuffle off.

At the check-in desk, I ask if I can have an aisle seat on the plane. "I have a broken arm," I say.

"Give me your boarding pass," the attendant says. "I'll hold it."

"You'll call me later?" I ask.

"Yes," she says, holding up the document. "See? I wrote 'Aisle' and 'Arm' on it."

I end up with a better seat, with more legroom, where I can stretch my feet and rest my arm at my side. The seat is much better than any I've had in the past. It's definitely an upgrade. But the pain grows as the flight goes on. I'd give up my elite seat in an instant to have a normal arm.

*

The doctor asks, "Are you sleeping through the night?"

"No," I say. "I wake up every couple of hours. I get up three or four times a night. Sometimes I'm awake for more than an hour."

"Are you doing the exercises I gave you?" she asks.

"I've just been standing and swinging my arm. That's what the physical therapist said to do."

"You've got to do my exercises! The three I gave you: lifting your arm with your other hand, pushing it to the side with a stick, and pulling it behind your back with a strap!"

The suggestion sounds counterintuitive to me. I wake up because my arm hurts. Why would I make it hurt more so I can go back to sleep? "I'll do it," I say.

"Do it for a couple of weeks," she says. "You'll start sleeping through the night."

Later, I try faithfully to exercise when I wake at night. I lie on the floor and do the lifts and pushes. Then I stand up and do the behind-the-back stretches. All of these motions cause sharp pain. After a couple of foggy sessions, I can't do them anymore. I just take an ice pack from the freezer, put it on my shoulder for a couple of minutes, and try to go back to sleep.

*

Sometimes I think my arm is going to get better, and I'm full of optimism. I think of the fun things I'll be able to do—ride a bicycle or drive a car, for example. And how about sex? Yes, how about it? I can't hug now; I can't lift my arm that high. Intimacy is limited to a one-armed kind of thing. I'm not spending much time in my bed with my wife, anyway. I'm usually in my own private sleeping hell, on the couch. But when my shoulder heals, I'll be able to do all sorts of things—push-ups over the mattress, for example, or the old arm-over-the-partner trick.

Other times, I think my arm will never get better, and I live in a dark vision of disability. I'm afraid my elbow will be permanently bent. Even without pain, that would not look good. Perhaps I'll never be able to lift my arm above the level of my shoulder. This would cut out a lot of activities, like writing on a blackboard. I like communicating by blackboard; it's a bold, abbreviated method. I'm worried that my arm will always hang useless at my side. As it is, the hanging weight pulls down on my shoulder joint and causes an ache. I can't stand or walk for long, until I have to sit.

*

"I have a goal," I say to the physical therapist.

"What's that?" she asks.

"I want to do my exercises until my shoulder is better. I don't want to have an operation."

"That's our goal, too," she says.

I'm glad she agrees. It's not that I'm afraid of general anesthesia. I just want to avoid it, if I can.

"I've heard an operation is quicker," I say, "but I don't really want one."

"No, you don't want it," she says as she starts to press and pull at my arm. "Push into me," she says.

"Which way?" I ask.

"Push into my hip."

I push as hard as I can, but my effort is nothing compared with the leverage she generates. She's got my shoulder locked, and she's using it as a fulcrum. I'm reminded of childbirth, but this time I'm on the other end, the giving end. I have nothing to help me, not even oxygen. I inhale through my nose, exhale through my mouth. I don't want to hold my breath—I don't want my blood pressure to rise. I don't want to faint. I hear my drill instructor asking if I'm OK. I hear myself saying yes. I don't look at her hair to see if it's coming loose from its bun. I take my free hand and squeeze around my eyes. I try not to fall off the table.

"Come back to me," she says.

*

I go to the doctor's office for a checkup. I don't know if I'll need a manipulation under anesthesia. I don't know if I'll have to be "put under" so the orthopedist can wrench my arm to break up scar tissue. I don't know how much progress I've made in physical therapy.

The doctor asks me to show her what I can do with my arm. I lift it straight over my head, bend it at the elbow, swing it to the side, put my hand up behind my back.

"You've done well," the doctor says. "Your arm is about 90 percent. It may never get better than that, but you're not a professional athlete, so maybe that's OK."

"It's OK," I say. "I'm not planning to pitch in any ball games. But my arm still hurts."

"The soreness and weakness could continue for a year and a half after the injury," she says. "The arm will hurt less as it gets stronger. You don't have to come back here or go to physical therapy."

I can't believe my good luck. All I'll have to do is continue my exercises at home and at a gym. I've learned a lot of moves from the physical therapist, the one who called me Honey. She knew I would make it just by stretching.

Strange Weather

I'm walking back to where I'm staying with my wife and daughter, and it is raining. The sky is unnaturally dark, as dark as night, but it is daytime. I walk under scaffolding so I won't get wet. The raised platform stretches for a couple of blocks. Beneath the roof, the sidewalk is cracked. I could trip on the cement, fall and fracture a bone. I don't want to slip and injure myself; I've done that once already. Whenever I think about the accident, my arm starts to hurt.

I want to stay under the sidewalk shed as long as possible. After I've gone about a block, however, I have to leave the shelter. Unprotected, I feel water dotting my pants and seeping through my shoes. I own no rubbers, though I had a pair when I was a child. My father bought them for me. I didn't like the word "rubbers"—it was embarrassing—so I didn't wear them.

Now, I walk quickly through the rain. I'm wearing a long coat, one that falls past my knees. I wish I had a motorcycle to go with the coat. They would look good together, the trench coat and the bike, and the bike would get me where I'm going faster than public transportation. Now, I have to find the nearest bus stop, so I ask a man for directions. He looks at me as if he knows I'm a foreigner, but he doesn't know where I'm from. I look somehow different, but I'm speaking his language. He can't figure me out: Am I Asian? Native Alaskan? Hawaiian? He wants to be polite but doesn't know what to say. He changes the subject. He tells me where I should go in the city, what I should see, but he doesn't help with where I want to go.

As I walk, I see a small whirlwind just above the ground. It picks up trash and spins it around. The wind isn't strong enough to do damage. I could walk through it unscathed. The wind wouldn't blow me off my feet.

*

I arrive at where we are staying—a house with two floors and a basement. We've left our daughter alone in the house, and I don't have my keys. She can't open the door from inside—the door is somehow double-locked—so I'm going to have to break in. I decide to go through the basement. I walk through the dark space toward the back of the house, then see a trapdoor in the ceiling that looks like it will open into the first floor.

When I reach the trapdoor, I have to take out the screws that keep it shut. I find a screwdriver, but my injured arm makes the tool hard to use. I can twist with strength, but after a short while my arm tires.

Presently, I'm aware of my wife arriving. We can hear our daughter screaming faintly inside the house. My wife has her keys; she can open both locks. I ask her to go through the front door while I keep working. I don't get all of the screws out, but the wood is weak. I tear the trapdoor off its frame and push my head through the opening to the floor above.

I look around to see what frightened our daughter. There is a dog in the house. Once, our daughter was bitten while she was walking with her school class, and her chaperone hadn't asked the name of the dog's owner. She had to get rabies shots. I see that this present dog is big, but it isn't unnaturally large. Its eyes aren't glowing red. It is not a hound from hell. I shut the animal in an empty room.

Outside, the wind picks up. I hear things—random objects, bottles and cans—clattering around the street. I hear people shouting, saying something about trouble, but when I look through a window I realize they are only trying to hail a cab.

*

In the morning, I go out through the front door. The rain has stopped, but the pavement is damp. I see moss growing in every fissure, and I understand that the concrete never dries. That's why the city is always green—the grass and flowers grow even when the air is cold. The water doesn't freeze.

I see that a major storm has passed through. It was stronger than a whirlwind; it might have been a twister. Pieces of garbage—brightly colored plastic bags—are stuck in the branches of trees. Parked cars have been moved by a great force; they are at angles to the curb. Leaves stripped from branches litter the ground. I pick up a leaf, take it inside and tape it to a piece of paper. I label it "From the hurricane."

My wife and daughter are asleep. It is easy to sleep here, because of the shift in time. We can't keep track of the hours—we rest and wake by internal clocks.

I say to the two who are sleeping, "Let's get up now. Let's get going."

At first, it seems that they don't hear me. Then they respond by moving deeper under their blankets.

"It's pouring out," they say.

After the Storm

I got on the phone to our utility company because I had a complaint. We'd been without power for days, and while I could live with this situation, I didn't think our child could. I thought she might have bad memories for years to come, and she might blame us, her parents, for not doing something about it. We could have taken her away from our lower-Manhattan apartment to a place that had electricity. We could have crossed to another borough, or gone to another state. We could have found a place with lights, hot water and heat.

But I took the easy way out—I called the utility company. Unfortunately, no one answered. As I waited on the phone, I was given several options for service—the main office, the new-business office, the mobile department, the steam-emergency division, the cancellation line, the operator—but each time I pressed a button, the original recording started again.

The lack of response led to a new complaint. I couldn't tolerate the phone system at our neighborhood utility. I mean, here I was, at a pay phone because I had no home phone—the storm had knocked out everything but the phone booths. I was freezing on the street, and all I was getting was a recording.

I was ready to flag down a utility truck and accost the driver. But who knew if it was a real utility truck and driver? Maybe these people were thieves posing as utility workers. Perhaps they'd neutralized the real workers and stolen their uniforms.

These people could have been sophisticated criminals, intent on gaining access to the apartments of innocent customers. In that event, I'd have a new complaint. I'd have to call the local police precinct and report that I'd been robbed.

I could have armed myself against the threat. Before the power fizzled, I'd heard a TV commentator say, "If you go out alone at night in a blackout, you might encounter people who are up to no good. When these people find you, do you think they'll engage you in polite conversation? Do you think you'll be able to reason with them? Or do you think you'll need to defend yourself? Maybe you'll need a firearm. And not just a peashooter, but the biggest assault rifle you can carry!"

The weapon option sounded like the quickest solution, but as a matter of principle, I owned no guns.

I knew things would be tough the moment our lights went out. Seeing all of the dark buildings around us confirmed my fear. Our daughter, however, was not convinced. "We could play board games," she suggested.

We did that: we played one board game—it was the game of Life—until rolling the dice, reading our fortunes, choosing careers and making financial moves became too boring to continue.

Fortunately, friends of my wife offered to take her and our daughter to their place for the night. I wasn't included because I was working late at my office (located in the powered zone). I was working too late to be picked up.

My wife's friends had driven through pitch-dark streets to get to our building. Once at the door, they were unable to use the buzzer or make a cellphone call. So they stood there, banging on the window of the metal entrance. A couple of floors away, my wife and daughter didn't hear the knocking. When they went downstairs to make a pay-phone call, they found their frustrated hosts looking in and waving their hands.

When I got home from work, I lit a couple of candles and turned on a battery-operated radio. I extended the antenna to its fullest, but could pick up only one station. Apparently, the station had a backup power source. I listened to a show on which the announcers were bantering about songs that were appropriate for floods. A country singer showed up at the studio. She'd walked from her home in Chelsea to the station in SoHo.

The hosts played one of the country artist's songs, "World Without Sound." She reminisced about making the recording and talked about living in the dark.

After more chatting, the announcers played the ultimate flood song, Led Zeppelin's "When the Levee Breaks." Too bad there were no levees in New York. A levee might have helped.

I slept alone that night, in the cold and dark. But I was OK. At least I had a roof over my head. In the morning, I heated water on the stove and poured it into the tub for a bath. It was the shallowest bath I'd ever taken.

The next day, I heard from my wife and daughter. They'd had a nice time at their friends' place in Brooklyn. In the morning, they'd gotten a ride to the far end of an East River bridge. They'd walked from there to Manhattan. "It was a long walk," my wife said, "The air was clear, and we could see the buildings of our neighborhood. It didn't matter that the lights were out. The city looked beautiful."

The Orgone Box

My injured arm sometimes feels like it's detached from its socket, as if it has no weight. I believe that if I try to lift the arm, nothing will happen. But I try anyway, and the arm responds. It rises from my side if I'm standing, or from the mattress if I'm reclining. But it feels loose and bubbly, as if its biological gears aren't meshing. I can lift it, and I can do more than that. I can comb my hair, reach a light switch, ride my bike, carry a bag of groceries, and turn a screwdriver. I have some strength now where I once had none. I can even throw something, like a stone. I can skip a disk-shaped pebble across still water. I don't have occasion to skip stones often, and I never was a good thrower, of stones or baseballs, even with a healthy arm. But I used to be a competent Frisbee thrower, and I believe I can still whip the flying disk.

*

I bring my daughter with me to the closest park, where we can pitch a Frisbee. She is a small person and doesn't have experience with this game, so that makes the two of us about equal. We stand a few yards apart and throw the disk back and forth, pausing when people walk between us. I snap the disk in an underhanded, wrist-flicking motion that comes up from my leg. We often miss our catches, and we change positions each time the Frisbee sails by and we have to chase it.

After some minutes, my throwing arm becomes tired. "That's all I can do," I say.

"That's it?" my daughter asks.

"I don't want to make my shoulder worse," I say.

I picture my arm deteriorating. Eventually, I might not be able to lift it at all. At that point, I will probably need surgery. Maybe an artificial shoulder. Does such a thing exist? The whole assembly, ball and socket? How many months of physical therapy would be required after that operation? Would I ever get used to a metal joint in my body? Maybe I should learn to live with a sore natural arm.

My daughter jumps over a metal fence to join other people in a grassy area. I can't flex my body enough to make it over the barrier, so I sit on a bench and watch her.

*

I go to my regular, family care doctor for an exam. I'm finished with the orthopedist, the one who helped with my shoulder fracture. I just need a checkup.

"You know," I say to him, "my arm always hurts, even while I'm sitting here."

"How would you rate the pain," he asks, "on a scale of 1 to 10, with 10 being your arm ripped off entirely?"

"About 2," I say.

"There's a new treatment," he says. "I'm working on it with scientists at the university. It's like the orgone box. Do you know what that is?"

"I've heard of it."

"It's as big as a shower stall," he says. "You sit in it. It's made of two layers of wood, with a layer of aluminum foil between them. The box is designed to trap 'bion' particles flying through the air. The bions bounce around in there with you, focusing the orgone force and raising your energy.

"Sounds scientific," I say.

"It works. Not the box; I mean our invention. We don't wait for the bions to float in; we use electricity and a new kind of wave. We hook you up to an oscillator, which generates bions. We energize your damaged joint. Not only will your arm feel better, your libido will get stronger. The life force will boost the sex force."

"I'm in," I say.

*

During my next appointment, I climb into the box. It reminds me of the outhouse next to my childhood home. When my family lived there, the outhouse hadn't been used in years, so it didn't smell terrible; it just smelled dusty. It had a small window, covered with wire mesh to keep birds and squirrels out. The walls were papered with old calendars from local service stations, with slick photos of scantily clad women leaning over cars. Some of the women were washing the cars; others were feeding them gas.

I didn't spend much time in my childhood outhouse; I spent as little time there as possible. If I got the backdoor trots, I didn't have to run out the back door. We had central plumbing, after all.

The doctor's orgone box makes me feel claustrophobic. While I'm sitting in it, I can touch the walls with my hands, but I can't see anything. I hear Eastern music playing softly. I don't feel any bions flying around me. I feel somewhat relaxed, but mainly bored. I suppose I could stand up and leave, but I don't think I'm allowed to do that. Now and then, the doctor knocks on the door to find out how I'm doing, and I respond in the affirmative. When I exit, he asks how my arm feels.

"No better," I say. "Maybe slightly worse."

"You were sitting too long," he says. "You need to stretch your arm, flap it around. That might help."

*

I lie on my back on our living-room floor to stretch my arm. The living room is the largest room in our apartment, but it is nonetheless small. My feet reach the couch, and my fingers reach the wall's baseboard. I bring my injured arm up over my head in an arc, then use a stick to bend it at the elbow. I roll onto my side and pull my weaker hand down with my other hand. Then I roll onto my other side and lift a weight with a reverse elbow motion. I do each of these things repeatedly.

When my daughter sees me, she says, "You have to do push-ups."

I haven't done push-ups since I broke my arm. "I don't think I can," I say.

"Yes, you can," she says.

I get down on my arms and toes, with my face to the floor, and I slowly flex my elbows. I am able to go down and come back up. I repeat the move a couple of times.

"Keep going," she says.

I do more push-ups.

When my wife comes into the room, our daughter says, "Look. He's doing push-ups."

I *am* doing push-ups. They are rather pathetic, but they are push-ups. The orgone box might have done its work. Now, I'm ready for the next step. I'm ready for the libido part to kick in.

*

I go around feeling permanently aroused. I can do normal things, like make a sandwich, type on a keyboard or stroll on a sidewalk. But my thoughts come back to images, like those on the old service station calendars from my childhood, that provoke arousal. There is no question in my mind that car washing can be sexy. The only problem is, I have no car. I do know how to drive, and if I had a car, I could get it washed. I could also get it gassed up. Once fueled, I could race down the middle of an empty highway at a hundred miles per hour.

It is more likely, however, that I will do my traveling by wheelchair. I can imagine riding a wheelchair along the streets. When I'm going downhill, I pick up speed. On level ground or on a slight upgrade, I can use my feet to push myself forward. I'll hang my feet over the sides of the chair and push against the pavement. The wheelchair will be low to the ground, as low as a kayak. I can bend forward and touch the ground with my hands. My injured arm will help to propel me forward. The pavement will slide by, under me, like water.

Road Trip

I have to get from one part of the desert to another. I look at a map for the quickest way. I see a road drawn as a dotted line and decide to take it.

As I enter the road, I see a sign that reads, "Unsafe in Winter Months." There is snow on the ground, but the pavement is clear. The route twists out ahead of me, but it seems safe. As I proceed, the road winds higher and holds patches of snow and ice. I go around those spots and come to where the pavement ends. The road changes to dirt that's completely iced over, and I see a sign that reads, "Impassable Beyond This

Point." I go a little farther and cannot continue. I can't even turn around. I put the car in Reverse and ride over the ice until I come back to the clear pavement.

*

I'm in a pit house—a shelter built over a circular hole dug in the ground. It's cold inside; there's no fire burning. And it's hard to get out; the house is a kind of trap. The only nice feature is an upholstered couch in the middle of the room. I lie on the couch and feel its comfort. My injured arm sinks into the cushion. I can handle living in this room with mud walls, as long as I can lie on the couch.

I'm tempted to start a fire to warm the place, but I know what could happen. The fire could burn out of control. The flames could reach the thatch that forms the roof. Not only will the roof burn off, but everything below the roof will go up, including the couch. I might escape, but when I return, I'll see a blackened pit, with no house over it.

With the couch gone, I'll have no place to rest my injured arm.

*

I go outside and see that the pit house is built on the side of a cliff. It's hundreds of feet to the top or the bottom of the sandstone wall. There is a short ladder from the top of the house to a rock ledge, but no steps leading from the ledge to the top of the mesa or the bottom of the canyon. I spot handholds and footholds, but using them won't be easy. Anytime I put weight on my arm, it hurts not just at the fracture, but all along its length. The pain goes from my fingers to my side.

I see a cactus pad lying on the rock ledge—someone has kicked it off its root. The inside of the pad is exposed, and the green flesh looks soft. I pick up the pad, thinking I'm avoiding the spines, but I don't see the tiny, hairlike needles. I feel an itching and see that the needles are sticking into my fingers. Some of them have entered the creases under my fingernails. I pull them out of my skin, but I can't reach the ones under the nails.

I realize I'll have to go up, not down, to get off the cliff. That's the easier way—I see a route between stones. Using my hands and feet, I take the steep path to the lip of the canyon.

*

When I come out of the gorge, I spot a group of men wearing hats. One of the men is with a woman. The woman is wearing a dress made of thick fabric. The man with a hat and the woman are arm in arm, crossing an open area between buildings. These buildings are low: they are in a region where low buildings are common: maybe the American Southwest, maybe Mexico.

The air is windy, but not windy enough to blow off the hats. Not one hat has left a man's head.

The people outdoors have somewhere to go. Some of them are moving on foot. Others might be doing business: they've stopped and are talking to each other.

The street is made of dirt. The people who are standing and talking might start walking soon. They might have decided what to do about the problems they are discussing. Nothing is holding them back now.

*

I look through a window and see a girl on a bed in a cluttered room. Her room is in one of the low buildings. Outside, a few adults are walking with children. Most of the men are wearing hats—maybe the style called the fedora, more likely the sombrero.

The girl on the bed doesn't seem to mind the clutter in her room: she might like to accumulate things, or maybe her parents prefer to pile things up. No one in her family is interested in neatness or throwing things away. Hoarding is what they do.

Maybe the people outdoors are discussing what to do with the girl on the bed. Maybe she is an orphan, and all the clothing and toys around her are not hers. Maybe they are contributions from people who want to help people in need. Maybe the girl is living in a children's shelter.

*

I have a conversation with the girl.

She asks, "Are you happy?"

"Sometimes," I say.

"Are you happier now than you ever were?"

I don't know what to say. Maybe I am happier now than I was when I was a child, or even when I was a young adult. Maybe I am more at ease with myself now. But when I think about it, I can't say I'm any more relaxed now. I mean, I still bite the ends of my fingers out of nervousness. I won't bite the fingers that have cactus spines in them, though.

"I'm happier now than when I was on the cliff," I say.

She looks disappointed by my remark, as if my having been "on the cliff" is a sign of uncontrolled behavior. She walks away from me.

"Come back," I say. But as I approach her, she moves farther away. I know that to get her to return, I should not pursue her. So I stay where I am, and after a time she comes back.

*

I'm traveling on the impassable road, toward where I started. I see familiar warning signs, red reflectors—objects I remember from my trip up. There's a place where a rabbit ran in front of me and onto the snow on the other side. At the end of the road is a four-lane expressway.

I see a fast-food place and pull in. I get a cup of coffee, sit at a Formica-topped table and look at a map. I could take the expressway north and reach a paved road that goes across the mountains. Or I could take it south a hundred miles past where I need to go and loop around. I decide to take the expressway north. The road across the mountains is not drawn as a dotted line. It should go all the way through.

Glass House

I have to take a standardized test at work, during my full-time day job. There aren't too many questions on the test, but they are hard questions, requiring thought. The answers are multiple-choice, so there's no room for interpretation.

I go through the test and think I got all of the questions right, but when my supervisor gives me the result, I see that I missed three of the eleven questions.

One young man gave all of the correct answers, but he doesn't even work in my area. The test covered my specialty. I find out this young man is someone I know from childhood. He works at a desk on the other side of the office—I wasn't aware he'd joined the company. I don't know what to say to him, but I know I should ask him to lunch sometime.

My score is the same as that of a colleague, someone I've considered less intelligent than I am. Obviously, I am less intelligent than I thought. This is the lesson for me: Whenever I think I am the best, I find out I'm not the best. I'm not even close.

*

At my part-time teaching job, one of my students tells me he has traveled to see my mother. I don't know how he found her or why he would drive a couple of hundred miles to visit her. Another student tells me she has also seen my mother. In fact, these two students were at my mother's house at the same time, by coincidence. I picture all of them in the kitchen, at the bar counter my father built, conversing.

The female student tells me my mother was afraid of her. The student looks South Asian; maybe her facial features frightened my mother. But why would my mother, who is East Asian, be frightened? Could it be that my mother is getting up in years and is easily startled?

I guess these students wanted to know more about me, so they went to ask my mother. Surely, my mother would have information to add to my biography. But what my mother would say and what *I* would say are two different things.

*

My wife, our daughter and I are living in a different apartment. It's next to a grassy area under an expressway. It's more like a storefront than an apartment. The front wall is made of glass. We'll need to have a metal gate to protect the front windows, but there is no rail to attach a gate to. Our place is vulnerable to anyone who wants to break through the glass.

*

My brother, sister and mother—the surviving members of my childhood family—come to stay with my present family in our apartment. The place is one big room. It's modern: a box with a sliding door leading outside, and carpeting on the floor. There's no furniture in it. My guests will have enough space to sleep, as long as they don't mind sleeping on the floor.

They are here to attend a wedding. I don't know whose wedding. I hug each of them in turn, even my mother. She feels thin and fragile in my grasp.

*

At my part-time job, I begin to teach a class, but I don't know what to say. I don't know how to fill the time with a meaningful lecture. I'm supposed to help people understand esoteric material but have no clue that what I say is coming across.

I see that an old friend is a student—I don't know what he's doing here, in the classroom. He's already well educated.

I hand back some homework papers, pointing out the good ones, but I don't know what the students have written about. I've forgotten the assignment, even though I'm the one who made it.

I look for a wire connection for the classroom computer; I get down on my hands and knees on the floor. While there, I suddenly see that my sister is beside me.

"How did you find me?" I ask.

"It's an emergency," she says. "Our mother has disappeared."

We can't go to the wedding without my mother. That's the whole purpose of my childhood family's visit, to attend this once-in-a-lifetime event. "Where has she gone?" I ask.

"Maybe she went to find someone."

Who might that be? My brother? I wouldn't be surprised. He often gets lost on purpose so people have to look for him.

*

I've been sleeping next to my wife for a long time, but we've had little contact. We have no privacy—there's a child around.

One morning, we start touching and kissing, and I can tell she likes this activity. She looks at me like she wants me to do something more, and I look into her face to see if I can. I'm not sure; maybe I can. But I am in a hurry—I have to get to my full-time job. My workday starts early in the morning.

"That's OK," she says. "I have to be somewhere, too."

*

On Christmas Eve, I'm called into an office room with several other employees. There's a man I worked with many years ago—what's he doing here? He's sitting with people I've never seen before.

We're told that we haven't been doing an essential part of our jobs. As a result, we are being let go.

The person speaking goes into detail about what each of us has been neglecting. I think about how this news comes at a bad time, just before a holiday. Some of the employees get tired of listening and walk out of the room.

I stay to find out what it is that I haven't been doing. It turns out I've never tracked how many people see the company's ads. The ads appear on computer screens, and each time someone views a display, the computer pings. There are different-sized ads on each page, and I'm supposed to determine which ones get the most views.

I won't lose my day job if I count the pings.

I focus on my computer screen and listen for pings. I make hash marks on paper to keep track. Soon, I have hundreds of marks.

I go to a meeting, ready to report my results. But the meeting is so crowded I can't even sit in the same room as the presenters. I have to sit in another room and watch the proceedings on closed-circuit television. In the separate room, I find an empty chair and settle in. I see the screen on the wall between my room and the place where the real meeting will start. I wait for the proceedings to begin. I can see and hear everything perfectly.

*

My mother has been found. She wasn't lost; she was just trying to round up my brother and sister for the event we are attending. Getting everyone in my family together is an almost impossible task. My brother has said he hates the city; yet here he is, in a place he doesn't like at all.

The big event turns out not to be a wedding, but a Bat Mitzvah for our daughter. I've written a brief speech, and I've practiced some lines of Hebrew with my wife. She knows how to pronounce the words and put them into song. I'm not good at mimicking her, but when the time comes, I muddle through. *"Baruch atah Adonai elohaynu melech ha'olam ..."* I sing.

*

A rumor that I'm leaving my job goes around my office. I'm aware of the rumor, and I know it's not true. At the end of the workday, people start to gather in my space. I have a very large room, with a desk in a corner. The room fills with twenty, then thirty people. They are wishing me well.

"But I'm not leaving," I say.

"Right," someone says to the assembled staffers. "If he were leaving, he would be gone by now."

Who started the rumor, I wonder, and why? I know who, but I don't know why. I don't know why this employee would take the trouble. She usually doesn't notice me at all.

*

There's a new chief editor in my office. He calls the staff into a meeting. He has the same name as the former editor, but he is not the same person. His hair is dyed red. I know this isn't what he wants to do—run a magazine. What he really wants to do is write books. He has written a book but doesn't know how to publish it.

After the meeting, I head outside with one of my few friends from the office. We get on the same city bus. "Are you going to your neighborhood?" he asks.

"No," I say. "We just moved to Brooklyn."

"When was that?"

"About three weeks ago," I say, but I'm not sure when we moved, and I'm not sure how I'll get to our new place. I'll have to change from the bus to a subway train, and when I get out of the subway, I'll have to walk. My trip home will take a long time.

And when I get there, who knows what I will find? Our new apartment offers no security; it's made of glass.

Hard Biking

It's raining, and I'm on foot, heading for my parked bicycle, when I see a bike go by with two umbrellas attached to it. One umbrella is over the main rider, and the other is over the back wheel, as if to protect a small passenger. Maybe there is a child in the jump seat, but I can't tell as the bike rolls away.

I have no umbrella. I have only a plastic jacket with a hood. Light rain falls onto my face as I start to ride home.

This isn't so bad, I think as my pants get soaked. At least the air is warm, and I don't have far to go.

I ride through deep water at the side of the street. With each pedal downstroke, one foot gets wet. Maybe I should get two umbrellas for my bike. They could protect me and my daughter, if she were still small enough to ride on the back.

*

Between the traffic and the curb, a cab door opens in front of me. I'm too close to stop. My front wheel hits the door, and I fall off my bike. I pick the bike and myself up as a woman gets out of the car's back seat and walks away.

I get back on my bike and ride, but when I'm out of sight of the cab, I notice that my hand hurts and something might be torn or broken. I realize I should have gotten the woman's name and phone number. She seemed totally unconcerned, but she would be concerned if I had her contact info. If my hand is injured, she should pay.

Then I remember: I couldn't sue when I fell and broke my arm a couple of years earlier. There was construction on the street, and someone had left a fire hydrant running. The water had frozen, but the ice looked like water in the dark. I was walking fast; then I was flying fast, briefly, through the air.

After my fracture diagnosis back then, I took pictures of the pylons and dividers, the flooded manhole next to where I fell. I studied the parked trucks, vans and heavy equipment. But I couldn't find the name of a responsible entity. It was nobody's fault but mine.

*

I notice a hole, or a series of holes, in the seat of my pants. The pattern looks like I sat on barbed wire. I blame my bicycle. My pants must have ripped when I hit the cab's door. Maybe I caught my pants on a metal clip that holds a cable. Maybe a seat spring was loose. My hand isn't the only thing that was hurt.

I examine the bike, but all I see is the relatively soft seat. No sharp pieces of metal are sticking out. It looks totally harmless.

*

Farther along, I see a rat squashed on the street with an orange circle spray-painted around it. Why is the rat marked? I don't stop to find out. Then I wonder, did I not see it correctly? I'm pretty sure I saw it for what it was—a squashed rat. There are other orange markings on the pavement where I'm riding. Maybe they indicate gas lines or water mains under the street. Construction is going on. Maybe the rat was flattened over a key piece of infrastructure and had to be officially marked. But I doubt it. I think the spray painter was just being whimsical with his can of orange pigment.

*

As I approach the block where I live with my wife and daughter, I see that the street in front of our building has been cordoned off. Police cars' lights are flashing, and no one can cross. People have gathered at the corners, as if waiting to see something.

Shortly, a motorcade goes by. A cheer goes up when the U.S. president's limo passes. The president must be in town for a television or fund-raising appearance. I see small U.S. flags fluttering on the hood of a car, but I can't tell who is inside.

The street has been narrowed by construction barricades—the same pylons and dividers from couple of years earlier. The street looks the same as it did when I broke my arm. So the motorcycles and limos have to follow a single lane, from one side of the street to the other. The vehicles slow down, then stop in a jam.

I want to write a letter to the president, complaining about the construction. "Dear Mr. President," I'll write. "The city has been tearing up our street for several years now. I can't even ride my bicycle on the street anymore. I have to ride on the sidewalk, where I am yelled at by pedestrians. Our tax dollars are paying for this project. Do you have jurisdiction to stop it, or order it done?"

*

I see a mushroom-shaped cloud between the earth and sky, but it isn't a nuclear blast. The lighter-than-air mass resembles a shape I've seen somewhere else, in another country. There aren't many, or any, mushroom-shaped clouds in this city, at least that I've seen. This cloud reminds me of where I've been, in a country where the air was smoky every morning. Later, the sun would come out and heat the air with incredible intensity, and the haze would slowly give way to blue sky.

*

Inside our building, I take my bike to the basement, stepping carefully down the narrow metal stairs.

On the lowest level, I see a freight elevator. It wasn't here before; it must have been newly installed. It is just below a pigeon's nest, which sits on an air duct. It looks like a contraption in a building where I used to live. The car of that elevator once fell on a man and broke both of his legs.

I get into the elevator, glad for not having to take the stairs. I push the handle and the car starts. It stops at the building's front hallway, but no one is waiting there, so I continue on. When I get to our floor, I stop the car by moving the handle. But the floor of the car and the floor of the hallway are not aligned, so I can't open the gate. I push the handle the other way, and the car moves a couple of inches. When the surfaces are perfectly aligned, I open the door.

I am back at the time I told my wife and daughter I would be.

"I'm not late," I say when I walk in. "Look at the time."

I can't see a clock from where I'm standing, but I'm sure that any timepiece would agree with me.

Code of Violence

On the subway, I see a boy who is about 10 years old; he's with his father. Both have red hair, but the boy has Asian features—a round face and pointy eyes. His father has a long face and Western eyes. Maybe this boy is something like me, a halfling.

"Do CIA agents use switchblades?" the boy asks his father.

The father makes no reply, and the boy says, "I think they carry hidden knives."

The boy continues, "There was a gun called Hitler's Buzz Saw. It fired three shots per second.

Again, the father doesn't respond.

"Are there still people with Ebola in Texas?" the boy asks. "Why don't they just make them drink poison?"

"Let's move to the back," the father says, and the two of them head for the seats above the bus's engine.

"Can you believe Hitler's Buzz Saw was that fast?" the boy asks.

I wonder if this is a typical boy, or if he resembles the young Adolf Eichmann. Is this boy a killer in the making? Or is he just a normal kid?

He looks like a normal kid.

*

After I get off the bus, I walk between buildings that house faculty for the local university. The well-lit street is lined with trees. Two young men are walking toward me. Perhaps they are students, going to meet a professor.

They stumble as they walk; they are off balance. I look at one as I pass; then I look away. He strikes the side of my head with an open hand.

"Hey!" I say. "Why did you do that?"

He comes at me with both arms hanging, gorilla-like, in front of him. His friend—if he is a friend—steps in and hugs the aggressor, pinning his arms at his sides. The first man struggles, says, "Let me at him."

"Leave him alone," the supposed friend says.

I hold my hand to the side of my head as I walk by.

*

I arrive at a club to have dinner with a friend. It's the kind of place I'd never visit on my own, but I've been invited. Inside, men wear jackets. My friend takes off his jacket to go to the rest room, and I take off my jacket, too, but I don't leave the table. A wait staffer comes over almost immediately and tells me to put my jacket back on. "You have to wear it at all times," she says, "but we'll make it cooler here for you."

I suppose she is going to adjust the air conditioning in our corner of the room. As time passes, however, I feel no comfort.

I tell my friend about the head-slapping incident.

"You were just walking by and he hit you?" my friend asks.

"Maybe I looked at him the wrong way," I say.

"I don't know what I'd do if that happened to me," my friend says.

He's a big guy, and I wonder if he means he would hit back.

"I might do something," he adds as he makes a fist on the table.

Near the end of the meal, an older woman comes over to our table. She knows my friend—they are both members of the club—but she wants to talk to me. "Let me see your left hand," she says. "Are you wearing a wedding ring?"

"Why?" I ask.

"I want to find someone for my daughter," she says. "I'm looking for a man of about 50."

Maybe I look like I fit the part. It doesn't matter, though; I don't want to be matched up with anyone.

"She's right there," the woman says.

Sure enough, there is a young woman at a nearby table. She is getting ready to leave. Her mother motions her over, and the daughter shakes my hand and says hello.

"She's a lawyer," her mother says, "but she doesn't practice. She works *pro bono*."

The daughter is attractive, younger than 50. Any bachelor in the club would be a good candidate for her.

Unfortunately, I'm wearing a ring, and I show it to the mother.

*

I take the subway home. I don't see the usual musician on the subway platform. The older man who plays a wooden flute and makes notes that sound like wind through trees isn't there. Instead, I see a man who has a poetry display. He has a cardboard table with papers on it and sign that says, "Published Poet, *New York Times*." Another sign is propped on the concrete floor. It says: "Watch TheLivingPoet on Youtube.com." The small text says he'll write poems for a fee.

When I walk toward him, he says, "I'm the poet."

I ask if he'll write a poem about violence.

He says he won't. "I'm a poet of peace," he says.

I offer to pay him.

"You should pay for peace, not violence," he says. "Where are you from, any-way?"

"I'm from Pennsylvania, but my mother is Chinese," I say. "She was a Chinese person living in China; she wasn't an American in China."

"What the hell are you talking about?" the poet says.

"Some people don't understand," I say, "so I have to clarify."

*

Later, I tell my wife about the potential match-up.

"Do you think they were playing with you?" she says.

"No," I say. "I think they were serious. I could have called one of them, the mother or the daughter. I could have made a date."

"You're going to give me bad dreams," my wife says.

*

The next day, when I go to the subway, I look for the published poet, but he is gone. The stairs where he lives and writes are swept clear. Apparently, it is not permitted to live and write poetry in the subway.

I wonder if he has gone deeper into the tunnel network. There's an unused station halfway to the next stop—I've seen it when I ride. No trains stop there, but some dim lights illuminate the platform. The walls are covered with graffiti. It might be a good place for a poet who doesn't want to be disturbed.

I look down the track from where I'm standing, and I think I see the glow of that ghost station. The published poet might be living there.

Between Places

I'm living in a rented house with my wife and daughter. We're sharing it with people we don't know. We have our own apartment, but sometimes we go into other people's rooms, and sometimes they come into ours. No one seems to mind this arrangement—people coming and going as they please. We're leaving the house soon, anyway.

*

There is material on my work-computer screen that I don't want other people to see. I look at a window on the monitor, careful that no one is watching me.

Someone comes to my desk to ask a question, then sits at my keyboard and starts to type. The private content is one layer below what shows on the screen. The person won't leave my desk.

But maybe I'm wrong. Maybe the secret material is on my home computer, not my office computer. I wouldn't put those kinds of images on my computer at work.

*

I'm copying Chinese text onto sticks. I'm holding half a dozen pieces of wood that look like tongue depressors. The Chinese characters are aligned in vertical rows.

I'm finding these words in a source book, and they are being duplicated automatically on the wooden sticks, as if by a Xerox machine. I don't have to do the copying by hand. All I have to do is make my wishes known.

I'll show these coded sticks to people and hope they understand the words.

*

My wife, daughter and I are moving out of our apartment. We have only a few boxes and bags to pack, but I can't gather all of them. Each time I reach for something, I find something else I need to bring. I pick up a plastic bag, and I begin to stuff it into a larger bag, but the larger bag is filled with cookies for our trip. I eat a couple of the cookies and leave the plastic bag alone.

The rooms now have no furniture, just carpeting and bare walls. I don't know what we slept on or sat on during our stay here.

*

My office has been moved to a new space, a sort of large terrace, with a slate floor. There is no office equipment, no desks or computers. There are some tables with wrought-iron legs—patio furniture.

The people I'm working with are new, too. They are taking over the operation. One is a woman—I used to work for a female boss. The new people seem nice enough, but I suspect they won't need me around much longer.

*

I decipher the Chinese characters I've copied onto sticks. The ideograms form a poem about drinking wine. It's a short lyric by a poet of the Tang Dynasty. In the poem, the speaker is spending the night outdoors and alone. He has no friends. After a few drinks from a jug, the moon and his shadow become his friends. The three of them do some singing and dancing. His shadow follows him along; even the moon travels with him. Then they go their separate ways, looking to life while sober.

*

I go back to the apartment we've moved out of to see if we've left anything behind. I find a number of things, mostly shoes. There are about three pairs of my wife's shoes on the floor, and one of her shoes that has no counterpart. I look into a closet and see a couple of pieces of luggage: a large backpack and a long, thin case for something like a fishing rod or a rifle.

I see that I can fit these things into my backpack. Somehow, the larger pieces are collapsible. I'm going to have to carry all of this stuff with me to work, then bring it home when the day is done. My wife will be surprised and happy to see the retrieved items.

*

Our new apartment's front door is flimsy. It's a folding door with a small knob in the middle, at the seam. It looks easy to break into.

I've forgotten where the subway entrance is. It is far from our apartment, but it used to be clear in my mind. Now, I can't find it at all. I walk along unfamiliar streets, looking for a lamppost that marks the stairs.

When I get home, I see that my Chinese texts have been defaced. Someone has written sarcastic comments next to the characters and made serious words into jokes. "Moon," a scrawled note reads. "Wine. Ha!"

Otherwise, I see no evidence of breaking and entering. Nothing has been taken.

*

I come out to the car I've rented for our move and see a traffic officer leaving a parking ticket on the windshield. "I'm going to move the car now," I say, hoping to avoid a fine.

It turns out not to be a ticket, but a crime report. "Someone broke into your car," the cop says.

I was carrying paintings in the car. The canvases were small, but some were valuable. I don't know where I got those paintings.

I look into the back of the car and see some jackets and hats—they haven't been stolen. Only the paintings are gone.

I'm waiting for my daughter. Obviously, I left the car parked too long. My daughter and I were inside a house, doing something, not paying attention to the car. Now, a lot has gone wrong.

*

Our daughter is going to China by herself. She is packing bags—she has several of them. They are not all suitcases. Some are shopping bags.

She has tasks here, where she lives. One is a big test in school. She has a series of exams coming up. But she'll miss these duties while she's in China.

If she needs our help there, we won't be able to go. I don't even know how we'll communicate with her. She has Chinese hosts, but I don't know them. I'm not sure if they are trustworthy.

I always knew there would come a time when she would move away from home. I just didn't know it would happen this way.

"Don't worry," she says to me. "I'm not leaving yet. We have time to play a game. You know, the one where you and Mom hold my hands and swing me up while we're walking."

I remember that game. We played it almost every time we were on the sidewalk. We would lift her between us, and she would kick her feet. "I'll try," I say.

*

When the Work Runs Out

I'm working in a divided city. As I go from one side to the other, the landscape changes, becomes more desolate. My assignment is to meet people in their apartments and find out how life is different on the other side. One person tells me life is not so hard on his side, except that when a lightbulb burns out, it's hard to find a replacement.

I have to meet a deadline to get back to the other side, my side. Travel ceases at a certain hour. I sneak through a corridor of the travel terminal, which straddles the border, and find myself back on the familiar side. I am not trapped, though I was afraid I would be.

In my apartment, I want to turn on the lights, but my room remains dark. I flip the switches on all of the fixtures, but the lights won't come on. One bulb glows orange, but it is too dim to illuminate the room.

I could reach up and turn on the lamp over my head; I could do that, but I don't, so the room stays dark.

*

My office has been redesigned. I see that my work area is on a new countertop. But it still isn't far from my supervisor's desk. Luckily, she doesn't spend much time at her desk, because she has to attend meetings.

At the end of the workday, I order some Chinese food to take home, but there is a misunderstanding. I receive two gallons of soup and some other dishes. I'm going to have to take a cab to get this amount of food home.

I go out to the street, walk a couple of blocks and realize I've left the food in my office. But I get lost trying to return to the building. I go through an archway and across a courtyard; the streets don't look familiar anymore.

In my work area, my supervisor is at her desk. I realize I'm leaving too early, even though it is after 6 p.m. I shouldn't leave while she is still working.

She talks about the article she's reading on her computer screen, complains about it. "We have to follow the guidebook," she says, "but nobody reads it. Have you read it?"

I admit I haven't.

I pick up my Chinese food. One carton of noodles is the perfect size and shape for my briefcase. I leave the rest of the food at my desk and head for the elevator.

*

I'm visiting friends at their apartment. It's strange to be at the friends' place, because I haven't seen this person and his wife in a couple of years. But they are nice enough. The problem is, I've left work too early and must go back to the office. Pages have been set up by others in my absence, but the elements don't fit on the pages. I call in on a telephone, but my supervisor can't explain the problem to me. Her voice trails off and goes silent.

"Hello?" I say. "Hello?" but she doesn't answer. Maybe she is listening without speaking, or maybe the line has gone dead.

I leave the friends' apartment and go out to the street to catch a cab. I see no cabs, so I start walking. Soon, I realize that I've been walking in the wrong direction; I'm way downtown and west, when I wanted to go uptown and east. There are no cabs because there's been a storm. None of the streetlights are working.

A cab stops with passengers in it. "Get in," the driver says. "I can take more than one fare when the power is out."

I almost don't respond, and he almost drives away. The cab starts to roll forward. I run to the car, rip open a back door and jump in.

*

When I get to work, I see that my desk has been moved to a separate building. My new room is big, like a loft space, but I have to share it with three other people. I'm the first one in, so I unpack my belongings. I have more than I need for the day: I have food, boxes of cereal.

My computer is just my laptop. When it's time to start working, I don't know what to do. I can't tell where the material is, on the computer. My supervisor is in the main building, not my building. I could go and ask her what to do.

I am cut off from the key people at the company. But I'm lucky. One woman in the inner circle has to wear chains to work, like a slave. I am not fettered, though I have nothing to do. I spend my time rearranging my belongings so they take up less space.

The chief boss comes over to my building. I look outside and see him approaching. But he's not coming to where I work; he's walking to a Buddhist temple next door. He sits on the flagstones in front of the temple and opens his laptop computer. He meditates on electronic documents; he's a spiritual man.

*

My supervisor says to me, "In two days, the company won't be able to pay you anymore, so you'll have to leave."

I understand I'll lose my job in two days. Forty-eight hours isn't much notice, but that's the way it has to be.

As the second day arrives, I go in to my office, but I don't speak to anyone. I don't say I'm leaving, and I don't say goodbye. I don't work very hard, either. I pretend to look at some charts—fever lines showing economic trends—but I have no suggestions for the graphics people. I have no changes to make.

I'm not sure what I'll do after my last day of work, but I figure I can collect unemployment pay for a while. I don't know how I'll take my possessions with me. I own some of the books on my desk. They are too numerous and heavy for me to carry all at once. Even so, I'm not planning to make another trip to get the rest of my things. I'm not coming back.

Secret Places

I take an elevator from a building lobby to a high floor. The elevator has glass walls, so I can see the lobby dropping away. I'm going so fast I'm almost frightened—not of falling, but of what I don't know. When I get to the office area, I find my way to a computer, where I'm supposed to work for my former company. If I do well, I might be asked to rejoin.

However, I can't get into the right part of the computer system. I see icons on the screen but can't find the proper queue. I'm working for new supervisor, a woman I don't know. She tells me that the chief editor is still there at the company and that "he'll never leave." He's on a different floor, she says, and I could go through the entire day without seeing him.

*

My task is to arrange a list of labels under the right headings. I look at strings of letters and numbers. Everything has to match, as in an outline for a research paper or the taxonomy of a species. But when I have the list in front of me, I realize I've left some items out. One missing piece will make the whole puzzle fall apart. It's like a house of cards.

I make a change to the overall heading. It is not a big change, but it is a key change. It adjusts the focus of the whole list. I hope it takes care of everything, but it might not. It might well not.

*

When I leave the office building late at night, I walk through unfamiliar corridors. The company has remodeled its space, and the passageways have clean lines—they are modern and airy. The walls seem made of Plexiglas. The windows are huge—if they were open, there would be no walls. I feel that I am in a maze, then I find the lobby and exit. I have not seen the chief editor all day. I wait outside, for what I don't know.

Unexpectedly, I see a young woman—someone I used to spend time with—leaving with the chief editor. She is wearing a lot of makeup, and her hair is wavy. She doesn't look like the person I remember, but she does look young. She looks like someone who places great importance on her appearance. She is hot, but beyond that, she is *hawt*. I can see that she and the boss are going to be intimate, if they haven't been intimate already.

This young woman also wants to work at the company, and she is going to get the job over me. There is no doubt about that. But I worry about the chief—he is a family man. What is his idea of commitment? Of fidelity? I know what he would say if I asked him. He would say he doesn't have to tell his wife what he's doing. His wife is asleep. It is late at night. Anything he does when she is asleep is his secret.

*

To my surprise, I am invited to a retreat with my former company. The gathering is at a hotel complex in a suburb. At the retreat, I'm scheduled to sing a karaoke version of a pop song. But I'm not a good singer. I picture myself starting to sing the words as they appear on a Teleprompter, and not getting the words out. So I look for someone else to do the singing for me. My plan is, the host can announce my name, then the name of the other singer. The other person can come up to the mic and perform.

I have to find someone who is willing to do it. I try to think of someone I know who's a good singer and available. The person would have to travel to the retreat—a lengthy trip. I can't think of anyone. I might have to put out a call on social media and alert hundreds of people to the favor I need.

*

I can't relax enough to sleep at the retreat. It's the middle of the night, and I'm sitting in a metal chair next to the hotel pool. The only light comes from underwater lamps. As I sit, I see an art director and a reporter walking toward the pool. When they get to the edge of the water, they take off all of their clothes.

The art director is a young Italian man who speaks with an accent. The reporter is American, and she has the odd last name of Girl. The two of them are crossing some kind of a line and arriving at the other side of good conduct.

I hope one else is around. There are some people who can't keep a situation like this secret. It might be only a matter of time before everything about the art director and Ms. Girl is known to everyone.

*

I'm on a bus that will take people back to the city from the retreat. The bus is waiting in a parking space. I get off the bus to go to a rest room, and when I return I see that the bus has left without me.

The dispatcher puts out an emergency call. "Don't worry," he says to me. "The driver will come back to get you."

But the bus doesn't come back. As I wait with the dispatcher, we look at a paper map of the city. I show him the neighborhood where I live.

"When I go the city, here's where I usually go," he says, pointing to an area I'm not familiar with. "I go to the rooftop pools. You wouldn't believe what goes on there."

I realize he's pointing to a secret place, a place that would be nice to visit, if one knew where it was. With the map I'm being shown, I could get there easily. All I'd have to do is set aside the time to make the trip. If I had some downtime, I could find those pools. I could take part in what goes on there.

The Path Back to Work

I receive an e-mail message that says, "If you're not doing anything today, come in to the office." The message is from my old job. But I have time off, so I head to my former office. I don't know what I'll do there—I'll have no reference books, no computer. What kind of work can I do sitting at a bare surface with nothing around me? Who will I talk to? How will I fill the time?

I walk toward midtown, which is not how I used to travel. I used to take the subway. As I pass through an unfamiliar neighborhood on the East Side, I hear an announcement through a public-address system.

"Ladies and gentlemen, ..." an amplified voice says, and announces a name I don't catch. It's the name of a celebrity—people on the street are getting excited. I wait with a crowd as a limousine arrives.

A woman comes out of the limo in a wheelchair. I look at her face—she's not old but not young. She has shoulder-length dark hair, no glasses; she could be someone I've seen before—but I don't recognize her. I don't know what all the fuss is about.

I go into a fast-food restaurant because I'm early, and I see people from my former company. Apparently, this is where they hang out before work, though I've never been here. While I'm sitting at a plastic table, I realize I have no desire to go back to my former office.

As it happens, I can't get out of the restaurant. I am somehow locked in. The main door is sealed shut. I see people moving on the sidewalk; I see vehicle traffic. I hear the rumble of a subway. I don't want to be trapped, so I go out through a window. In the restroom, there is an opening just large enough for me to squeeze through. Head first, hands clenched, I crawl out and jump down.

On the street, I turn and head in the opposite direction. Then I hear a woman calling to me from far away. She's someone who knows me from my former job. "I'm not there, either," she says.

"Where is that?" I ask. Her face looks familiar, but I can't place her. Maybe she has a different hair color now, or shorter hair.

"The company where we worked," she says as I come closer. "We were on the same floor."

Now I remember. I was dismissed earlier than she was. I wasn't around to find out what happened to her.

She walks back into the pedestrians. "Do you like your new job?" she calls.

I can't see her through the people on the street, but I shout back over their heads, "I'm not working yet."

*

I meet a man I used to work with. We are both unemployed, so I ask him how he's doing. "I'm doing well," he says. "I started my own business, and I have good clients."

He looks young, as young as he was when I worked with him years ago. It doesn't seem possible that he didn't age. Maybe I have only one version of him in my mind and can see only that.

He and I want to take a cab, and at first it looks like there are none available. Then we see one with a truck rig attached. We slide into a small front seat. The driver explains the cramped space by saying, "There's an oil tank behind us."

As we ride through narrow passageways, I don't think the vehicle will be able to make the turns, but it does. The driver navigates without hitting anything.

Then I realize my companion didn't work with me where I was laid off. He worked with me at a previous job, and he wasn't even employed there. He was a freelancer, not on the payroll. When they asked him to come in and work at a desk, he refused. He stayed outside the office. He went from place to place, doing his job, taking photographs. He was so skillful, he didn't have to come in.

The cab stops, and the driver gets out to use a restroom. We wait for him to come back. We're sitting in the cab, with an oil tank behind us, watching traffic go by. The cars slow down as they go around us. Some of the drivers honk their horns angrily. There are toys and bright-colored blocks on the dashboard and the floor. A child would have something to play with here.

*

I am on foot again, pounding the pavement with my shoes. I want to take a triangular path to get to a job interview. I want to find the hypotenuse, the shortest way. Usually, when I navigate the city grid, I go one way, then turn 90 degrees and go another way, turn 90 degrees again, go straight for a while, veer to the right or left yet again, until the zigzags fill my brain and I no longer know where I am. On this day, I don't want to follow the two legs of multiple triangles.

Where are the hypotenuses in the city? Was this city was planned by "experts" who had no sense of geometry? Did these experts forget the teachings of Euclid? Euclid of Alexandria would never have stood for this street pattern. He would have added some hypotenuses. And if Euclid couldn't get the mayor and the City Council to adopt his plan, he would have brought in the big gun. He would have called on Ptolemy. A heavyweight like Claudius Ptolemy would have straightened out the local politicians and planners. This goes without saying. It is axiomatic.

While I'm walking, I hear a woman calling from the other side of the street, "Can I go?"

I notice she is sweeping the sidewalk with a cane. No one answers her, but she keeps walking.

I cross the street to her and say, "Do you need help?"

"Can I cross?" she asks.

"Of course," I say.

"I'm going to the theater," she says. "Am I almost there?"

I see the theater up ahead. A banner with the theater's name hangs over the sidewalk. "Yes," I say. "You have one long block to go."

"Are there any more streets before I get there?" she asks.

"No," I say, and I wonder why she asked. Then I see that she is walking next to a parking lot. She must have thought she was in an intersection. But these parked cars aren't going to come at her, even if a traffic light changes. They have no drivers; their engines are cold. They can't run over anyone.

*

During a job interview, my potential new boss asks if I know someone from a previous job. I can picture the woman. She was solid and fierce. She ran a small department separate from the one I worked in, a department of maybe three people.

"Yes," I say, "I saw her every day."

"Anyone who worked with her is OK," the potential new boss says. "She's a great person."

Shortly afterward, I'm offered a job. I accept it, but before I start I have to be screened for security. I cooperate with the background check; I tell everything I can think of about my work history. Next, I submit to a drug test. At a clinic, I wait my turn, then enter the inner lab. I produce a urine sample while a nurse makes sure I do not cheat. She stands guard, waiting for me. Later, I learn that I passed both tests. I am no threat in terms of substance abuse or false statements. I'm not going to get high and lie about my past.

After I start, I try to contact the person known by my new boss and me. I don't know if the new boss asked her about me. Maybe it was enough for me to have recognized her name. Whatever the case, I look her up on social media. On her home page, she looks the same as she did years ago. I send her a message, thanking her for vouching for me, but she doesn't answer. Maybe my message went into her "other" folder. Maybe the computer marked it as spam. Maybe she knows nothing about my new job, or the fact that the woman I work for and she are friends. Maybe she thinks I am just sending her a weird message that makes no sense and deserves no answer. These thoughts run through my head as I work hard at the office to learn a new routine.

Getting There from Here

I worry that burglars will ransack our apartment. When I'm out on the street, I can see our windows. The windows are propped open with sticks. One floor below, there is scaffolding for work that hasn't begun yet. A thief could climb the fire-escape ladder to the scaffolding platform and get a boost up from a cohort to an open window.

Inside, the thief would work fast, but he wouldn't be able to get out the front door because it has an illegal lock that requires a key on the inside. He will have to pick up items and throw them (gently) out the window to his friend waiting on the platform. Then they will both have to jump down to the sidewalk and run. On one trip, they could carry a couple of thin computers and a flat-screen TV. If no one stops them, they can stash the first batch of stolen items in a fence's warehouse and come back for seconds.

I picture myself coming in, seeing an open window, and noticing empty spaces where objects had been. I'll look out the window and see a man with a large box on his shoulder vanishing into the crowd. I'll grab some kind of weapon—a wrench, a hammer (I own no guns)—and run to the street, but the thief will be gone.

*

I imagine that our child is missing, but I don't know what to do about the situation. Should I act as if everything is OK? Should I go about my business, which on this occasion is shopping? In this vision, I'm looking for items to replace the ones supposedly stolen from our apartment, mostly electronics—no books, of course. No thief wants books.

I could continue looking at merchandise, assessing the relative appeal of various televisions and cameras, or I could start screaming our child's name at the top of my lungs. But even if our child were within earshot, she would ignore me, as is her habit.

I hear the crash of an appliance hitting the store floor. What has the child done? Is she signaling her presence in the electronics aisle? Why am I rooted to my spot, when I should be rescuing the undamaged items from her curious hands?

Maybe I should pretend that the child isn't mine, and that everything is OK. I won't deny that I heard the crash; I'll just pretend I had no involvement in it. Someone else's child broke whatever it was that got shattered.

But no, this is not the adult way. I must claim the child as mine, and I must comfort myself with the belief that someday, hopefully soon, she will no longer feel the need to test the law of gravity.

*

I'm in a market in a part of the city that resembles an undeveloped country. I'm by myself, but my family is nearby. I see a table that holds a couple of crocks of liquid. The liquid is on fire; it is giving off smoke. The ceramic containers are filled with hashish, and a hit costs a lot—many dollars.

I'm encouraged by the vendor to take two tokes. "It's smooth and rich," he says.

I want to inhale the substance, even though I quit the practice long ago. I don't really have enough money, but I'm willing to spend what I have. I think that two doses will make me high, and I want that feeling in my head. I want to be lost in the clouds. I'll hide my altered state from my family. I don't know if I'll succeed at hiding it, but I'm willing to take the risk. It will be a private high.

*

We are moving to a new place, but we can't get our things out of our old place in time. When we empty a room, there is another room, another set of cabinets, another chest of drawers that holds things we need to pack. There are things of ours in the basement of the building. We didn't even know we had things in the basement, though most of the books and files there turn out to belong to a neighbor.

We find out the front gate is locked and we don't have the key. We need to open the gate to carry large pieces of furniture out. We've been using the side door for years. I didn't even know that the door we were using wasn't the main door, until now. I find a key, and I know it will work because I've tested it in a lock that's identical to the front-gate lock. When we are ready, we will be able to go out through the front gate.

*

In a car, we come to a large lake at the end of a road. The lake is so big we can't see its boundaries. The road becomes one lane of tarmac, zigzagging along the shore. My wife is driving. I look out and see a huge deer shape over the water, made of vapor and ice crystals. It turns out to be more like a wolf jumping over the water. "Look," I say to my family. "It's a wolf."

We have no place to stay for the night. My wife pulls into the parking lot of a fast-food shop—a low building with a serving window. "Not here," I say. "Don't stop here. They won't be able to tell us where to stay for the night."

*

Our new place is large, but it is occupied by a co-resident, the owner. He has decorated all of his own rooms well—they are perfect down to the last detail. They are furnished; the walls are painted; the ceilings are high. Our space, on the other hand, is cramped and unfinished.

I make a model of how I want the rooms redone. I put up a wall to create a new room, but the wall has no door. It also has no support. I'm going to have to hire a contractor to build real walls, with two-by-fours.

Meanwhile, our daughter spends time in the common areas, the areas we share with the owner. She finds a comfortable chair in an alcove by the single window. The rest of the space stretches out into the distance, like a subway platform.

I ask the owner if he can help with our space.

"I can refer you to someone," he says.

If we can't find a contractor soon, we will have to move again.

*

We are traveling to another planet. There's plenty of room inside the fuselage of our interstellar ship, but our child wants to go outside. I look out a porthole and see her floating in space. She is tumbling slowly through the nothingness, but she is breathing. After a time, she comes back in.

"How is this possible?" I ask. "How did she survive?"

"There are clouds of oxygen floating outside," her mother says.

I look into the void and see clouds, like those of water vapor. Apparently, a human can float in them and breathe.

When we arrive on the planet, the landscape is alien, at least compared with where we used to live. There are tall mountains and a rocky plain. Luckily, we are on a flat surface. I look across the empty land to a row of trees. There are a couple of monkeys swinging through the trees. The animals are dark, bearded and large. Their size makes them unlike the monkeys on Earth. The trees are different, too. They have smooth trunks, and they are bigger than the trees we're used to.

"Where is this?" I ask. "Where are we, really?"

No one seems to know, but our daughter takes this opportunity to film a video. She gives me her handheld camera and runs across the ground toward the line of trees. When she gets near where the monkeys live, I hear one of them screech out a warning, but I don't see any of the lesser primates. They have vanished into the trees. I follow her with the camera lens as she runs back to me.

Fear of the Dark

Our daughter asks me to check her closet, to see if anyone is hiding there.

"Where would someone be hiding?" I ask. "There's no space in your closet."

"Behind the clothes," she says.

"How would someone get in there?" I ask.

"From the fire escape, through the gate." She means through her window, which has an ironwork gate over the glass.

"Do I have to check?" I ask.

"You have to," she says. "Otherwise, I can't sleep. I'm too afraid."

I go into her room and open the closet door. I see many clothes hanging from a bar, boxes on the floor, more boxes on a shelf above the clothes. "There's no one here," I say.

"Look behind the clothes," she says.

I put my hand between the hanging shirts and dresses. I'm starting to get a little frightened myself. I push the fabric aside and see only darkness. "No one," I say, but I'm not 100 percent sure. I walk over to the window and look at the gate to the fire escape. I turn the knob to see if it's latched. I pull on the bars. The gate doesn't budge. I look through the window, but it's too dark to make out anything. I can't see the plants growing out there. A prowler might be staring me in the face, and I wouldn't be able to tell.

I remember seeing a horror movie when I was in high school. In it, a woman is thought to have died, but she hasn't really died. She just looks like she has died, and so she is entombed in the basement of a mansion. Later, she shows up alive, but she looks much the worse for being entombed. At that point, the whole mansion collapses into a pit.

As a teenager, trying to sleep, I was afraid that dead/alive woman, or a woman like her, would show up outside my bedroom door.

"Well, you can sleep with us tonight," I say.

I don't mean in the same bed with me and her mother. I mean she can sleep on cushions on the floor, near me and her mother. It won't be comfortable, but it might be less scary, and it's the best we can offer.

*

I try to hypnotize her to put her to sleep. I use a method I've seen on television. I have taken no classes in psychology. I am no doctor, not even a quack. I just flutter my fingers in front of her face and chant, "Your eyelids are getting heavy. Your eyelids are closing. You're feeling sleepy. Sleepier and sleepier. You're asleep!" I should have a pocket watch on a gold chain to swing like a pendulum in front of her face, but I don't have one.

On television, I've noticed, people receiving such suggestions will drop into unconsciousness. In their sleep state, they can be made to do things against their will, such as lie between two chairs like a board. Once they are there, between the chairs, the hypnotist can sit on them or jump on them, and they will not bend.

I don't want to paralyze my daughter or petrify her; I just want to put her into a peaceful state of sleep. I keep up my chant, my relaxing mantra, but she just looks at me. She meets my eyes with her eyes. She doesn't waver, and she doesn't go under. When she sees my fingers fluttering in front of her face, she just slaps my hand away.

*

Something falls onto the floor at night, makes a *clink* as it hits. It's something small and not powerful, not as powerful as a mousetrap going off. I didn't set a mousetrap, anyway. After the sound, the *clink*, I hear our daughter's voice from her bed in the next room. "I heard something," she says.

I wonder if she thinks a robber has entered, picked up a fork and dropped it. Or if she thinks a ghost has lost a piece of jewelry. Both scenarios could explain the sound. Or maybe our pet turtle has gotten into something metallic, something like an empty tuna can. Turtles like to eat fish. But the turtle should be safely in her tank, and we haven't left any food cans on the floor.

My wife gets up, goes into our daughter's room, comes back.

"Did you find out what fell?" I ask.

"No," she says, "and I'm not going to look for it now."

I don't want to look for it, either, in the middle of the night. It is probably a small object, invisible to the tired eye.

In the morning, I don't see anything that fell. In fact, I've forgotten that something hit the floor during the night. I'm not thinking that a spirit helped itself to a meal and dropped a fork. Or that a ghost threw dice in a game of supernatural craps. I'm not thinking about the sound at all until my toe touches something foreign by the sink. It's a plastic clothes hook that I'd stuck to the freezer and wrapped a rubber band around. I'd rigged the freezer door to keep it shut. The rubber band must have exerted enough force to rip the hook from its adhesive base. The hook must have shot off like a pebble from a catapult. It must have ricocheted off some surface—a wall or a cabinet—before it hit the floor with a *clink*.

*

She calls me into her dark room. I climb the ladder and sit on the top rung, on the edge of her bed. "Tell me a boring story," she says.

"I bought a pound of coffee today," I say. "The counter woman automatically gave me the sale brand. She knows I always get the cheapest kind. Today, it was mocha java. Then I caught a bus home. The driver tried to keep me off the bus by saying, 'I'm only going to Houston Street,' but that was fine with me because we live on Houston Street."

My story is not boring enough. She looks at her clock, which reads "11:33."

"I'll never get to sleep!" she cries. "This is the worst day of my life."

I go to her mother, who is in bed, and say, "She needs you; she is freaking out."

Her mother goes up to her bed and comes back a few minutes later.

"Is she asleep?" I ask.

"No," her mother says, "but she is calmer."

Her mother and I try to sleep, but after a few minutes, I hear footsteps approaching. Soon, our daughter's head appears above the edge of the mattress on our loft bed. "Can I sleep here?" she asks. "I won't take much room. I just need a corner."

"No," I say, but she climbs over us to a narrow area next to the wall.

"I can't sleep here," I say. "Three are too many in the bed."

Truth be told, I don't think the bed is strong enough to hold the three of us. I put it together, and I don't think the frame is solid. It's made out of relatively thin sticks of wood.

I take a blanket and a pillow and proceed to the couch. My body doesn't fit entirely on the cushions because the couch is too short. I lie there in the dark for a while in a fetal position and realize I'm not going to fall asleep. It's not the worst day, or night, of my life, but it's close.

*

In the early morning, before the sky is light, I hear the local weatherman say, "Just before sunrise, you'll see it. It's not a star. It's Venus."

I look out the window and see an orange glow to the east. The clouds are horizontal, and they are brighter near the horizon. I scan the line between the buildings and the sky until I spot a point of light that must be Venus, the morning star. It is the same object that shines in the west in the evening, at other times. It signals the rising of the sun on some days, the setting of the sun on other days. It took people centuries to figure out the physics, but I have been treated to an immediate lesson.

I'm glad I have seen Venus on a sun-rising day. I've seen the symbol of the goddess of love, and not just of love, but of beauty, sex, fertility, prosperity and desire, all those good things. She shines there just before the main charioteer makes his appearance. I mean the driver of the solar bark, who will blast through the red dawn and arc across the sky on a steady path, blotting out everything else in the sky with unimaginable brightness, before making his way down and giving way to Venus on those days when she is in the west.

Acknowledgments

These stories originally appeared in the following publications:

"Painted Ladies" in *Blotterature*

"Guess and Check" in *Your Impossible Voice*

"Out of Fashion" in *Ragazine*

"Animal Sightings" in *Connotation Press*

"The Mountain Man" in *The New York Times Opinionator*

"Under the Guns" in *Euphemism*

"On the Go" in *Still: The Journal*

"Sweet Music" in *Free State Review*

"In Our Nature" in *Vermillion Literary Project*

"Speaking into the Microphone" in *Bluestem*

"City Visit" in *Minetta Review* and *In Like Company: The Salt River Review and Porch Anthology* (Madhat Press).

"Wild Birds" in *Faultline*

"New Friends" in *Fox Chase Review*

"Taking Hits" in *Sou'wester*

"Making Progress" in *Little Patuxent Review*

"On the Way Out" in *Phoebe*

"Great Leap Forward" in *A Gathering of the Tribes*

"Brush-Offs" in *Crab Fat Magazine*

"Absent Without Leave" in *BigCityLit*

"Pardon My French" in *Sensitive Skin* and *Paris, Etc.* (anthology, Serving House Books)

"Mentorship" in *Empty Sink Publishing*

"On the Move" in *Evergreen Review*

"An Urban Weapon" in *Before Passing* (anthology, Great Weather for Media)

"Bad Matches" in *Liars League NYC* and *Shale: Extreme Fiction for Extreme Conditions* (anthology. Texture Press)

"Kehena Beach" in *Asian Cha*

"Warts and All" in *Potomac Review*

"Riding the Rails" in *Two Cities Review*

"Good Eggs" in *The New York Times Opinionator*

"Family Life" in *Eleven Eleven, Five Willows, Estrellas en el Fuego* (anthology. Rogue Scholars Press) and *Child World* (chapbook. Red Glass Books)

"Toasted" in *The New York Times Opinionator* and *The International Herald Tribune*

"One Degree of Separation" in *Marco Polo Arts Magazine* and *The New York Times Opinionator*

"Appointments" in *Fiction International*

"The Stupidest Thing I've Ever Done" in *Compose: A Journal of Simply Good Writing*

"After the Storm" in *Misfit Magazine*

"Road Trip" in *Connotation Press*

"Glass House" in *Cooper Street*

"Code of Violence" in *Sensitive Skin* and *Digging Through the Fat | Ripping Out the Heart*

"Between Places" in *Timber: A Journal of New Writing* and *Shale: Extreme Fiction for Extreme Conditions* (anthology. Texture Press)

"When the Work Runs Out" in *The Understanding Between Foxes and Light* (anthology. Great Weather for Media)

I would like to thank the New York Foundation for the Arts. the Virginia Center for the Creative Arts and the Writers Room for supporting this work.

About the Author

Thaddeus Rutkowski grew up in central Pennsylvania. He is the author of the books *Violent Outbursts* (Spuyten Duyvil Publishing), *Haywire* (Starcherone Books / forthcoming from Blue Streak Press), *Tetched* (Behler Publications) and *Roughhouse* (Kaya Press). *Haywire* won the Members' Choice Award, given by the Asian American Writers' Workshop in New York. He teaches literature at Medgar Evers College in Brooklyn and fiction writing at the Writer's Voice of the West Side YMCA in Manhattan, where he lives with his wife, Randi Hoffman, and their daughter, Shay. He received a fiction fellowship from the New York Foundation for the Arts. Visit him at www.thaddeusrutkowski.com.

Photo by Buck Ennis.

More from Gival Press

Tina Springs into Summer / Tina se lanza al verano by Teresa Bevin
The Tomb on the Periphery by John Domini
Twelve Rivers of the Body by Elizabeth Oness

For a complete list of Gival Press titles,
visit: *www.givalpress.com.*

Books are available from Ingram, Follett, Brodart,
your favorite bookstore, the Internet,
or from Gival Press.
Gival Press, LLC
PO Box 3812
Arlington, VA 22203
givalpress@yahoo.com
703.351.0079

CPSIA information can be obtained
at www.ICGtesting.com
Printed in the USA
LVOW11s0924121017

552034LV00007B/919/P